# Therapeutic Partnership

**Carl Goldberg, Ph.D.,** is Assistant Clinical Professor of Psychiatry, George Washington University Medical School; a consultant in Marital and Family Psychotherapy at Saint Elizabeth's Hospital; a consultant in Group Psychotherapy to the Portsmouth (Virginia) Psychiatric Center; on the teaching faculty of the Virginia Institute for Group Psychotherapy in Richmond, Virginia; and on the Board of Advisors and Visiting Faculty of the New York Center for Psychodrama. In addition, he has a private practice in psychotherapy in Silver Spring, Maryland. Dr. Goldberg is former Director of the Laurel Comprehensive Community Health Center and the Northern Mental Health Team, Prince George's County, Maryland. He has taught at the University of Virginia in Northern Virginia and at Antioch College in Columbia, Maryland; has been on the teaching staff of the Group Psychotherapy program of the Washington School of Psychiatry and a lecturer in Group Therapy of the Psychiatric Institute Foundation in Washington, D.C. He is a Fellow of the American Group Psychotherapy Association and a member of its Standards and Ethics Committee.

Dr. Goldberg has written four previous books, including one that was a main selection of the Psychotherapy and Social Science Book Club in 1971, and a second that was an alternate selection in 1976. Their titles are: *The Human Circle: An Existential Approach to the New Group Therapies; Encounter: Group Sensitivity Training Experience;* and with Howard W. Polsky and Daniel S. Claster, *Social System Perspectives in Residential Institutions;* and *Dynamics of Residential Treatment.*

Carl Goldberg

# Therapeutic Partnership

## Ethical concerns in psychotherapy

Springer Publishing Company
New York

Springer Publishing Company, Inc.
200 Park Avenue South
New York, N.Y. 10003

77 78 79 80 81 / 10 9 8 7 6 5 4 3 2 1

Designed by Patrick Vitacco

$RC 480.8$

$G 66$

**Library of Congress Cataloging in Publication Data**

Goldberg, Carl.
    Therapeutic partnership.

    Bibliography: p.
    Includes index.
    1. Psychotherapist and patient. 2. Psycho-
therapy ethics. I. Title. [DNLM: 1. Psychotherapy.
2. Physician-Patient relation. WM420 G6157t]
RC480.8.G66      616.8'914      77-24604
ISBN 0-8261-2350-3
ISBN 0-8261-2351-1 pbk.

Printed in the United States of America

# Contents

# Foreword

The proposition, which I advanced more than twenty years ago, that mental illness is not a disease but is a name we give to certain behaviors, has gained wide acceptance in and outside of the mental health field, save among devout psychiatrists. Since ideas have consequences, the idea that mental illness is a myth also has consequences. One of these is the conclusion that there is not, and indeed cannot be, any such thing as mental treatment or psychotherapy. Why? Because if mental illness is not an illness, then mental patients are not sick. If there is no sickness, there is nothing to treat; and if there are no patients, then there is no one to treat. The great merit of Carl Goldberg's *Therapeutic Partnership* is that it is one of the first works in the history of psychotherapy to be written from a point of view that takes these propositions seriously.

To be sure, the view that there is neither psychopathology nor psychotherapy presents certain problems for the psychotherapist. These problems, however, are troublesome only for those devoted to protecting the vested interests of a guild of medical psychotherapists. The fact that mental illness is a metaphor does not mean that persons called mentally ill do not differ from those usually not so called. Similarly, the fact that psychotherapy is a metaphor does not mean that persons called psychotherapists do not do anything different from those usually not so called. Actually, the psychotherapist purveys human services—in particular, conversations and behavioral rule-settings. Psychotherapists belonging to different schools of psychotherapy thus sell somewhat different services, and even therapists officially belonging to the same club often sell different services, depending on their own personal preferences, values, and life styles. Exactly what kind of conversation or rule-setting a psychotherapist sells is usually well disguised by the professional jargon in which his role and behavior are couched.

In *Therapeutic Partnership*, Carl Goldberg departs from this self-serving style of dealing with psychotherapy. Instead of considering it as a technical process, he writes about psychotherapy as a human enterprise conducted by intelligent and informed adults who agree or contract with each other about what they are going to do and why they are going to do it. As Dr. Goldberg rightly views it, so-called emotional disturbance usually entails some inadequacy in the "patient's" capacity for negotiated relationships with significant others. To be effective, so-called psychotherapy must, therefore, help the client to improve his abilities as a negotiator. Hence it is essential that client and therapist play collaborative roles, the contributions of both determining the outcome of the "therapeutic partnership."

Since the term "psychotherapy," like the term "mental illness," is now an accepted part of our vocabulary, it is convenient to call such a relationship "contractual psychotherapy"—which is what I have called it in the past, and what Carl Goldberg calls it in the present volume. Although this term is serviceable for the moment, I believe it should be used only temporarily, until psychotherapy, too, is fully demedicalized and demystified. When that day arrives, if it ever does, the activities of psychotherapists will be designated by their plain and proper names — that is, the names of various religious, rhetorical, or repressive acts. Carl Goldberg's *Therapeutic Partnership* is a pioneering attempt to bring that day a little nearer.

THOMAS SZASZ, M.D.
September 1977

# Preface

Man was born free, but is everywhere in bondage. This or that man believes himself the master of his fellow men, but is nevertheless more of a slave than they. How did this change from *freedom into bondage* come about? I do not know. Under what conditions can it be rendered legitimate? This problem I believe I can solve. . . .

In any case, social order is a right—a sacred right, which serves as the basis for all other rights; *it does not, that is to say, flow from force.* Yet it does not flow from nature *either.* It therefore rests upon agreements.

Our task here is to find out what these agreements are. . . .

— Jean-Jacques Rousseau

The issues addressed in this book should be of serious concern to all those who engage in the practice of psychotherapy—its recipients no less than its practitioners. It is an interpersonal partnership between therapist and client that is being promoted in this volume. For client and therapist to operate in a climate of informed consent, not only the practical considerations, but also the underlying existential and philosophical assumptions of the conduct of psychotherapy need to be revealed to the client. This book has two major themes: the quest for meaning in human existence through therapeutic encounter, and client-therapist collaborative endeavors in establishing a therapeutic alliance. These two endeavors are, in my view, joined. Therapists who equate freedom and autonomy tend to ignore interpersonal partnership as central to the therapeutic encounter, for if man is an autonomous agent, he must then free his solitary will, as encounter and Gestalt practitioners exhort, to assert himself in seeking happiness, meaning, and security (Linthorst, 1975). In my contrasting view, the journey into self requires the presence of another. We come to know ourselves through the other. The journey into self is most productive in a climate in which each partner is in the process of seeking an increased awareness of his own identity. This book is devoted to a quest for meaning in consort.

As a frame of reference for the practitioner, I have written the kind of text I would have liked to have had available when I began my psychotherapy practice but had instead to gather piecemeal from a variety of sources. For the past 15 years I have trained mental health practitioners on the firing lines and taught as well in medical schools, graduate and undergraduate psychology programs, and professional institutes. I have been concerned about the dearth of texts that relate the therapist's struggle with his own humanity to sound conceptualizations of psychotherapy, personality development, and psychosocial education. To date, existentially oriented psychotherapists, who share with me a deep concern about the therapist's struggle with his own humanity, have described the therapeutic encounter in poetic but generally rather metaphysically vague terms. Specific and practical aspects of these encounters are left to the imagination of the reader. In this volume, I have attempted to spell out the specifics of therapeutic encounters by focusing upon how the therapist may best utilize himself as a therapeutic agent in giving balanced attention to theory, technique, intuition, and the therapist's being-in-the-world, that is, how he employs his own humanity with those with whom he works.

Whereas this text is addressed to all psychotherapy practitioners, it probably will be read primarily by the serious young practitioners and those still in training and in graduate studies. Frankly, I am pessimistic as to how receptive experienced practitioners are to requestioning the existential premises upon which they predicate their work.[1] It is unfortunate if this is an accurate appraisal. No practitioner is without existential anxiety and concern. In the words of Frieda Fromm-Reichmann (1953), as practitioners "we differ from our patients not in kind but only in degree." Accepting this realization gives practitioners the humility and common ground to be together in a meaningful way with those with whom they work (Mullan, 1955). Consequently, I intend this book to be an integral part of the training and the personal reexploration of all

---

[1] This may be seen even in such apparently insignificant matters as when a practitioner takes a vacation. When surveyed by *Time* magazine in 1975 as to why so many psychotherapists chose August for their vacation, replies were given such as "because Freud did" or "because it is built into your training from the start. Your analyst took August and so you start doing so yourself."

those practitioners, of all mental health disciplines and theoretical persuasions, who are able to be concerned about significant ethical and existential issues too frequently ignored in the conduct and training of psychotherapists.

I also intend the book to be helpful to clients who seek to establish a therapeutic partnership in their quest for meaning in their existence. For the current and prospective consumer of psychotherapy, I have provided an appendix recommending guidelines for selecting a therapist and a treatment program. Too many people enter psychotherapy without giving sufficient consideration to the complexity and risk of a meaningful psychotherapy experience. There are, of course, vast differences in styles, training, and competence of practitioners. Unfortunately, there are few reliable guidelines available to prospective clients for assessing the appropriateness of practitioners' conduct and the efficaciousness of treatment programs without having first invested their time and money with a practitioner.

I have made recommendations for establishing a therapeutic partnership through developing guidelines for negotiating and contracting for roles, tasks, and responsibilities in the therapeutic encounter. I have also proposed ways of rationally terminating psychotherapy. Where problems develop in a therapeutic relationship, I have recommended guidelines for utilizing consultation in dealing with these issues. The use of consultation is a poorly understood and neglected dimension of psychotherapy. Consultation, when jointly employed by both therapeutic agents—therapist and client—has the value of demystifying the nature of psychological amelioration and reducing the omnipotence of the therapist.

Finally, this book should be of interest to all those who refer to, work with, consult with, or are curious about psychotherapy practitioners and the basis for their conduct. The pervasive influence of psychological manipulation on society deserves serious concern. Psychologists, psychiatrists, and the techniques of both are involved in virtually every facet of society. Psychologists reportedly have helped to win several important jury trials (e.g., the Mitchell-Stans trial, the Joanne Little trial, and the Wounded Knee Indian trial) by enabling attorneys to select jurors most psychologically responsive to their client's situation. Drivers in Venezuela need to convince a psychiatrist that their aggressive propensities are within acceptable limits in order to gain a license to drive an automobile. Bartenders in Racine, Wisconsin, are being taught by psychologists and hairdressers in Miami, Florida, are being taught by psychiatrists to improve their ability to listen empathetically to their customers. A successful tennis instructor in Maryland has described his approach as a counseling process that deals with students "where they're at," using meditation and body exercises to help them overcome the neurotic cycles they are locked into. Edifices that exude a "therapeutic environment" are being created by an interdisciplinary team of Yale University psychologists and psychiatrists in collaboration with architects, administrators, and interior decorators. At the same time, whereas thousands of books and tens of thousands of professional articles, reports, and papers have been written on the craft of psychotherapy and its application to everyday life, few practitioners have deemed it necessary to explore the ethical concerns in the conduct of psychotherapy and its societal implications.

# Acknowledgments

My interest in the ethical basis and the existential conditions of the psychotherapeutic relationship has been inspired by a number of thoughtful mentors. I am particularly indebted to Dr. Thomas Robischon, who was my philosophy mentor during my undergraduate days, and to Drs. Solomon and Karen Machover, whose clarity of clinical perspective I am still in awe of many years beyond the year of clinical internship I spent with them. I am especially appreciative to my wife, Merle Cantor Goldberg, M.S.W., for clarifying my concepts and practices in the use of contract negotiation in marital and group psychotherapy through our work together as co-therapists and co-trainers of other psychotherapists.

# Therapeutic Partnership

# chapter 1

# Ethical concerns in
# the conduct of psychotherapy

One must not forget that the relationship between
analyst and patient is based on a love of truth, that
is, on the acknowledgment of reality and that it
precludes any kind of sham or deception.

— Sigmund Freud

When a therapist and a patient meet for the first time, each comes to
the encounter with an implicit set of fantasies, expectations, and
demands about what will happen as a result of their meeting together.
When these expectations remain hidden or inappropriately addressed,
there results—as the situations and cases in this book attest—an unproductive impasse, if not an outright vitiating consequence for either or
both the patient and the therapist. This state of affairs may seem to be a
strange and unjustifiable occurrence in psychotherapy—the reputed
sanctuary from deceit, pretense, and inhibition; the supposed setting
par excellence for the baring of the naked truth. The practice of
psychotherapy, however, is a complex and difficult endeavor for its
practitioners, no less than for their clients. Like their clients, practitioners are as often arbitrary as reasonable, stupid as perceptive,
timorous as courageous, irrational as rational—all the while, merely
human. To be sufficiently cognizant of the existential dilemmas and
ethical implications of his behavior in psychotherapy, to say nothing of
being willing to face up to the implications in order to avert counterproductive conduct, is an onerous task for even the best of practitioners.
I am not speaking of deviation from ethical practices, which can only
occur in situations in which clear ethical guidelines are available. Far
more frequently, in my experience, the ethical implications of
psychotherapeutic practice are equivocal and open to dispute
(Goldberg, 1976a).

1

My primary focus in this volume is not the violation of existing codes and standards of practice. In my view, serious departures from ethical standards of practice are relatively rare, as compared to the more subtle and elusive evasion of the existential contract between therapist and client. Ethical questions in psychotherapy that are relegated to legal considerations seem to me to be generally beside the point. Psychotherapy practitioners are not attorneys or legislators, nor are most of the ethical abuses in the practice of psychotherapy violations of professional ethics, as these ethical standards are now constituted. There are substantive reasons for exploring ethical concerns in the conduct of psychotherapy beyond the desire to establish guidelines in order to inhibit exploitative and psychologically deleterious conduct. Ethical concerns in psychotherapy are not limited to therapeutic situations that pose questions of improper conduct. It is of primary importance that practitioners concern themselves with what they know of successful therapeutic practices and in what ways these successes relate to therapist-client values and conduct. This endeavor requires an intensive exploration of the basic philosophical and existential foundations of therapeutic practice.

In short, I believe that there is an urgent need to review the basic assumptions upon which psychotherapy is predicated and to pursue the implications of these assumptions in the practice of psychotherapy and in psychotherapy education and training. In particular, there is a need to discern lucidly the implications of such salient therapeutic concerns as the unspoken power of the psychotherapist, the restoration of the client's power, the rendering of psychological services with and without specific and agreed-upon goals, roles and relationships, the lack of guidelines available to prospective clients in selecting a competent therapist and therapy program, the divergent views among practitioners as to how to develop a therapeutic alliance, the paucity of guidelines for assessing progress and elucidating the difficulties arising during treatment, and the rational termination of psychological treatment.

I am not, of course, the first psychotherapy practitioner and educator who has become concerned with how vaguely the psychotherapy establishment deals with ethical issues. A former member of the Board for Social and Ethical Responsibility of the American Psychological Association, Michael Scriven, proposed at a board meeting that "every psychologist offering psychotherapy to the public [should] issue a disclaimer to potential patients warning that his or her services cannot be relied on to produce any demonstrable benefits. . . ." Other members of the board did not go along with Scriven's cautioning proposal to prospective clients (according to a story in the American Psychological Association *Monitor*, December, 1975). Despite the lack of support for Scriven's proposal, there appears to be abundant evidence, which I will explore in this book, to support Perry London's statement that "there are reasons to think that psychotherapy has gained more of a social respectability than of intellectual integrity" (London, 1964, p. v).

*Ethical issues*
*as existential concerns*

In my view, the principles and concepts that comprise an ethical position in the conduct of psychotherapy must be based upon a serious grappling with the existential conditions of human existence, as well as upon sound clinical methodology. In its most important sense, ethical abuses in psychotherapy are breaches of faith between the therapist and his client in their failure to deal with the existential concerns that bring the client into encounter with the therapist. The client entering therapy suffers from an inability to address adequately his existential responsibility. It is a person's existential responsibility to give direction to his own existence. Without this direction a person suffers from a lack of experienced meaning in his existence. His suffering is exacerbated by the therapist's collusion in avoiding addressing these concerns in their encounter together.

"Ethical concerns" will be defined in this book as those inquiries which seek to explore whether the conduct between the agents involved in the therapeutic encounter are consistent with their explicit agreement as to why they have come together and what they seek to derive from their relationship. If the dialogue between the agents fails to elicit or unclearly elicits the objectives and goals for their coming together, such conduct begs the question of psychotherapy. It is imperative in my view that the reasons for being in a therapeutic encounter be clearly understood and agreed upon by both agents, not merely inferred by one or the other. When I asked an analyst acquaintance of mine whether she and her patients have some explicit agreement about what they are working on together in therapy, she gave me an incredulous look. This highly trained, intelligent, and kind friend tolerantly pointed out to me that "neurotics don't know what they want! How do you expect them to work on goals in their analysis? Instead, I point out to them through my interventions what it is they are working toward." This paternalistic attitude, in my view, is existentially an ethical violation of the therapist-client relationship. In short, to leave unexplored the reasons for the therapist and client being together is a collusive endeavor that prevents the client from struggling with his ontological responsibility. These collusive relationships also have an antisocial implication. (Antisocial may be a strong term, but it is valid to the extent that a therapeutic relationship takes the client out of the larger social world without better enabling him to deal with this sphere after he begins psychotherapy.) The individual's human condition demands that he address his ontological responsibilities if he is to make available to himself an informed choice in the conduct of his existence. (This concern will be discussed in some detail in Chapter 4.)

I am, of course, using the term *ethical concerns* in a different sense from that generally implied by practitioners. Unethical conduct in psychotherapy is generally construed as violations of particular professional codes or even of legal statutes. Ethical conduct as I will be exploring it in this book subsumes, as well as transcends, legal, theoretical, and clinical positions. I am concerned in this book with meaning and purpose in human existence and how practitioners struggle or fail to struggle with these existential concerns in their therapeutic encounters. The book is written to be practical as well as theoretical. It is essential that practitioners develop some rather lucid guidelines for the conduct of psychotherapy. Practitioners have not always been straightforward in establishing codes of ethics. Many instances of blatant violation of the ethical standard of the mental health professions appear to concern other professionals more because they wish to protect the reputation of psychotherapy from its detractors than because of concern with the misconduct per se. A number of practitioners, for example, argue privately that sexual relations between therapist and client may be legitimate and useful in some instances, although in public they uphold these behaviors as misconduct.

If practitioners do not establish effective and meaningful guidelines for their conduct for themselves, it is evident that outside interest groups (e.g., governmental agencies) will impose rules and regulations on them. There has been considerable public clamor and pressure from the professional sector to police the practice of psychotherapy. In recent years several serious inroads into the once exclusive therapist-client relationship have been imposed.

### Modification of the once-exclusive therapeutic relationship

As psychotherapy in the past has been integrally tied to private health insurance, it is evident that the future of psychotherapeutic practice is closely related to the development of national health insurance. Advocates of national health insurance, who are concerned with the growing amounts of payment for psychotherapy, are insisting upon peer review of clinical cases covered by third-party payment. Peer review has begun to have an impact upon medical practice. It will be only a short while until its influence is felt by practitioners of other disciplines, as well. We, as practitioners, decry the long arm of governmental bureaucracy interfering with the private practice of psychotherapy. Nonetheless, until practitioners responsibly justify the conduct of psychotherapy as a private arrangement between a client and a practitioner with whom he chooses to work, psychotherapy as an exclusive conclave of client and therapist may soon be largely an anachronism. Already third-party payment has had marked effect on the type of treatment offered, created problems of confidentiality and diagnosis, influenced the nature of the transference relationship, and raised complex issues for client resistance (Meltzer, 1975; Chodoff, 1972; Halpert, 1972).

Unsettling to clients and practitioners alike are reports that the Medical Information Bureau, a computerized center for medical data set up by the insurance industry, makes data available to hundreds of commercial companies. The same is true for the Multistate Information Systems, which contains complete mental health histories and furnishes them to psychiatric hospitals, clinics, and outpatient centers in the New England area. What are the implications of this ready accessibility to psychiatric data? Benjamin Lipson, a Boston insurance underwriter, surveyed a thousand New England doctors, and according to a report in *Moneysworth* magazine, found that most of the physicians believed that insurance companies breach confidentiality. Apparently, patients share the same belief. Lipson reported that many of the patients of the doctors surveyed are paying for their treatment out of pocket, rather than fill out medical insurance claims.

Private health insurance carriers claim in their own defense that mental health services are being "overused" and "abused" by their subscribers, making it essential for the insurers to have easy access to medical records to review mental health practices. Insurance companies have, as a result of such practices, created strong pressure toward the formation of peer review committees to oversee the practice of psychotherapy. These committees of colleagues will be utilized by the insurance carriers and by professional (e.g., state and county) associations to review the treatment plan and treatment rationale of the practitioner in his work with patients where third-party payment is involved. Malcolm Meltzer (1975) mentions an acquaintance who confided to him that his psychiatrist's bill for the past month was $2,900. He indicated that he visits the therapist four times a week, his wife twice, each of his children individually, the children as a group, the family as a whole, the parents as a couple. He, of course, would not be able to afford to be so involved in psychotherapy unless the insurance coverage was at the 80 percent level. Meltzer, a clinical psychologist, indicates that the family he is describing is intact and middle class, and the members are capable and functioning. To justify expensive treatment, some therapists have distorted diagnosis and altered clinical data.

Mental health experts on social legislation believe that peer review committees to monitor the private practice of psychotherapy will also be an integral component of national health insurance. Indeed, there are strong indications that state psychological associations, as have their medical colleagues, will be initiating peer review committees even prior to the enactment of national health insurance. It may well be that these reviews will be required even in instances in which the client is paying the entire cost of treatment out of his own pocket. The responsibility of the practitioner in cases under review will be to specify intended therapeutic outcome, and he also will be held responsible for arriving at these objectives within a specified period of time. Such a state of affairs will clash with the notions of clinical responsibility implicit in psychotherapeutic practice—even when the practitioner is a nonphysician.

Elliot Friedson (1976), a New York University sociologist, argues in his book, *Profession of Medicine,* that two assumptions have been regarded as fundamental to the healing professions in the United States:

(1) once a patient has placed himself in the doctor's care, the practitioner has sole and complete responsibility for his treatment, and (2) clinical experience is the foundation of medical responsibility. Healing is regarded as an art rather than a perfected science. Cures cannot be effected by choosing the right procedures by objective appraisal of the patient's medical history. Parenthetically, this rationale denies that peer review committees are in a position to ascertain proper clinical procedures. Each doctor, Friedson writes:

> builds up his own world of clinical experience and assumes personal, that is, virtually individual responsibility for the way he manages his cases. . . . [In this way, the work of healing] gives rise to a special frame of mind oriented toward action for its own sake (p. 172). . . . Such action relies on firsthand experience and is supported by both a will to believe in the value of one's actions and a belief in the inadequacy of general knowledge for dealing with individual cases (p. 178). . . . [The healer] feels that his work is unique and concrete, not really assessable by some set of stable rules or by anyone who does not share with him the same firsthand experience. (p. 180)

In requiring justification for the goals of treatment, peer review committees probably will operate from a different set of assumptions. Their rationale will assume that in claiming a genuine ability to influence clients, the psychotherapist must reasonably assume at least some of the responsibility for the nature of that influence, as well as being accountable for the manner in which that influence is conducted.

*Political and societal*
*implications of psychotherapy*

Despite sufficient evidence to the contrary, the psychotherapy establishment has permitted societal institutions to assume and affirm that psychotherapists have the capacity to protect society from the "dark secrets of the mind." As a consequence, in such decisions as *Landau v. Werner,* the courts have ruled that a psychiatrist may be held culpable for malpractice for the destructive behaviors of his patients. The fact that multitudes fill our large state hospitals attests that, in actuality, practitioners have little control over the dark secrets of the mind. Only when drastic controls are placed on a patient's environment or severe alteration of his neurology or body chemistry is rendered, is the practitioner able to modify appreciably the resistant patient's behavior.

These practices, of course, raise serious ethical concerns. Today there is considerable concern among the populace about the utilization of psychosurgery, behavioral modification, and involuntary hospitalization. Concerns have also been raised about the use of insanity in criminal defense; megavitamin therapy for schizophrenia; the vast expenditures, intrusiveness, and inefficiencies of community mental health; the dangers of the new therapies; and the implicit fraud in the conventional therapies. The conventional therapies have been called antifeminist, proestablishment, antiworking-class, prointellectual, and so forth. At the same time, a considerable number of therapists are anxiously scurrying around looking for newer, more exciting, more "relevant" techniques without seriously grappling with issues and values being called into question. Shepard, in his book *Marathon 16* (1971), for example, makes the claim that he is willing to try with his patients any behavior that he regards as not physiologically harmful to himself. In subsequent books he seems to be eagerly pursuing this challenge and promise in his psychotherapy practice.

The responsibility for the failure to seriously grapple with the issues and values upon which psychotherapy is predicated cannot be attributed to any single factor. Yet it is evident that although psychology is today the most popular college subject, as well as the leading source of scientific literature and college texts (London, 1974), and although countless books, movies, television dramas, and popular conversation broadly "portray" what happens in psychotherapy sessions, psychotherapy lies behind a mystique. It is not that practitioners don't know a great deal about influencing or changing human behavior, but that practitioners often behave like romantic poets who believe that the power and efficacy of their practice resides in its mystique. Many psychotherapists, for example, have been annoyed by the publication of such books as Eric Berne's *Games People Play* (1964) and William Glasser's *Reality Therapy* (1965). The overt reason for this is the undue oversimplification of psychological conflict and its amelioration as presented in these books. Covertly, in my opinion, psychotherapists object to the demystification of the psychotherapeutic process presented by such books.

There are even more serious implications of psychiatric mystique. *The Washington Post* reported in December, 1975, that a research psychiatrist at Saint Elizabeth's Hospital, a large psychiatric hospital run by the federal government in the nation's capital, acknowledged that patients involved in psychological research at the hospital frequently do not understand what they are being asked to do. The concept of requiring informed consent from human subjects, according to Schwitzgebel (1975) appears to have emerged primarily from the German war trials: "The investigation of German medical experiments by A. O. Ivy served as a basis for the 1946 decision of the Judicial Council of the American Medical Association to require for the first time the 'voluntary consent' of research subjects." When a profession, on the other hand, permits the practice and conduct of its practitioners to remain implicit and mysterious, while at the same time requesting the trust, the financial resources, and the difficult personal modifications of persons in distress and confusion, for me this profession raises many serious ethical concerns.

Unfortunately, there are no clear guidelines for the review of psychotherapeutic practice. Psychotherapy is not always a circumscribed ameliorative endeavor intended to heal the individual's emotional wounds. Psychotherapy has subtle social and political implications. Some psychotherapists openly affirm psychotherapy as a political activity (Halleck, 1971). The practitioner's prerogative, in their view, is either to encourage the client to rebel against an oppressive environment or to accept and adjust to his present condition (Blatte, 1973). Various programs of behavior modification and psychosurgery are the hallmark of adjustive treatment philosophies. In their more insidious forms these programs are conducted in the absence of the informed consent of those who are being subjected to their influence. This practice gives some men the power to directly impose their values and points of view over others. In Jackson, Mississippi, for example, a neurosurgeon used a mutilation operation on hyperactive children as young as five years old. The surgeon reported that the children whose brains he coagulated with electrodes were postoperatively more easily managed by staff on the psychiatric ward. They were also intellectually deteriorated from their preoperative functioning (Breggin, 1973). Breggin (1973) reports that the U.S. Justice Department has granted $500,000 for the first year and $1 million for the second year to a group of Boston psychosurgeons to develop "screening methods" to search out and find citizens who are "violence prone" and employ psychosurgery to control them.

Legal and ethical concerns further complicate the treatment of persons who are experiencing psychological distress. Several of the children who were operated on in the case reported above were black. There are no precise studies, but the First National Minority Conference on Human Experimentation held in January, 1976, at Reston, Virginia, reported that about 80 percent of all research is conducted on members of minorities and the poor. In the state of North Carolina, unlike people accused of other "crimes," a person involved in an insanity hearing has to prove that he is not insane. The reader should not be surprised to learn, then, that a Baltimore pipefitter told a Maryland legislative committee considering a bill to abolish the controversial Patuxent institution in March, 1975, that he "submitted to this joke called group therapy" to secure his release from the institution after he realized that "if I didn't capitulate I would spend the rest of my life there" (Baker, 1975).

Despite the controversy these practices have evoked, some 10,000 patients of private practitioners and at least 50,000 inmates of hospitals, prisons, and training schools are being subjected to behavior modifying treatment, according to Dr. Bertram Brown, director of the National Institute of Mental Health. NIMH currently allocates $2 million a year to behavior modification programs. The Federal Alcohol and Drug Abuse Agency contributes an additional $1 million to these programs. With so many people having to have their personalities modified to meet the demands of our society, the practitioner must begin to question whether society should expend more effort in dealing with the nature of socialization in the present society rather than devote so much money and effort to resocializing society's "failures."

Where does the social scientist begin in studying the nature of socialization in society? In my view, the psychotherapeutic situation provides an unrivaled opportunity for the study of the most basic psychosocial processes influencing personality development and interpersonal competence. Participants in a therapeutic relationship carry out relationships vis-à-vis each other by rather direct and intimate interaction to an extent not found in the events the social scientist is usually witness to in society at large.

The reader may ask as a result of my alluding to the study of socialization in psychotherapy, "Are you proposing to write a book on the study of social interaction or the establishment of ethical guidelines in conducting therapeutic practice?" My answer is that it is impossible to write an intelligent book on the latter without a firm grasp of the former. I am in agreement with Thomas Szasz (1969) that psychotherapy is meaningless without an articulated ethic—an explicit statement of intent. It is my belief that ethical guidelines should not be based upon external criteria; for example, what is impolite in a social situation is not automatically prohibited conduct in psychotherapy, and what is unsafe conduct in a discussion in a competitive business situation is not equally inappropriate in psychotherapy.

As the reader is undoubtedly aware, techniques and methodology involved in some of the newer psychotherapies require the therapist to initiate treatment options that, while potentially beneficial to the individual client, chafe against conventional morality. An example is the utilization of surrogates in sex therapy.

> Is the surrogate sexual partner a therapist? Or is she a prostitute, since she exchanges sexual services for money? . . . Pandora takes her referrals from various physicians and psychiatrists around town. She started out charging $500 for a set of twelve sessions, spread over a fourteen-day period, three to four hours per session. She has just raised her fee to $750 and has found no decrease in the demand for her services. (Wolfe, 1974)

The study of interpersonal influence and interaction is essential to the establishment of guidelines for exploring ethical concerns in psychotherapy. Ethical considerations for psychotherapy must rest upon the conditions that insure an effective working relationship between therapist and client.

## A frame of reference for psychotherapy

Psychotherapy, like all other interpersonal relationships, consists of a host of complex and interacting dimensions and parameters, certain of which stand out in importance. In order to develop more fully the therapeutic encounter as a meaningful human endeavor, practitioners need to know how these factors interact and to appreciate more clearly the particular shape these parameters take in a wide range of different psychotherapy and clinical situations. I will not try to maintain that I or anyone else knows for certain what all these factors are, but I will insist that practitioners know more than critics of psychotherapy generally claim. I also feel that practitioners have not been as straightforward and steadfast in looking at the crucial philosophical issues behind the more apparent clinical problems. My approach, while admittedly subject to numerous potential errors of inclusion and exclusion, some ignorance, some presuppositions, and a bit of hope and apprehension, will, I believe, help systematize what practitioners do know about psychotherapy—helping to posit the essential factors to be considered in evaluating psychotherapy, and perhaps most important in the long run, helping to postulate a set of hypotheses to be tested empirically.

The approach I am proposing explores psychotherapy and other clinical situations as an interpersonal dialogue in which certain conditions, in particular interactions, occur. Successful psychotherapy, from this orientation, results from the sufficient articulation of these interpersonal dimensions. Curiously, the research literature, as I read it, does not emphasize interpersonal conditions in psychotherapy, but focuses instead on what appears to be a sum total of desirable therapist and client personal attributes. This appears to lead to the notion that successful therapy results from the proper client-therapist matching. Moreover, whereas the personal trait model may be useful in the selection of therapists-to-be-trained (because of supposed probability of "success"), such an approach does little or nothing to help the already practicing psychotherapist. This model merely points to personal traits the practitioner either has or does not have. It does not help him become aware of the important conditions that must be fostered and issues that must be struggled with in psychotherapy. In short, personal warmth, congruence, genuineness, accurate empathy, and unconditional positive regard may be essential personal traits of the effective therapist (as Rogers, 1951, and Truax, 1968, have demonstrated), but it is not simply because some therapists possess these traits that they are conducive to successful treatment. These personal traits are important only to the extent that they are useful in fostering certain crucial conditions in a therapeutic relationship. It is these crucial conditions that I propose to study in the quest for meaning in the psychotherapy encounter.

The thesis I will develop in this book is that if practitioners are concerned about the plight of the individuals in distress with whom they work, they must first uncover the issues that predicate the individual's place in the social order. Emotional disturbance, as I will argue in the next chapter, is a result of deterioration and disequilibrium of equity and balance that an individual experiences in relationship to significant others in his normative system. If equity and balance are essential interpersonal dimensions for maximizing one's place in society, the client must be taught how to negotiate directly for restoration of these relations in his interpersonal and societal transactions. To seek out the reasons why the client has feared to ask for equity in his object relations is not sufficient. For the client to become a more responsible ⟵ and effective person, he needs to be given responsibility for collaborating in his own emotional growth. This endeavor requires a partnership between therapist and client. The practitioner serves as a role model ⟵ The client will be no more willing to struggle for meaning in his journey into self than he senses the practitioner is in his own personal and interpersonal journeys. As such, psychotherapeutic practice requires a rationale and a methodology that are based upon a realistic assessment of the ontological conditions in the therapeutic encounter. This rationale and methodology must enable the practitioner to get in touch with his own, as well as his client's, loneliness and despair, to address the conditions that present themselves in a therapeutic encounter in which therapist and client take each other seriously. To the extent that a practitioner does not consciously experience his struggles with his own humanity in his encounter with a client, he tends to regard the therapeutic relationship as a function. The therapeutic relationship under these conditions becomes an abstraction, appropriate for description and convenient for observation, but at the same time unavailable as a meaningful human encounter in which client and practitioner share concerns in regard to their being-in-the-world. The traditional therapeutic model:

> holds that the therapist, having already had his training, has little need to grow experientially in the therapeutic situation. He must, in fact, specifically guard against experiential rather than cognitive, rational involvements, for failure to do so is generally regarded as overinvolvement or "countertransference." Thus, although disclosure of self is an inherent part of the traditional model of therapy, it is almost all one way, from patient to therapist. (Dublin, 1971)

I will further argue in Chapter 3 that all transactions between people are contractual. The therapeutic relationship I propose differs from that of other interpersonal situations in that the contractual obligations of the agents involved in a therapeutic encounter are or should be based upon a voluntary, intentional, informed, and goal-directed agreement as to how each will conduct himself with the other. By focusing upon the transactional and contractual dimensions within the therapeutic relationship, the therapist has the opportunity to become aware of the effect his own values and sentiments have upon shaping the client's behavior in ways the client may or may not intend. To foster a relationship in which the client can learn to contract for his wants in an effective and responsible manner, the therapeutic partnership needs to be viewed as an autonomous system. Neither therapist nor client can be beholden to any third party in their dealings with one another. Where the practitioner is a double agent—representing the state or a school of psychotherapy and its dogma or being reimbursed by a third party— there is serious intrusion upon the partnership relationship. In my therapeutic model, the client is not relegated to the role of victim of his inscrutable nature and circumstance and in need of being taken care of by the therapist. The therapist's function is not to change the client but to help him discover his intentionality so that he may have more conscious choices about how he lives his existence. My model supports the theoretical positions of Szasz, Haley, and others who hold that conventional psychotherapy based upon a medical model, whether conducted by physicians or nonmedical practitioners, creates an implicit status relationship that serves to exacerbate the client's denigratory sense of self. The model I am proposing requires speaking and dealing personally with clients. For too long, Schaffer (1974) argues, practitioners "have been content automatically to use a fundamentally impersonal diction: it seems so safe and effective, so tried-and-true. But working only in that way no longer seems adequate to the variety of situations we encourage or arrange."

Psychotherapy as a contractual partnership offers the client a fair, reasonable, and efficacious treatment modality. It may not always be a welcome prospect for the client, however. Unlike the traditional medical model, in which the client places a blind trust in the practitioner's knowledge and healing powers, contractual psychotherapy replaces magic with hard work. The client may initially feel it is unfair to assume collaborative responsibilities when he is feeling confused, exhausted, and distressed. Because he experiences himself as inadequate, he willingly pays a therapist to resolve his difficulties. Only from the practitioner's willingness to share his own humanity with the client does the client come to the realization that he cannot escape his ontological responsibilities if he is to find meaning in his existence.

# chapter 2

# An interpersonal foundation
# for psychotherapy

Justice is one of the most highly respected notions
of our spiritual universe. All men—religious
believers and non-believers, traditionalists and
revolutionaries—invoke justice, and none dares
disavow it.

— Charles Perelman

The magnitude and comprehensiveness of modern technology is such
that a relatively few scientists and technicians can serve the physical
needs of the entire population. A century ago, over 50 percent of the
American population lived in rural areas and were engaged in agrarian
endeavors. Today, perhaps less than 10 percent of the population
resides on farms, but our food production is many times in excess of that
of a century ago. A factor contributing to our persistently large unem-
ployment rate is the obvious fact that we do not require the large
unskilled labor force of less technological yesteryear. Moreover, as the
crises in our large cities demonstrate, a minority of the denizens support
the needs and economic well-being of the majority of the cities' populations. In New York City, for example, more people do not work for a
salary (e.g., are welfare, disability, or retirement payment recipients;
are minors; or simply have someone else to support them so they are not
"required to work for a living") than do work for a living. An individual's
existence today may be freely egocentric and asocial, to a degree not
tolerated but a short while ago. Each individual today is not actually
required, except perhaps in a moral sense, to maintain a trade and a
lifestyle forged on supporting immediate and extended family. In the
past, a man's destiny had always been his family. They were the root and
essence of his existence. He could no more evade this commitment than
obviate the realization that he had produced offspring who required his 15

care and protection. Today, with the high rate of changing families, through divorce and remarriage, a man may not be required by law to support the woman he took in matrimony and the children their union produced. If other persons do not take up his financial and social responsibilities, there are public agencies designed to do precisely that (Goldberg, 1973).

## The quest for meaning
## in America today

These considerations suggest that the individual in American society has been set emotionally adrift by the dissolution of the traditional anchoring institutions of his social system. In the past, these venerable ethical, social, and occupational concepts and beliefs of religious, family, and work-guild membership served to define the role and function of each societal member. The individual who was able to internalize these societal concepts derived a sense of identity and value as a member of society. Today, our anchoring societal institutions are no longer able to absorb the intellectual and emotional energies of the populace. The individual must define for himself his place in an ever-changing world. Morality is now regarded as situational, tentative, and open to revision. Public and private commitments are no longer absolutely binding as they were within the more ordered and less questioned societal guidelines.

The individual today is forced to question for himself the meaning of life: Who am I? How did I get this way? Where shall I go? The more the individual must rely upon his own resources for solving personal difficulties, the more he is in touch with feelings of self-denigration, frustration, and anguish. The individual today feels that he is ailing, possessed by a sickness neither physical nor psychiatric, but rather a malaise of spirit, a sickness of alienation, no less epidemic and socially contagious despite the absence of an organic etiology.

The existential practitioner views this malaise of spirit as an ontological condition underlying all emotional and social disturbances, be they characterological or due to a brief situational crisis. The individual today seeks more than the perpetuation of his existence; he yearns for personal and transcendental meaning for his existence. Individuals possessed by ontological malaise frequently have attempted conventional forms of treatment and remedial actions and languished in these situations, more frustrated and disillusioned than when they entered. Many clients think conventional psychotherapy takes too long, is uninvolving, and does not provide enough give-and-take between client and therapist to encourage them out of their alienation and characterological disillusionment (Goldberg, 1973). Many therapists have a difficult time reaching clients who appear to function adequately in their daily activities but who at the same time are detached from their surroundings and have minimal involvement with any other person and no firm commitment to any endeavor (Ruitenbeek, 1970). Insofar as these practitioners develop aversive reactions in their ephemeral struggles with these clients, conventional psychotherapy proves to be counterproductive for persons afflicted with ontological malaise (Goldberg, 1977).

### Dimensions essential
### to psychotherapy

The psychotherapist needs to feel that in some real sense he is a necessary and responsive agent of healing for those who petition him with their burdens of distress and uncertainty. Long years of experience and proven expertise generally do not blunt this deeply felt need. Being intimately involved in an ameliorative endeavor, with its heightened human drama, its challenges, its penetrating philosophical issues, its tragedy and personal pathos, no less than its exulting moments, is comparable to being involved in the creation of the world's greatest art. In short, in addition to his wish (need) to assist others, the psychotherapist is both personally and intellectually curious about the intricacies of human drama. It is a most exciting, albeit often ungratifying, experience. The experienced practitioner learns to balance his own frustration about ungratifying aspects of the therapeutic process against a satisfaction derived from his increasing understanding of his role in this process.

The inexperienced therapist, on the other hand, views the clash and interchange of divergent, conflictual, and dystonic forces within a therapeutic session and marvels at the compatible, syntonic, and facilitating energies and behavioral modalities that take shape from their union. Struggling with uncertainty as to whether he possesses the required attributes to induce these enabling processes, he of necessity queries how these complex processes come about.

The experienced therapist, on the other hand, is often so busy doing whatever he feels needs to be done to facilitate the therapeutic process that he may not have the opportunity to figure out what happened in a particular session and why it happened as it did, but as an inquiring and critical person, he too questions the complex and obscure venture that constitutes his daily professional endeavor. Successful as he may be relative to his colleagues, he is forced, nevertheless, to acknowledge resistive and befuddling failures both in particular cases and at various junctures with every client with whom he works. To transmit to younger colleagues what he has learned through the years, no less than to become more effective in what he does, he draws generalizations from his many "successes" and "failures." In this way, he tries to parcel out the specific problems and procedures that have contributed to particular therapeutic outcomes. He can never be certain, of course, that his generalizations are substantial and valid. In canvassing his therapeutic endeavor, he is forced by sheer evidence to admit that those clinical procedures that appear to him to contribute to a successful outcome with some of his clients are the same procedures and conditions that seem to stultify effective work with other clients.

At this juncture, the clinician may abandon objective assessment of his therapeutic procedures as fruitless labor replete with epiphenomenological implication, and he may revert instead to introspection in search of subjective truth. Aside from a diminishing number of operantly oriented behaviorists, most clinicians posit that there is something about the existential "being together" between client and therapist that is necessary but generally not sufficient for the client to come to grips with himself and achieve increased psychological maturity. The designation of that particular of the being together of patient and therapist that most therapists would agree upon as an essential condition of successful therapy has proved as difficult as the determining of effective treatment procedures by objective assessment (Goldberg, 1973). In this chapter I will attempt to locate these dimensions from data obtained by empirical research as well as from my own experiences as a clinician and from the self-reports of clients with whom other therapists and I have worked.

A balanced emphasis needs to be accorded both to the transactional relationship between client and therapist and to the systematic theory, the clinical skills, and the procedures necessary to turn an interpersonal relationship into a therapeutic and enabling one over and above its inherent influential, educative, and affective qualities. How does the practitioner or the research investigator move from current principles of psychotherapy—some of which have already arrived at the status of truisms, some coming from personal intuition and soul searching, others the result of unique client populations and characteristics, and still others the result of unique therapeutic styles and personalities—to guidelines for the conduct of psychotherapy? Clearly some systematic frame of reference is required. I will discuss in this chapter the conceptual considerations that have shaped my clinical thinking in the last few years and that I believe will generate a frame of reference for developing guidelines to assess the therapeutic relationship. This model will focus on the interactional aspects of the clients' situation and the consequences of those aspects for the therapeutic relationship.

In attempting to develop this model, I found the clinical literature of no immediate assistance. Concepts discussed in the literature appeared to be descriptive in a unidimensional way—as explanations either of pathology or of psychological health. I decided therefore to canvass the various dilemmas and complaints of the clients with whom I had worked, both in the private and public sector, as phenomenologically as I could. I would initially suspend any tendency I had to reduce these issues to existing psychotherapeutic systems. Having done this, I reasoned that if the dilemmas of my clients emanate from universal principles of social interaction, they must also be present in the complaints and dilemmas of persons who have never been psychotherapy patients. Particularly noteworthy would be those persons who, having suffered, had found solace and come to terms with the conditions of their existence. I decided to explore the dilemmas of prominent historical and fictional characters because their case histories were easily accessible for exploration. An underlying personal struggle always stood out among the dilemmas of the heroic and tragic figures I was studying. Each of these figures seemed to be struggling to find a system to explain and give meaning to his personal anguish, for example: Don Quixote sought the knight's antiquated code of conduct because he regarded it as more just than the customs and mores of his day. Hemingway's protagonists resent death as a dirty trick because death can neither be predicted nor conquered. Job's anguish was derived from his inability to comprehend his fate. He had been led to believe that pious men prosper and, as a pious man, he felt his plight to be undeserved.

Like these literary and historical figures, the clients with whom I have worked are lamenting that the world in which we live is a big, booming, buzzing confusion. Man craves a sense of meaning and unification to his existence (Lecky, 1969). In order to survive, each of us attempts to make some semblance of meaning from our experiences by creating standards to live by, thereby regulating and ordering an otherwise inexplicable world. Thus, Oedipus dashed out his own eyes. In a particularistic sense, he could not be held culpable for his tragic deeds. He had not known his father prior to his fateful encounter on the road to Corinth. Moreover, he had slain his father in an act of self-defense. But in a universal sense, Oedipus realized that patricide was an unpardonable crime. He had done the deed. A price had to be exacted. He realized that it was just.

All groups, subcultures, and societies establish normative systems that regulate exchanges among their members. These exchanges may be regarded as psychosocial formulas for social utility. Without such systems of exchange, interpersonal relations would be bombarded with haphazard, chaotic, and unexpected demands and consequences. When the standards of the system are not shared, or when they cease to function as they were intended to, individuals experience difficulty communicating with one another, are unable to make sense of their existence, and fail subsequently to function harmoniously. With these considerations as my context, I asked myself what standards and motifs lie at the heart of all human endeavor, regardless of whether these endeavors are directed toward the world of ideas or natural phenomena or are rooted within the framework of interpersonal relations. In short, I was searching for dimensions of object relations that are so basic that they cut across all interpersonal and relational situations. As a psychotherapist, I am concerned with finding ameliorative modalities that most closely touch man's existential being. An understanding of the basic motifs in psychological life will enable me, as a practitioner, to explore the problems that lead to interpsychic and societal disturbance.

*The importance of equity*
*in object relations*

I found that my clients were espousing complaints similar to those of the historical figures described above, though perhaps doing so in less articulate and attractive ways. Gorman (1974) has argued that "the sense of justice is a universal psychosocial 'obsession.' " It is my impression that patients I have seen in community clinics and psychiatric hospitals, as well as in private practice, essentially are seeking either justice from the social institutions that regulate their lives or *equity*[1] (fairness) in their relationships with significant others. Although intellectually they may be asking for help in psychodynamically changing themselves, at an emotional and functional level, they prefer that others change in regard to them because they experience others as treating them arbitrarily and unfairly. For example, when working with a married couple, one marital partner will experience the taking of increased responsibility for resolving the marital conflict as arbitrary and unfair unless he experiences his partner as taking increased responsibility also.

In addition, I observed that conflict between alienated and troubled significant others, such as parent and child, husband and wife, employer and employee, is exacerbated and perpetuated by the infusion of each agent's personal system of equity into the interpersonal system. It is my impression that each of the agents in chronic conflict operates from an arbitrary moralistic structure that implicitly suggests that the other agent is supposed to act in particular ways. For example, in cases of spouses or parent and child, each agent expects actions that indicate respect, consideration, caring, morality, and so forth. When the other agent fails to act in the prescribed manner, he is blamed for causing conflict. The blaming agent tries to induce guilt and anxiety in the other. In turn, the blamed other generally reacts with anger and resentment. With some persons, the reaction toward the blamer is a passive-aggressive one and the issue in conflict cannot definitively surface so that it can be dealt with and resolved. With still others (and this is most often manifested in marital conflict), reaction to blame and manipulation takes the form of a tit-for-tat retaliation in which the major payoffs are hurting the other or learning skillful strategies for slipping out of the attack. None of these strategies, of course, effectively deals with the issues at hand or harmonizes the relationship.

My study revealed the concept of *fairness* as a ubiquitous motif

[1] The reader might assume that social scientists would have shown a great deal of interest in a concept of interpersonal life as essential as equity. However, in canvassing the *Psychological Abstracts* in 1975 (which cover the psychological literature from 1927 to the present), there was not a single reference to the subjects of fairness or equity. Even justice, a closely related concept, received scant mention.

underlying human interaction. It is a basic issue that runs through the course of history. Indeed, it is rather difficult to conceive of any issue that is more fundamental to the transactions of persons involved with one another than fairness, be these exchanges in brief encounters or in durable, lasting relationships. People tend to perceive the universe in terms of their early relationships with significant others. Individuals who were made to feel powerless and incapable of establishing fair exchanges with significant others tend to perpetuate these feelings into contemporary relations. As long as an individual believes that he is incapable of freely contracting in a fair manner, he must either remain dependent, as a patient or as a child, or be involved in aggressively active manipulating or changing of the rules to his own advantage. The individual's "awareness of the existence of injustice in the world comes from infantile feelings of deprivation, a recognition of all the frustrations inherent in being human—the child in each of us still expects *automatic justice,* a spontaneous gratification of its feelings of unfairness" (Meerloo, 1959).

Most of our actions are based upon *justification.* That is to say, our behavior has reference to some standard or guideline that legitimizes our actions. So often in our conversations, to say nothing of our thoughts, we employ concepts of "deservingness," "reasonableness," "justice," or "fairness." The individual who refuses to refer to and abide by shared standards of conduct and common justifications—i.e., I do whatever I want; I don't need anyone to tell me what to do—is regarded as dangerous to a regulated society. Sanctions are applied to such persons to induce them to provide socially acceptable justifications for their behavior—i.e., I just ask that you give me a good reason for the way you treated me!

Even among societal deviants, it is well substantiated that a need for justification exists; these individuals feel that they experience mitigating conditions that require them to bend or break societal codes. The drug addict justifies his palliative on the grounds that he was born weak; the alcoholic his imbibing, because he is misunderstood; the criminal his violation, because he has the courage to do what other men only dare in fantasy. By justifying the violation of social codes, the "exploiter" restores psychological equity. Rosenquist (1932) indicates from his study of Texas convicts that the vast majority of the prisoners directed their excuses for their crimes at society at large, and they felt that their excuses either completely exonerated them or strongly mitigated their guilt for their crimes. This is hardly an isolated instance. Joost Meerloo, a psychiatrist, reports (1959) that "one of my most astonishing experiences as a prisoner of the Nazis during World War II was observing the appeal made by both prisoners and jailors to the abstract principle of 'justice.' The masters of the torture chamber spoke more of their 'sacred rights'—justifying their crimes with various mythical theories, than the victims themselves." Apparently, then, even those who violate serious social mores are concerned with the need for justification.

According to recent equity theory, after an exploitative encounter—a situation in which one individual (the exploiter) takes a relatively larger outcome than he deserves—both the exploiter and his victim experience discomfort. Equity theorists maintain that the discomfort both victim and exploiter experience emanates from two sources. According to Walster and Walster (1975):

> When children exploit others (or allow themselves to be exploited) they are sometimes punished. Soon the performance of exploitative acts comes to arouse conditioned anxiety. This distress may have cognitive correlates. Harmdoers may attribute their distress to a fear that the victim, the victim's sympathizers, legal agencies, or even God will retaliate against them. Victims may attribute their distress to a fear that their colleagues will ridicule them or consider them "a pushover" or "fair game" for subsequent exploitation. Discomfort emanating from these sources is labeled *retaliation distress*.

> Exploitation may produce discomfort for another reason. In our society there is an almost universally accepted (if not followed) moral code that one should be fair and equitable in his dealings with others. . . . When a normal individual violates that code by participating in a profoundly inequitable relationship, he violates both his self-expectations and accepted ethical principles. . . . Discomfort emanating from this source is labeled *self-concept distress*.

Research studies (Glass, 1964; Brock & Buss, 1964; Sykes & Matza, 1957) support these theories. The experimental evidence from these studies indicates that in order to maintain the belief in a just world, people attempt to establish an appropriate fit between performance and reward so that even fortuitous reward is construed as justly deserved, while aversive behaviors and characterizations are attributed to those who suffer unpleasant fate (Lerner & Simmons, 1966; Lerner, 1965). How do I account for people who appear not to require equitable treatment in their object relations? A psychodynamic explanation suggests that they may be suffering from manifestations of a sadomasochistic complex. These unfortunates have incorporated into their person cruel object introjects, which they split into active and passive components and then identify with alternately. In sociological terms, incorporating introjects is the acclimatation to status socialization (see Chapter 3). In this process the individual, fearing loss of protection from the social order, feels compelled to control his instinctual reactions and keep them within behavioral latitudes, which he experiences as cruel and unjust restriction. This self-imposed control leads to intolerable feelings that he renders more tolerable by legitimizing the injustice he experiences. He does this by convincing himself that he has violated a moral code, whether or not he knows what code he has violated. When he identifies with the sadistic component of his introjection, he is forced to experience the full, uncontrolled fury of his impulses, which has been fed by his previous self-constraints. To gain control and regulation over his urges, he tries, by becoming involved in cruel and outrageous actions toward others, to force others to set limits on his behavior.

In some of these people, the masochist component identifies also with struggles that occurred early in life between the individual's parents. Through compromise and identification with both parents, he tries to eliminate the biological differences between the sexes and the struggles thereby implied. In his fantasies about the primal scene, he fears that one sex suffers more from biological differences than does the other. He tries to achieve equity by sexual neutrality, which leads him into passive and vulnerable relations with others (Calet, 1950).

Our emotional being, then, is integrally related to our evaluation of the equity and inequity on the part of others in their actions toward us. We perpetually ask whether we are being treated justly. Instinctually, we react in terms of gross threats to our physical survival. However, these instinctual reactions have become modified by social compromises. The philosopher Rawls (1971) has pointed out that "if men's inclination to self-interest makes their vigilance against one another necessary, their public sense of justice makes their secure associations possible." This means, for example, that potentially, every angry gesture by another person, every sign or display of force or coercion, poses a threat to our physical safety. The socialized individual, however, has been led to believe that his physical survival is in jeopardy from others only at such times as he intentionally or seriously violates society's codes. "What is 'justice'? Only a legal code of mutual behavior" (Meerloo, 1959). Consequently, as long as he abides by social codes vis-à-vis others, he expects that others will not subject him to harm. On the other hand, when he meets with hostile or uncaring treatment, which he believes is undeserved in terms of his understanding of social convention, he feels betrayed and unprotected by the social order.

If an individual cannot derive desired commodities in accordance with what he has come to regard as his referent system of equity, then frustration, resentment, and finally acting in or acting out behavior occurs. At such times as these, he experiences the urge to return to instinctual, that is primitive, manners of survival. Emotionally and socially disturbed behaviors are, from this perspective, attempts by the individual to restore protection to himself in situations in which the social order has treated him unjustly. Kregarman and Worchel (1961), Pastore (1952), and others have provided some empirical foundations for this thesis. They have demonstrated that whether or not aggression appears after a frustration depends upon whether or not the frustration was expected and whether or not it is perceived as arbitrary. The more nonarbitrary, the less the response of aggression.

The concept of fairness appears to me to have universal application. Indeed, standards based upon inequality are generally justified by means of equity. Thus, in ancient Persia, to take a somewhat remote example, since the monarch was regarded as a descendant of God and was therefore a special person, it would have been inequitable to treat him equally with a common-born person. More recently, in Nazi Germany, a similar situation prevailed between "Aryans" and "non-Aryans." In the United States, whereas the Constitution declares that all men are created equal, societal authorities deem it proper to impose quota requirements on employment, education, and housing in such a way that minority group members, who don't have equal opportunities, are given added opportunity (an advantage) in competing with other citizens. (In short, social and economic inequalities are to be tolerated if they work to the betterment of the least advantaged. Implicit is the notion that it is unfair to expect citizens disadvantaged in education and socioeconomic resources to compete equally with those of greater advantage.) Basic to institutional attempts to regulate equality is the assumption that a standard for regulating exchanges—interpersonal and material—is, in and of itself, more equitable than having no standard at all.

Not only are our societal institutions based upon regulated systems of expected and sanctioned, proper (that is, fair) exchange among social units, but a person's choice of life-styles may, as well, reflect his own struggles with the meaning of equity. This was certainly true of my choice of a professional career. I was encouraged as a college under-graduate to pursue a medical career, but that was emotionally unaccept-able to me. I have always felt uncomfortable with persons who are severely physically disabled, particularly if they were born that way or if they could do little to improve their condition. I felt uncomfortable because I could not discern in what way these persons were responsible for their afflictions. If they were not responsible, then their condition seemed to me to be grossly unfair. I am more comfortable with persons who suffer from emotional disturbance. Their condition has greater clarity and meaning for me because I can generally discern how they are "responsible" for how others treat them. Because emotional distress had greater meaning for me than physical illness, I felt that I could be helpful to persons suffering from the former to a far greater extent than to those suffering from the latter.

Closely related to the concept of equity is the concept of *balance*. The principle of balance in interpersonal relationships is basic to human functioning. Structuring of experience is a universal tendency. We tend to see definite forms and patterns and make of them definite images. Over time, our memory of these entities and events may be modified and transformed, structuring our experience still further. Heider (1957) has described this psychological tendency toward structuring of experi-ence as *cognitive balance*. A state of harmony exists if entities that, in our experience, belong together are all positive or else all negative. If closely related entities are perceived to be of different valences, then a state of tension or disharmony is experienced by the perceiver. Jordan (1953) experimentally demonstrated that when a person finds himself in an unbalanced situation, psychological forces within act upon him to achieve balance. The traditional power-behind-the-throne, manipula-tive roles played by women with their husbands and sons may be regarded as attempts to balance their societally deficient power roles. Unable to realize their ambitions by their own endeavors, women often seek satisfaction of their objectives through the pressures they bring to bear on the men in their lives (Gelb, 1972). It does not follow, of course, that people seek or desire relationships that are perfectly balanced. Fiske and Maddi (1961), on the basis of a large number of diverse psychological studies, argue that the human organism inherently seeks novelty and excitation. Perfectly balanced relationships would result in states of stagnation and boredom.

*Equity and balance*
*in interpersonal relations*

The roles of equity and balance in object relations suggest to me a number of important principles that have serious implications for interpersonal relations, including, of course, therapist-client relationships. The result is three psychological premises that order my conceptual frame of reference.

First, both aberrant and emotionally disordered behavior are generated by disturbances of regulated and common systems of expected and proper (equitable) behavior between significant persons. If an individual cannot derive desired material and emotional exchanges in accordance with what he has come to expect and feel entitled to from the referent system of equity under which he operates, aberrant or emotionally disordered behavior results. George Homans (1950), in canvassing numerous sociological and anthropological studies, arrives at a somewhat similar concept underlying social behavior.

> [I] envisage human behavior as a function of its payoff—social behavior [is] an exchange of activity, tangible or intangible and more or less rewarding or costly, between at least two persons—the more to a man's disadvantage the rule of distributive justice fails of realization, the more likely he is to display the emotional behavior we call anger. (p. 75)

A second psychological premise that orders my conceptual frame of reference is that the reestablishment of a mutually acceptable and equitable system of conduct between persons involved in conflict and emotional upheaval tends to lessen conflict and harmonize interpersonal exchanges. Moreover, for those individuals who have had early developmental experience pervaded by psychological exploitation and inequity in interpersonal relations, training in skillful negotiation with others is an effective ameliorative endeavor. The concept of equity in object relations is a natural bridge to a psychotherapy that emphasizes the establishment of a working contract and the development of skills in negotiating and strategizing for need satisfaction. When the individual lacks effective negotiating skills, interpersonal accommodation, that is, the matching of his personal needs with the resources to satisfy them, clearly becomes difficult to attain.

Third and most important, equity can best be achieved in interpersonal relationships when the relationship is balanced. In a relationship in which one person gives more of himself than does the other, the recipient becomes less valued both by the provider and by the recipient himself. Quite recently, social psychologists have attempted precisely to define equitable and balanced relationships by means of a "mathematical" formula. The formula says, in effect, "Two people are in an equitable relationship when the ratio of one person's outcomes to inputs is equal to the other person's outcome/input" (Walster & Walster, 1975). For my purposes, however, a phenomenological statement is preferable: A balanced relationship is one in which both agents perceive that they have something of value to give to the other and something of value to receive in return. According to Homan's analysis:

> [The] more frequently persons interact with one another, the stronger their sentiments of friendship for one another are apt to be. (1950, p. 133)

> [The] more frequently persons interact with one another, when no one of them originates interaction with much greater frequency than the other, the greater is their liking for one another and their feelings of ease in one another's presence. (1950, p. 243)

In summary, the concepts of equity and balance offer an understanding of the maintenance and deterioration of interpersonal relationships. Persons in significant relationships who are regarded by their partners according to arbitrary rather than explicitly negotiated standards of conduct experience their relationships as frustrating and unfair. In order to restore balance in the relationship, they react with retaliatory mechanisms. These observations suggest to me that attention to the normative system structuring the client's relationships must be combined with psychodynamic formulation in working with clients involved in conflictual interpersonal relationships. Similarly, attention to the normative system is essential to an understanding of the therapeutic relationship.

The purpose of this book is to explore specific ways in which practitioners and their clients can effect a meaningful therapeutic partnership by being cognizant of and responsive to the manifestations of equity
and balance in their relationship. The following factors are, in my
experience, integral to a meaningful therapeutic encounter:

1. attention to the manifestation of equity and balance in the
   therapeutic relationship,
2. exploration of the manifestations and utilization of power in the
   relationship and its effects upon the feelings of adequacy of each of
   the agents,
3. clarity of contractual roles and responsibility,
4. clarity of therapeutic goals,
5. exploration of how permission and informed consent are manifested in the relationship,
6. exploration of how each of the agents communicates and meets
   needs in the relationship,
7. clarity about the administrative contract,
8. exploration of how the above-mentioned issues are negotiated for
   in the relationship,
9. provision for review, evaluation, and modification of the working
   relationship.

# chapter 3

# Psychotherapeutic partnership through contract negotiation

A mind conscious of integrity says no more than it
means to perform.

— Robert Burns

Every therapeutic encounter represents a series of contractual obligations that client and therapist have agreed to enact vis-à-vis each other.
This statement may sound absurd to a reader who regards a contract as a
highly articulated legal document, but contracts may be viewed within
a broader context from which all social relations may be regarded as
contractual transactions (Pratt & Tooley, 1964). Man, finding himself
not self-sufficient, has found it necessary to make promises and
agreements with others to exchange material and emotional resources
for mutual advantage. He is able to establish agreements with others
because of his capacity to create and utilize signs in establishing rules,
language, and interpersonal games (Havighurst, 1961). By means of
language games, men pledge themselves to employ mutually accepted
signs and sign obligations in fulfilling promises and agreements.[1] As a
consequence, interpersonal influence is possible whether or not the
agents involved have ever encountered, or even have prior knowledge
of, each other.

Demands and expectations of another are generally predicated upon
rules, roles, and sanctions experienced with others in previous situations approximating the emotional requirements of the present situation. Communication difficulties arise when men differ in their

[1] It is hardly surprising that we regard the schizophrenic who violates language
rules and signs as infrahuman.

31

willingness and ability consensually to validate and comprehend the interpersonal agreements and promises they have made with others or the intrapsychic agreements and promises they have imposed upon themselves. Each of these contractual modes may be characterized by varying degrees of explicitness and informed consent. Contractual arrangements among men are, as a rule, more frequently implied than explicit, unconscious than conscious, coercive than voluntary, unilateral than mutually endorsed. Accordingly, contractual arrangements may harmonize relations among some men, while antagonizing and creating tensions among others.

Contractual behavior, although a fundamental human capacity, has only in recent history achieved social significance in everyday life.[2] A contract is, by and large, an arrangement between equals that, when explicitly formulated, rejects coercion and fosters personal freedom (Havighurst, 1961). As such, contractual relationships stand in sharp contrast to status relationships. Every type of discrimination that categorizes another person, such as those that regard a person as "sick" or "well," makes use of status relations. Every discriminating act toward another person deprives him, by transforming him into the occupant of a predetermined status category (e.g., "patient" or "victim"), of his right to contract as to how he will conduct his relations with others.

Psychiatry before Freud may be characterized generally as the administration of a curative methodology to a disease entity—a status type of relationship. One of Freud's most significant contributions to the practice of modern psychotherapy was his penetrating exploration of the therapeutic encounter as an interpersonal process. He clearly recognized the need for joint participation in the therapeutic encounter, an endeavor that has come to be referred to as "the therapeutic alliance." As early as 1925, Freud established contracts with patients or with their families (Pfeiffer, 1972).

Of further importance to the development of the therapeutic alliance, Freud and his followers have been rather encyclopedic in recording their insightful observations of the ways in which patients, through transference mechanisms, and therapists, through countertransference mechanisms, unwittingly resist the development of effective therapeu-

---

[2] The sacredness of contract is integral to the American character. It is zealously guarded by American courts, beginning with the landmark *Dartmouth College v. New Hampshire* decision in 1819.

tic alliances. Nonetheless, description of resistance does not by itself enable clients to assume therapeutically efficacious roles. Strategies for effecting interpersonal partnership are required. Until recently, these therapeutic strategies have remained at a primitive stage. Eric Berne (1964), George Bach (1968), and several other practitioners concerned with regulated interpersonal relations have lately catalogued a variety of strategies and games played in psychotherapy and other interpersonal situations. They have also suggested a number of therapeutic ploys to gain the client's cooperation. Berne regarded a game as a transaction in which the agents involved could, by knowing the rules, become skilled in strategizing to handle the moves of the other agent in such a way as to obtain a fair shake and a predictable outcome. (Berne's notion appears to be concordant with the role of equity in object relations discussed in Chapter 2.) When the practitioner appreciates the client's need for an equitable and predictable exchange in psychotherapy, the requirement for an explicitly contractual relationship becomes an ethical necessity. It will be my task in this chapter to come to terms with the contractual issues involved in a therapeutic partnership.

*The literature on contractual*
*arrangements in psychotherapy*

The idea of mutual participation by means of a contract is not widespread in the field of psychotherapy. More often than not, there is simply a tacit understanding between therapist and client, based upon an implied rather than an explicit agreement, on why they are convening. The classic formulation of psychoanalytic psychotherapy (derived from the medical model) may be characterized as a situation in which the physician, defined as an expert in the specialty of psychoanalysis, agrees to provide his time and services in exchange for a fee. "If the patient fails to pay, the physician may recover the value of his services by suing for breach of contract. The physician reasonably assumes he will be paid and the patient will follow instructions, not conceal symptoms, etc. Conversely, the physician will conduct the treatment with at least ordinary skill and care." (Schwitzgebel, 1975). This model is well represented in Karl Menninger's (1955) work in which he focuses almost entirely upon the unwitting, involuntary, and psychopathological participation of the patient in the analytic relationship.

As far as I am aware, Thomas Szasz (1969) is the only analyst who proposes psychotherapeutic work in terms of explicitly contractual and mutual participation of client and analyst. The aim of psychoanalysis, according to Szasz, is "to increase the patient's knowledge of himself and others and hence his freedom of choice in the conduct of his life [by means of] the analysis of communications, rules and games, and lastly, by its social context—a contractual, rather than a 'therapeutic' relationship between analyst and analysand" (pp. viii–ix).

Behavioral therapy and transactional analysis practitioners, in their writing, have devoted some attention to negotiated contracts. Robert Stuart's (1969) writing well represents those behavioral practitioners who employ behavioral agreements as a means of scheduling the exchange of positive reinforcements between two or more persons. With this approach, Stuart claims that it is "possible to make known the behavioral expectations of anyone involved in a particular interpersonal interchange or series of interchanges, and allow each person to evaluate the losses and gains accruing to himself out of the contractual situation." (This sounds very similar to the Walster & Walster (1975) formula for equitable interpersonal relations discussed in Chapter 2.) For this system to effect change, Stuart indicates, each of the agents must clearly understand: (1) the privileges that he expects to receive after fulfilling his responsibilities, (2) how he needs to respond in order to secure each privilege, (3) the system of sanctions that will be incurred by him for failure to meet his responsibilities, (4) the feedback system that will be utilized in order to record the rates of reinforcement given and received, and (5) the bonus clause that assumes positive compliance with the terms of the contract.

For transactional analysis (TA) practitioners, a therapeutic contract is an overt agreement, arrived at by negotiation between a client and therapist and, in a group situation, with the other group members, about specific items of behavior the client would like to address within the therapeutic encounter. In this contract, the therapist agrees to call specified behaviors to the client's attention when he observes them occurring. He may also agree to assign "homework" to the client to modify his transactions within himself and with others. TA practitioners claim that contractual arrangements are productive of rapidly effective therapeutic change (Hollister & Holloway, 1973).

In the field of group therapy, Mainord (1968), and Mowrer (1968), most notably, formulate contracts with their group clients. Mowrer's contract contains three major provisions. The prospective client agrees:

(1) to be completely open about himself with the other group members in regard to both current and past events, (2) to take personal responsibility for how he fares in the group experience, and (3) to interact and become involved (with the other group members). Mainord's contract resembles that of Mowrer. Bach (1966) has promulgated a general contract for participants in his marathon groups. Its provisions are referred to by Bach as the "ten marathon commandments" and are designed to create an "intensification and acceleration of transparency and genuine encounter by a deliberate instigation of group pressure focused on behavior change" (Bach, 1966). Egan (1970) argues that "[t]he success of such therapeutic communities as Daytop Village and Synanon and of Bach's Marathon groups rests, in part, on the fact that the participants contract, more or less explicitly, to confrontation. They know what they are getting into, but their desire for change outweighs the pain they foresee" (p. 326). A group contract, insofar as it defines the expected (or even required) ways that each group member is to involve himself with others, prevents group members from avoiding important modes of interpersonal experience.

The concept of formulating a written contract between therapist and client, according to Adams and Orgel (1975):

> grew out of a method of evaluation developed by Kiresuk and Sherman called Goal Attainment Scaling in which client and [practitioner] write down each problem area specifying what the possible results of therapy may be—from best, to expected, to worst possible outcome. Later authors such as Lazase, et al., and Toussieng used the method as an adjunct to the therapeutic process, as well as a method for diagnosis and measuring the outcome of therapy (success/failure). (p. 35)

The significance of formulating a contract in psychotherapy has been supported by a number of studies on discontinuance. Levinger (1960), from his survey of studies on discontinuance, reports that "in order to profit from the relationship it seems that P [person] must be able to share H's [helper's] goals for the treatment and have a realistic conception of the therapist's role and capacities." Lake and Levinger (1960) found that 82 percent of the continuers at a child guidance clinic agreed with the therapist's definition of the problem and the services offered. Lennard and Bernstein (1971) report that "dissymmetry of expectation not only interferes with the therapeutic task, but can actually lead to premature death of the therapeutic system. For example, in two therapist-patient pairs that discontinued after a few sessions, the patients expected to be cured in a few sessions and the therapists expected a long treatment process." In reviewing the literature on discontinuers, Seabury (1976) reports a study by Mayer and Timms (1964), who found that discontinuers had:

> totally different expectations of the casework process from those of their caseworkers. In this study the clients who discontinued treatment did not understand what the caseworker was doing nor his reasons for certain behavior. Studies reveal that to resolve this incompatibility in expecta-tions, clients would make up harmful expectations that the worker was not concerned about them or was unable to understand their problems and unwilling to act on their behalf.

Schmidt (1969) found that "an absence of discussion about purpose [characteristic of cases in which workers did not formulate interview goals] may lead to considerable client misperception of the worker's objectives for the session and, conceivably, also some misperception by the client of what is relevant to his problem." In a study by Overall and Aronson (1963), the investigators found that "those patients whose expectations were most inaccurate were less likely to return for treat-ment." Finally, in a study conducted at a Los Angeles Department of Social Services center, Hosch (1973) compared two groups of clients for their capability to engage in and successfully complete a contractual arrangement for social services. This study demonstrated, as we might suspect, that "the voluntary client is better able to use the contract approach, while the involuntary or mandatory client will find it more difficult to formulate a contract or complete the required tasks." Similar difficulties arise with the severely disturbed and retarded. Seabury (1976) has recommended the involvement of family members and other responsible agents in developing contracts with these populations. The practitioner who works with involuntary clients needs, of course, to be even more scrupulous in his use of power than he might otherwise be.

*Relationship as contract*
*in psychotherapy*

Ideally, what differentiates the therapeutic encounter from other inter-personal situations is that the contractual obligations of the agents involved are based upon a voluntary, intentional, informed, and goal-directed agreement as to how each will conduct himself with the other.

Szasz and Hollender (1956), in their now-classic discussion of the basic models of psychotherapy, argue that the main intellectual and educative value of psychotherapy lies in the kind of model the analyst fosters to induce mutual and informed participation within the therapeutic relationship. Informed consent, the eminent psychiatrist Fritz Redlich indicates, "is the basis of all psychiatric intervention and . . . without it no psychiatric intervention can be morally justified. . . . [T]he medical profession's exclusive hold on its system of ethics no longer exists. The fiduciary system, in which a patient puts his trust in the physician's ability and willingness to make crucial decisions, is being replaced by a contractual system" (Redlich & Mollica, 1976).

A therapeutic contract, then, is a promise or a set of promises, the fulfillment of which each agent involved has agreed to assume as his duty. Existentially, a therapeutic contract is an attempt to enable each agent in a therapeutic encounter to inform the other agent involved of his responsibility in addressing the former's ontological concerns. Client and therapist need to explore together the questions: Why are we here? How did we get here? Do we need to be here? and Where do we go from here? To the extent that either agent fails to address these concerns, the client's quest for meaning is appreciably thwarted.

As my discussion of the literature should suggest, a therapeutic contractual arrangement is an attempt to combine the best aspects of a clearly defined set of work goals with a method for continual reassessment and review of the work in progress (Adams & Orgel, 1975). By "contract," then, I am not referring to a cut-and-dry, written document that either client or practitioner insists upon at the commencement of the relationship and that is referred to again only at such times as one of the agents experiences the other as violating their agreement. I mean that goal setting and negotiation is an essential part of viable therapeutic work and goes on throughout the course of treatment. Insofar as a contractual relationship divests psychotherapy of mystique by defining its specific purposes and procedures, it increases the accountability of both agents for what transpires in their work together. A contract is a tool that clarifies the client's goals by enabling him to take an active role in deciding on goals and meaningfully pursuing them. A client will derive as much out of psychological treatment as he personally invests.

The therapist who suggests or supports the notion that psychotherapy is only a preparation for life—that the psychotherapist's office is the place where the client learns about psychological skills he someday may use to become the kind of person he would like to become—does his client a serious disservice. Psychotherapy is life. To encourage precaution in living in the immediate world, rather than active courage in facing up to one's responsibilities, is to reinforce and entrench the difficulties the client has brought with him. In this sense, some modalities are more insulated from the immediacy of the client's concerns than are others. Family and marital psychotherapy has the distinct advantage of enabling the client to work directly with significant persons in his life with whom his relationships are in conflict. Group psychotherapy enables the client to negotiate with other people who evoke conflictual feelings similar to those he experiences with significant others outside of therapy. In dyadic sessions, the client generally has greater control of the process than in other therapeutic modalities. Working out conflictual feelings may be more easily avoided in dyadic than in group or family sessions, unless the practitioner focuses upon the immediacy of the transactional relationship of therapist and client. By definition, a contractual arrangement focuses squarely on the transactional relationship. In this endeavor, there is a need to interface what the client is working on outside of therapy with what the therapeutic agents are working on together in their therapeutic encounter.

In addition to its pragmatic purpose, contractual psychotherapy has, of course, an ethical intent. The only certain way of effectively dealing with ethical concerns in psychotherapy is to focus upon the transactional and contractual dimensions of the therapeutic relationship. How can the practitioner be aware that his own values and sentiments may be shaping the client's behavior in ways contrary to his becoming the person he intends to be, unless open discussion, assessment, and negotiation about what the client is working toward and about the roles and responsibilities required of both agents become integral components of the therapeutic encounter? In short, for the client to become a more responsible person, he needs to be given responsibility for collaborating in his own living experience. In contractually oriented psychotherapy, the therapeutic relationship is "determined neither by the patient's 'therapeutic needs' nor by the analyst's 'therapeutic ambition,' but rather by an explicit and mutually agreed set of promises and expectations which is called the 'contract' " (Szasz, 1969, p. 7).

*The contractual phase
in psychotherapy*

Many practitioners appear to view contract negotiation as an endeavor
that takes place when the agents first convene but is put aside once the
client's objectives have been established. This attitude regards the work
of psychotherapy as two distinct steps: first, trying to establish goals;
second, striving to reach those goals. In fact, a viable therapeutic
contract is a developmental process that is continually being negotiated
and periodically being reviewed throughout the entire course of treatment. In most instances, the goals of psychotherapy are better understood and can, therefore, be more specifically stated as the therapeutic
encounter unfolds. In discussing the role of contract negotiation in
social work, Seabury (1976) states that the following stages usually
characterize a therapeutic contract:

1. *Exploration and negotiation phase.* In this preliminary phase, both
agents are sizing up and testing out each other. They are attempting to
understand what the purpose of their encounter is and what each one's
obligations are in this endeavor. In this phase, each agent explores what
he needs to know about the other in order to develop a working
alliance.

2. *Preliminary contract phase.* There is in this working phase a tentative agreement as to why each of the agents is in the encounter with the
other and how each expects to be treated. This agreement is generally
characterized by considerable reservation and ambivalence.

. 3. *Primary working agreement phase.* The terms and conditions of the
therapeutic relationship are clarified as to what the specific task and
time limitations are and how each has agreed to treat the other in this
relationship. This phase gives rise to a variety of secondary, as well as
behaviorally specific, contracts. Moreover, there is some agreement in
this phase as to how the outcomes can be evaluated and reviewed and
how provision can be made for grievances.

4. *Termination phase.* After specific actions have been taken, both
agents evaluate the outcome of their attempts to achieve their agreed-
upon goals. Mutual agreement is given for terminating the working
relationship or continuing with new goals.

According to those who have surveyed the practice, few practitioners actually employ written therapeutic contracts, unless urged to do so by their clients (Adams & Orgel, 1975). The following are the components that The Mental Health Study Group (Adams & Orgel, 1975) suggests should be contained in a written contract:

*Elements of a Contract*

1. Name of each agent.
2. Date of beginning and end of agreement.
3, 4. Length of each session.
5. Goals of sessions stated as specifically as possible.
6. Cost per session and when payable.
7. Definition of services provided by psychotherapist (stated as clearly as possible).
8. Provisions for cancellation:
   a) no penalty for termination.
   b) amount of time necessary for warning therapist of cancellation.
   c) protection for therapist against willful no-show on part of client.
   d) provision for unavoidable and unforeseen events causing client to be unable to attend session.
9. Renegotiation at end of stipulated period.
10. Allowance for changing goals within stipulated period.
11. Definition of nature of services; no guaranteed results; guarantee of intention and good faith.
12. Establishment of access by client and therapist to documents which become part of client's records; guarantee of confidentiality and control by client over medical record and its contents and use of any information therein.

In my view, a viable, contractually conducted, therapeutic relationship does not require a written contract. There is, after all, a major distinction between a therapeutic and a legally defined relationship. Evidence or proof of stated intent will not alone enable therapist and client to act responsibly in a relationship. Proof and evidence are the strengths of a written contract. What seems to me to be more important to a viable therapeutic relationship is an evolving awareness of what each agent is asking for, an awareness that proceeds from implicit (silent) hopes, fears, and expectations into explicitly (directly) articulated and openly negotiated roles and responsibilities. This kind of process is difficult to capture in a written document. When documentation is desired, audiotape and videotape are expensive, but preferable. My own concern is that a contractual negotiation process should take place in psychotherapy, not that it can be documented once having occurred.

Contractually, the client's roles and responsibilities in psychotherapy are similar, with one important exception, to his roles and responsibilities in buying a house, contracting for its construction, and securing proper services in its maintenance. A buyer is entitled to the commodities and services he purchased, not because he is lonely, nor because he is upset or has emotional problems, but because he has requested them, because the seller has agreed to deliver them, and because a fee was exacted to validate their agreement. A person would be imprudent to buy a house without investigating the market for the best available houses and without obtaining information about what he should attend to in a well-constructed and functional edifice. The one exception is that, while a customer would be foolish to purchase a house without obtaining a written contract guaranteeing the specifics of the negotiated agreement of what the purchaser has bought, since the goodwill of the seller cannot be sensibly presumed, he can enter into a therapeutic arrangement with a therapist without benefit of a written contract because the goodwill of the therapist is generally not suspect.[3]

*Outline for establishing*
*a therapeutic contract*

1. Clark (1975) recommends that the initial task in a therapeutic situation should be an exploration of the *relationship* issues and concerns. This proposal makes infinite sense to me. Clark states:

> Ordinarily clients use the first session to discuss the problems they feel are causing their difficulties. Partly because they want relief as quickly as possible, partly because they think the therapist expects them to explain why they have come to psychotherapy as fully as possible, most clients submerge the questions they have about psychotherapy. This is a mis-

[3] "Unlike the businessman who aims to sell products, compete and make a profit, the professional's first goal is to perform a service. Therefore, society gives the professional certain privileges based on the expectation that professional ethics will prevent exploitation" (Shore, 1973).

take. The best way to use the first session is to outline, with the therapist, the basis for the psychotherapy relationship. (p. 75)

2. For the client to get as much as he can from the therapeutic relationship, he must assume that the therapist is there to hold up a mirror, but the therapist must rely on information from the client since he is not able to read the client's mind (Viscott, 1973). The client should be ready to present himself actively rather than wait to be drawn out by the practitioner's inquiry.

3. It is essential in formulating a therapeutic contract to avoid use of technical terms and complex concepts. Operational terms, such as how the client might look, feel, and act at the conclusion of the therapeutic relationship, may be employed and should be made as specific as necessary for each of the agents to be cognizant of what is being asked for and what each has agreed to fulfill.

4. A contract must define the nature of therapeutic work by addressing such concerns as: Why are we here? What are our expectations of one another? What do we have to offer one another? What would we like to gain from our experience together? and What is the meaning of asking help from the other? In this dialogue, the therapist seeks to ascertain the client's notion of psychotherapeutic work and replies in terms of his own beliefs and also according to the best evidence he has available about psychotherapeutic endeavor.

5. I am aware that in their initial discussions many practitioners are unwilling to inform the client fully of how the therapeutic experience may be of help and, particularly, of its possible limitations. This may be due to the therapist's awareness of unconscious material he believes the client either cannot tolerate without serious psychological repercussions or is not psychologically receptive enough to acknowledge early in a treatment relationship. In my view, this is not a therapeutically useful attitude. It is the therapist's responsibility to provide an assessment of what he foresees as the conditions of the work ahead for each of them. (This is referred to as a "prognosis" in medical-model terminology.) The practitioner's assessment is based upon what realistically can be accomplished in regard to:

a) the client's hopes, wishes, demands, and expectations of the therapist and psychotherapy, in terms of the client's problem-solving capacity and his personality attributes,

b) the client's strengths and limitations, with specific regard to the transference object(s) the therapist may likely evoke for the client and to the client's complementary role relationship with the therapist (based upon the client's family system),

c) the therapist's skill, expertise, and personal attributes,

d) their combined ability to influence environmental conditions that would lead to the most favorable outcome.

6. The conditions of the contract must be equitable and realistic. The requirements must be within the capability of each agent. Both agents are responsible for the relationship. Since the client is the ultimate judge of his own needs (as the therapist is of his own), he cannot allow the therapist to withhold "threatening" material from his awareness. In this endeavor, the client must hold the therapist responsible for answering such questions as:

a) How does the therapist see the situation that the client is bringing into treatment?

b) What does he hear the client asking to accomplish in therapy? That is, what does he perceive to be the hopes, wishes, demands, and expectations the client has of the therapist and of therapy?

c) Which of these appear to be conscious but unarticulated, and which are presently beyond the awareness of the client?

d) What does the client seem willing to do so that the therapist will meet his expectations?

In developing a contract, it should be noted that the therapist may assume that he has both a responsibility to the client at the present (C1) and to the client at some time in the future (C2). Consequently, the therapist's perception of the client's needs may differ from that of the client or he may conceive of the client's goals in ways the client might not recognize. Many therapists feel that it is legitimate to sell a suit to a client who is only asking for a hat. For example, the client "might want to erase his stutter, rash, or anxiety, while a psychoanalytically trained therapist might see these as symptomatic and manifestations of repressed hostility, and might formulate his own goal as freeing up the patient's impounded aggression. In effect, he sees C1 as different from C2 and works his contract with a C2 who does not yet exist, trusting that when C2 arrives he will be happy with the results" (Michaels, 1973).

7. The practitioner has a responsibility to the client to explain:

a) if diagnostic tests are to be performed, the nature of these tests, the reason for their being employed, and any significant risks involved;

b) if medication is recommended (by the practitioner or by another practitioner the client will be referred to for medical supervision), the expected results and possible adverse effects;

c) which techniques (in terms the client can understand) he intends to employ and the expected results, risks, and complications, as well as other techniques appropriate to the client's concerns and the reasons he has decided not to employ them;

d) the alternatives and options to psychotherapy should the client refuse treatment or decide at some point to discontinue therapy;

e) the expected outcome of therapy (in terms the client can relate to in his everyday existence), if the client stays with it for the period of time therapist and client have agreed on.

The following is a tragic example of a client uncritically accepting the medical mystique, in which the contractual considerations I have been discussing were disregarded. A 30-year-old Louisville woman was blinded by a prefrontal lobotomy operation. In a lawsuit brought against her surgeon it was ascertained that the patient was lobotomized for pain of psychological origin without the surgeon first giving the patient the opportunity (and the patient, herself, not requesting the opportunity) to explore the problem in psychotherapy (Breggin, 1973). I do not have sufficient details in this case to explain why this Louisville woman accepted her doctor's risky procedure when there would appear to be other options available, but I will explore in the next chapter the difficulty other clients have in selecting a competent practitioner and treatment program.

8. A therapeutic contract must specify the negotiable and nonnegotiable aspects of the therapeutic relationship. The psychotherapist cannot let the client decide for him how he is to meet the needs the client wishes to have addressed. These considerations require an intensive exploration and negotiation in which the concerns of both agents can be explored. Let me illustrate this from a common phenomenon in psychotherapy that might aptly be referred to as the "purchase of love." There are probably few practitioners who have not encountered clients who demand love. The client pleads from need and desperation that he or she deserves unquestioning love, not labor. The therapist may well ponder whether he has agreed to give love or sincere endeavor. If he has

contracted to give love, what kind of love has he agreed to? Has he agreed to make the client more important than others in his life, or is he promising only partial love, such as sexual involvement or paternal support? Meaningful love, of course, cannot be rendered on demand, however deserving the client may be.

I have sometimes responded to the attractiveness of some of these offers and the reasonableness of still others in the following way: "Where did you get the idea that I agreed to give you my love? I agreed to give you my unselfish attention and the product of my understanding of your situation and its effect upon me. Are you not asking me for my love as a substitute for what you have not found in your life? In any case, I will not be a substitute for you. To do so would mitigate your attempts at genuine love outside of this special situation. If I experienced love as freeing you, I would give it as best I could, but love will not free you as long as you are a prisoner of your fears and silent dreams. Indeed, only when you experience your own internal 'permission' to care as much for me as you need or want to without my having to care as much for you, will you free others to care for you as you need or want them to. I, too, have some of your fears. I refuse, however, to fall into your illusion. I have committed myself to struggle with these fears—in you, and in myself. You may choose to join and work with me or you may choose not to work with me. This is your prerogative! Mine is not to mask my fears and yours with an illusion!"

Aware of the dangers of seductive patients in an emotionally charged relationship, Freud (1915) wrote that a love affair would be a great triumph for the patient, but would be a complete interference with the cure. It is genuine love, not love on demand, that the client seeks. As such, the client deserves more than an illusory relationship. Whatever the therapist is promising must be made clear early in their relationship.

9. A viable therapeutic contract must have provisions for its fulfillment and a modus for addressing grievances and dissatisfactions. For example, a second opinion or consultation should be encouraged by the therapist before rendering heavy medication, electric shock therapy, hospitalization or, indeed, any therapeutic intervention about which the client is deeply concerned. The terms of the contract should be flexible enough to be renegotiated whenever client or therapist believes that the terms are nonproductive.

10. There must be a clearly understood means for terminating the contract and psychotherapy. The practitioner should be sincerely will-

ing to deal with termination as a real issue at any time this concern is raised by the client. What hangs up many therapists is the notion of a complete analysis. With the exception of Ferenczi, even the psychoanalytic masters did not believe that a complete analysis was possible. Freud was certainly pessimistic about complete analysis. Nonetheless, the practitioner's omniscient wishes may transcend this reality.

Emotional disorders, because they are expressions of disorientations to reality, are also disturbances of time. The psychotherapist has a dual function: not only is he expected to enable the client to call forth repressed and dissociated impulses, he must also serve as a "representative of reality who tries to reeducate the patient to an optimal reintegration of reality" (Weigert, 1952). In this endeavor, each agent must be clearly cognizant of how he uses or misuses therapeutic time. Objective time is a dimension of reality that both agents share. It is also the quintessence of reality upon which all other dimensions of reality depend. Time, in this sense, predicates the possibility of human meaning and purpose. Toward this aim, client and therapist must struggle with termination and its implications for nonbeing.

What implications does this orientation have for time structure in psychotherapy? The role the therapist assumes differs from the roles and relationships the client has taken with others in that, from its very beginning, psychotherapy is a process of preparing the client to take over for himself, vis-à-vis significant others in his life, those functions the therapist is assuming at that time and place. The more uncertain and vague the period of treatment and the goals to be worked on, the greater the influence of irrational and magical notions and attitudes the client may have toward therapeutic work. The more specific the period of treatment and the goals to be worked on in treatment, the more appropriate and rapid the confrontation with these refractory attitudes in the work to be accomplished in therapy (Goldberg, 1975c).

11. Therapist and client need to reach some initial agreement about how upsets and acting out by the client will be handled by the therapist. The practitioner should inform the client the controls he is willing to assume. In a word, will the practitioner become personally involved when a client becomes inordinately upset, or will he handle it by medication, hospitalization, or termination of the relationship?

12. A therapeutic contract must begin with an outcome; only then can it be decided which procedures are needed and how to evaluate

what happens. The goals of the therapeutic relationship must be evaluated mutually, even though evaluation is a term that makes many practitioners anxious. Standards for assessing therapeutic progress must be decided upon before evaluation of results.

13. Proper evaluation concerns itself with both internal and external criteria. The therapeutic contract is just part of the client's life contract (to be discussed in Chapters 5 and 11). The therapist must continually draw the client back to the interrelated concerns of What have I learned in therapy that can help or is already helping me with concerns in my daily existence? and conversely, What am I learning from my relationship with others that can help me with my work in therapy?

14. There should be an understanding and agreement about the relationship (which could run the gamut from phone calls to intimate involvement) or nonrelationship of the agents outside their ascribed therapeutic sessions. A similar understanding must be reached among members of therapeutic groups about their relationships with one another, as well as with the therapist.

15. In summary, a therapeutic contract must establish a mutually agreed-upon and explicitly articulated working plan (in medical-model parlance, a "treatment plan"). The working plan consists of the following six elements:

a) the goals client and therapist have agreed upon working toward,
b) established means for working on these goals,
c) a prospectus on the ways the therapist plans to intervene in or stay out of the client's issues, based upon how the client tries to draw the therapist into this struggles,
d) a prospectus on ways the client has agreed to work on his issues,
e) means for reviewing and evaluating the therapeutic work,
f) means for addressing dissatisfactions in the working alliance.

## Contract negotiation between therapist and client

My methodology for teaching contract negotiation is derived from a theoretical model delineated in terms of the consequences of the participants' expectations and obligations upon their cooperative or conflictual transactions with others. My methodology emphasizes both those articulated benefits the individual expects to derive from a training or treatment encounter and those benefits he is unable or unwilling to identify consciously. Sager and Kaplan (1972) indicate that there are three levels to contracts between persons involved in an intimate relationship:

1. *Conscious and verbalized expectations:* the hopes and demands that each agent expresses to the other in clear and understandable language.

2. *Conscious and nonverbalized expectations:* the expectations, plans, beliefs, and fantasies that each agent withholds from the other because he is fearful or ashamed to express them to the other.

3. *Unconscious expectations (wishes beyond awareness):* needs and desires that frequently are contradictory and unrealistic, initially not accessible to the client's awareness.

Obviously, to the extent that the client's or participant's expectations remain implicit rather than clearly articulated, it is unrealistic for the participant or client to expect them to be fulfilled by others.

My training and treatment methodologies attempt to delineate how the people I work with seek to achieve, maintain, or avert a position of equity with significant others. An important focus in my work is to indicate how the people I work with use the equity issue in the forms of justification, rationalization, illness, and weakness to assume positions of inferiority, passivity, and irresponsibility or, on the other hand, domination, oversolicitude, and overresponsibility (Goldberg, 1973).

In brief, in negotiating for a contract, the first step is to make explicit what is implicit in the expectations and wants of those involved in the ameliorative endeavor. The second step is the establishment of balance: A successful contract cannot be rendered unless each agent feels he has something of value to give as well as something he wishes to receive. This necessitates a period of work in which the therapist and client (or trainer and participants) discuss what they want from and can offer each other. Basic agreements are set down for the giving and receiving of assistance, and the consequences and handling of broken agreements and dissatisfaction are discussed. This gives the client (or trainee) confidence that his feelings and behavior are being responded to in a nonarbitrary way. There are, as a result, clear dictates about the consequences of his behavior and that of the persons with whom he is working. I believe that this collaborative structure, conducive to establishing feelings of equity and balance in the working relationship, is an essential component of an effective therapeutic contract. The final step is that of negotiating the exchanges among those involved in the ameliorative endeavor.

In sum, the contract negotiation approach I have delineated is intended to enable the practitioner to help the client clarify from the onset what he is seeking help for, what roles and responsibilities he and the practitioner are willing to assume, and how they, together, can implement the client's goals. Once having reached these goals, client and practitioner then decide together the next step in the client's quest for psychological maturity.

*Structured exercises*
*for contract negotiation*

In exploring the contracts people make with themselves and others, I have employed many different types of contract negotiation approaches, ranging from nondirective to directive verbal techniques, and to various action modalities. In the following pages, I will explore various methods I have employed for helping the client examine, in his own life contract, those implicit expectations and demands he has imposed upon himself and others. In working with a therapeutic group of people who don't have serious psychological disturbances, I have found that the well-known psychodramatic magic shop is a valuable tool. It enables participants to ask themselves and others directly for those commodities they require in order to maintain a constructive life contract (Goldberg & Goldberg, in-press a; Goldberg & Goldberg, in-press b). The protocol of the magic shop technique illustrates a method for teaching participants how to negotiate for their wants by helping them get in touch with issues that are getting in the way of their making unambiguous and unambivalent requests of themselves and others.

In my use of the magic shop technique for contract negotiation purposes, the director (psychodrama therapists are called "directors") assumes the role of shopkeeper, setting up a fantasy shop in which each group member can enter and purchase what he most wants that the group can help him to obtain at that moment. The member is then asked what price he is willing to pay (what he is willing to give up) for what he wants. Negotiation follows. Various other members of the group are called upon to represent parts of the shop. The following example of the use of the magic shop technique is from a workshop conducted by my wife, Merle Goldberg.

DIRECTOR    This is my Magic Shop. You can buy anything you want here. Our shelves are filled with everything imaginable, in every size, shape, and color. (*Director begins to walk around room, delineating the physical dimensions of the magic shop.*) These are the walls of my shop. Who wants to be a wall? (*Two students volunteer and assume positions on either side of the room.*) Here is the door to my shop. (*A student volunteers to be the door and assumes hands-on-hips position.*)

DOOR    I'm a swinging door. I open and close fast, so if you want to come in, you have to push hard and enter quickly.

DIRECTOR    This is the inside of my shop. It can look any way you want it to. My counter is here and my shelves are back here. (*Student rushes in to be a shelf.*) I usually stand here, behind the counter. Well, it looks like we're all ready for business. Anyone have anything they want to buy today?

CONNIE    I do. (*Tries to enter through door, but it won't open.*)

DOOR    You have to push harder than that. (*Connie pushes hard and rushes in as door closes rapidly. Walks very slowly and hesitantly around shop, looking.*)

DIRECTOR    Welcome to the Magic Shop. Can I help you with anything?

CONNIE    I don't know. I'm not sure what I want, but I do know that I wanted to come in.

DIRECTOR    Perhaps you might want to look on the shelves over here for some ideas. We have many things here.

CONNIE    This is a nice shop. Let's see . . . (*looks on shelves, slowly*). I don't see what I want. It's not there.

DIRECTOR    What are you looking for? Maybe I can help you. (*At that minute door bangs open and Ken rushes in.*)

KEN    I know what I need. If she can't make up her mind, I can make a purchase.

CONNIE    (*Looks sad and withdraws to side of shop.*)

DIRECTOR    Welcome to the shop. I'm glad to see you. I'm waiting on Connie right now, so perhaps you can look around a few minutes.

KEN    Okay. *(Moves rapidly around shop.)*

CONNIE    I think I know what I want . . . some confidence. I thought about it some more when Ken came in.

DIRECTOR    Lots of people have come in asking for that lately.

CONNIE    I knew you didn't have it. I've looked everywhere and no one seems able to give it to me.

DIRECTOR    You've been looking for confidence for a long time.

CONNIE    Oh, yes. And it seems so hard to get.

KEN    *(Rushing over and almost knocking Connie down.)* I have lots of confidence. I can give you some.

DIRECTOR    *(To Connie)* Want to wait while Ken makes his purchase? Then maybe we'll have some more of what you want.

CONNIE    Okay, I'll wait.

DIRECTOR    *(To Ken)* You saw what you wanted?

KEN    Yes, there it is on the shelf.

DIRECTOR    Which one? What does it look like?

KEN    That one. The mason jar with the heavy lid. It's not very big, but it's very full.

DIRECTOR    Here, let's get it down and put it on the shelf. *(Moves it.)* How does it look from here?

KEN    It looks great, filled with hundreds of pieces of paper with writing on them.

DIRECTOR    What is the writing about?

KEN    It's all the knowledge that I need about working as a therapist with children. I really want the contents of that jar.

DIRECTOR    You know that to buy something in this shop you have to pay for it by giving me something. Usually people try to pay me by giving up whatever stands in the way of what they want to buy. You mentioned wanting to give up some confidence. How does that tie in?

KEN    Wow, I don't know! *(Walks more slowly around shop; stops and looks at imaginary mason jar; looks up.)* Gee, I guess that's right! A lot of people tell me I think I know it all, that I'm always sure of what I'm doing. Maybe giving up some of my confidence would let me be less sure of myself. That way I could have more from other people.

DIRECTOR    How much confidence would you want to give up?
*(Ken indicates large amount.)*

That's a lot. It may be a little difficult for you to give me so much all at once.

KEN   It may be a little scary. It's important for me to act confident, but it may be worth it. That part of my attitude may really stand in the way of my learning from others. It seems like a fair trade to me.

DIRECTOR   Why don't you set aside some of your confidence for awhile and see if it really does buy some of the knowledge you want. Take this mason jar on loan. If you don't feel the trade is working, you can always come back next week to the shop.

KEN   That sounds fine. Thanks a lot. (*Takes jar and exits, more thoughtfully.*)

DIRECTOR   Well, Connie, it looks like our shelves are well stocked with confidence now. Want to buy?

CONNIE   You know, I've been thinking and I've begun to change my mind. Instead of confidence today, I want a good feeling about myself. Oh, yes, there it is! That beautiful glass bottle filled with purple flowers. Can I have it?

DIRECTOR   Let's take it off the shelf and put it here in front of us.

CONNIE   It looks wonderful. But I guess I'd have to give up feeling bad about myself to get it.

DIRECTOR   That would be hard?

CONNIE   I guess so. I know what feeling bad about myself is like. I'm used to it. It's not much fun but it's reliable and a comfortable pattern. I'm good at it besides, and it gets me lots of attention from the other guys here. Feeling good about myself would be new. I'd have to let the people in here know about my accomplishments as well as my weaknesses.

DIRECTOR   It's been hard for you to show your accomplishments in here?

CONNIE   Sometimes I found it hard to feel good about myself and show my accomplishments in here. I don't know how the others would respond to me then.

DIRECTOR   If you want, you can decide you don't want to buy it today. That the price for what you want is too high at this time. Or you can purchase it on loan and try out the new behavior.

During the course of the magic shop negotiation, a contract may not always be reached. During a workshop in New York City, a well-dressed young man named Bill quickly volunteered to enter the magic shop. He glibly explained that he desired to purchase a master's degree. Although he was able to articulate his wishes with some fluency, something was missing. Even Bill seemed confused as to why the degree seemed out of reach. Further exploration revealed that getting his degree meant giving up his present playboy life-style. As he negotiated for his degree in the magic shop, it became clearer to him that he just wasn't ready to make a move out of his current life-style. At that time, the tradeoff was not worthwhile for him. He made a decision to stop his outflow of graduate school entrance applications and frantic search for admittance until a later date when he might be more ready to make the move.

Though it is easy enough to impress practitioners with the importance of contract negotiation in psychotherapy, it is quite another matter to enable hard-to-reach clients to articulate their fears and implicit expectations. In my practice, in addition to the usual exploration of goals through dialogue or action techniques like the magic shop, I employ several structured fantasy exercises to elicit these data with more reticent and psychologically blocked clients. I will touch briefly upon three of these exercises. I have found that an exercise I refer to as "future projection" is a relatively unthreatening and efficacious means of assessing contractual considerations early in a working relationship. In this exercise I first create a mood of free fantasy by having the client sit back, close his eyes, and give his mind free rein. After a few moments, I suggest that our work together has terminated. It is now 6 months or a year into the future. The client is speaking with someone who is quite significant to him. He is telling the significant other what he derived from our work together. I suggest that he discuss such topics as the following in his fantasy with the significant other:

1. Psychotherapy with Dr. Goldberg was _____ experience.
2. What I derived from our work together was _____.
3. What I did not get from therapy was _____.
4. What I liked about Dr. Goldberg was _____.
5. What I disliked was _____.
6. If I had to do the therapy all over again, this time I would

_____.

With recalcitrant or intellectually rigid clients, I couch my inquiry in terms of what I refer to as "future self." I ask specifically what the client would like to look like, feel like, sound like, and be like at the end of our work together.

I have found both of these exercises rather useful because they reveal, rather vividly, not only the goals the client wishes to achieve in therapy but, just as important, his underlying attitudes and sentiments toward the therapeutic endeavor. The future projection exercise brings out the client's attitudes toward learning and working and elicits a definition of his conception of "meta-learning," that is, what he assumes are the roles, practices, and responsibilities of the agents involved in achieving the goals of psychotherapy.

The third exercise explores in depth, experientially, the role into which the client will cast the practitioner in the therapeutic encounters to follow. In order to get at preconscious feelings the client has toward how he wishes the therapist to help him with his place in the world, I have employed a projective exercise that I refer to as the "free flight situation." The therapist asks the client to imagine that he has embarked on a free-flight parachute jump. The client and the therapist will be leaving the airplane together. The client is asked in the session to freely fantasize, out loud, what this experience is like for him. The therapist is attentive toward how the client experiences himself in the free flight. How, for example, does he experience the therapist's presence? The therapist notes how the client goes through the flight. Several clients to whom this exercise was given suppressed the practitioner's presence in their fantasies; still other clients acted as if they were heavily dependent upon the therapist for their safety. I am also concerned whether the client takes into consideration what he believes the therapist is experiencing in the flight. Finally, I am most interested in whether, and if so how, the client makes clear to the therapist how he wishes to relate to him during the flight. Obviously, these considerations forecast the initial course of the therapeutic relationship.

*Implementing a contractual approach*
*with difficult clients*

Obviously, techniques do not resolve characterological client resistance to therapeutic work. Psychotherapists are not infrequently faced with deciding whether to treat, and how to treat, the unwilling client. Generally, clients come into encounter with a psychotherapist because they are "overwhelmed by anxiety" or, contrastingly, they are concerned because they "feel nothing." In either case, they are generally dissatisfied with the direction their existence has taken. In other instances, people feel "forced" to enter therapy by the persuasion or coercion of others, and these clients resist treatment. I have found that the contractual approach need not be abandoned in these instances.

The contractual partnership model is the ideal psychotherapy prototype for which I aim in my practice. I realize, nonetheless, that clients are, in varying degrees, characterologically unwilling or unable to assume a responsible relationship with me. If they could, they probably wouldn't be seeking psychological amelioration. To varying degrees, clients generally prefer to assume positions of confusion, helplessness and inadequacy, or indifference—in order either to be saved by the omniscient magic of the therapist or to have fulfilled their belief that their personal situation is without remedy so that they can legitimately continue to harbor resentment and hurt and react with retaliatory mechanisms toward themselves and/or others. I try, therefore, to work from whatever attitude the client comes with to engage him in a relationship in which I provide him with the opportunity to negotiate for becoming the kind of person he wishes to be. I will illustrate my strategy with an example of my work with a most recalcitrant client.

Mr. Jones had reluctantly consulted me as a private practitioner on the advice of his attorney. He had been charged on two occasions with sexually molesting small children. He would shortly be brought to court on criminal charges. His attorney advised him that the court would probably look more favorably upon him if he voluntarily sought psychiatric help and entered into a treatment program. His attorney also advised him to consult a psychologist or psychiatrist because a doctor held more weight with the court than did other mental health workers. Mr. Jones, a poorly articulate and ill-educated person, was a passive-dependent person of around 50 years of age who had a chronic alcoholic pattern. Both incidents supposedly occurred while he was intoxicated. He saw no need for psychological treatment. He claimed that he recently began seeing an alcoholism counselor who had helped him stop drinking (as a "result" of two sessions). Since both incidents occurred while he was intoxicated, he claimed, his desisting from further imbibing would guarantee that these incidents would never again occur. But, Mr. Jones added, he would go along with my recommendations.

A few months after I began seeing Mr. Jones he was given a 5-year suspended sentence by the court. His probation was based upon the provision that he be "under a doctor's care" for the period of probation. The terms of the "doctor's care" were left vague and ambiguous. I did not feel entirely comfortable with continuing to work with Mr. Jones once he had received a sentence. I had no doubts that he would have discontinued psychotherapy had his probation not required it. Consequently, he had not freely contracted to work with me. Upon thinking about this, however, it occurred to me that this was overly idealistic and inane reasoning. Freedom and choice cannot realistically be conceptualized as absolutes; they are only possible within a defined situation. Although there were serious consequences for our actions, Mr. Jones and I still had the freedom to discontinue working with each other. Mr. Jones did not have to accept me as a therapist, the area in which I practice is saturated with psychotherapists. I chose to work with Mr. Jones because he was paying me a reasonable fee and because I felt that I might be of help to him. Despite his inarticulateness and stubbornness, I found him likable. Though I could have chosen to delimit Mr. Jones's freedom if I acted as a representative of the legal system that had the delegated power to control his behavior, I chose instead to be in no way responsible to report Mr. Jones's behavior inside or outside therapy to anyone. Nevertheless, because his freedom from a prison sentence was dependent upon his attendance in psychotherapy, I agreed to report his attendance at sessions to his probation officer, but only if this information was requested of me.

Given psychotherapy as an alternative to prison, Mr. Jones had more of a choice in how he would use the sessions than in whether he would attend them. Since he was paying for the sessions, it was his prerogative to use them as he wished. It was my responsibility to explore with him, in language he could relate to, my notions about what psychotherapy was about and what it could and could not reasonably accomplish for him. Mr. Jones had grown up in a rural mountain area. I made frequent analogies to raising crops and animals and educating young children for responsibility to relate my notions about psychotherapeutic work to experiences with which Mr. Jones could identify. I made specific recommendations about how he might use the sessions in terms of the difficulties he was experiencing in his marriage.

Mr. Jones expressed more annoyance than guilt about the events that had caused him legal difficulty. He blamed them on the abuse he received from his wife and his stepchildren. With minimal insight, and even less guilt about his behavior, a scrutiny of Mr. Jones's developmental history could well have taken up the 5 years of probation without necessarily modifying his character structure or leading to mastery over his marital situation, so I suggested that the focus during the sessions be contemporary. Because he was a very withdrawn person whose only significant, albeit conflictual, relationships were with his wife and his stepchildren, I recommended that his family join him in his sessions. He readily agreed because he maintained that it was his wife's neglect of him that forced him to commit the acts that required him to see me for psychotherapy.

He spent most of the sessions complaining about his wife's mistreatment of him. In reaction, Mrs. Jones expressed frustration and resentment that he was not willing to articulate or demonstrate any caring for her. Ironically, despite the legal and moral difficulties he found himself in, Mr. Jones was a person with a strong sense of justice. Indeed, his morality conflicted with his wife's childish, impulsive, and irresponsible system for relating with others. It was at those times when his wife treated him unfairly, depriving him of sexual and affectionate caring, that he became intoxicated. Mr. Jones, in turn, used his lack of emotional expression to punish his wife. He refused to express caring for her because he claimed, "It ain't do any good!" She retaliated by impulsively spending money on commodities he regarded as "junk." Mr. Jones became more resentful and withdrawn. Mrs. Jones in reaction refused to attend any more therapy sessions. Their respective systems of equity came into volatile conflict in her justifying her withdrawal from therapy by saying, "The court told you that you have to go to treatment. I don't have to go to the doctor. Only you do!"

Their marital relationship was based on a revenge contract. They were implicitly saying to each other:

MRS. JONES   If you don't express caring for me, then I won't give you any emotional support. I will not only withhold sexual relations, I will also make you suffer your psychotherapy treatment as punishment rather than attend sessions so that we can work as partners in a relationship.

MR. JONES   If you don't treat me fairly, I'll withdraw from you, get drunk, and withhold money from you, since that is all you seem to want from me.

The revenge contract in their relationship resulted in a "Mexican standoff." As each basically mistrusted other people, neither would retract his or her wont to hurt sufficiently so that the other could take a psychological risk and express caring. Neither of the Joneses had had sufficient experience in a trusting relationship in their personal development. Each required immediate payment in order to give to another person.

To resolve this difficult impasse, several contractual issues had to be dealt with. For Mr. Jones, money had a punitive value within the therapeutic situation. He was paying me for treatment, which in his perception was punishment for having committed a socially unacceptable act. On casual observation, the reader may regard Mr. Jones's situation as atypical—a resistive client having to pay for treatment he prefers not to receive. If the reader looks more closely at the function of money in psychotherapy, he soon realizes that money is frequently an unintended but quite real punishment, even for clients who willingly and enthusiastically pursue treatment. In short, meaningful and productive psychotherapy is less expensive than incompetent and unproductive work. In productive contractual psychotherapy, client and practitioner arrive together at goals and pursue them in a mutually agreed-upon fashion. Their work is efficient because they have agreed on what they are seeking and how to evaluate what they achieve together. In unproductive and uncontractual therapy, the therapist is rewarded for his inefficiency until such time as the client finally has enough sense to terminate the relationship.

Mr. Jones had less freedom to terminate therapy than do other clients who are not having their attendance monitored by a governmental agency. If he dropped out of treatment, his behavior would more likely be regarded as his unwillingness to be helped rather than as a result of my incompetence. Moreover, because Mr. Jones appeared to trust me more than he did most other people, he was unlikely to seek another practitioner regardless of how ineffectual I might be in handling his situation. Thus, I could continue to see him and have him pay me every week regardless of his progress. Indeed, I could reap more financial rewards for his lack of progress than from having him improve sufficiently that the requirement of psychotherapy might be removed from his probation. Consequently, to restore power to Mr. Jones, I had to transform money from a vehicle of punishment to a source of reward. To do this, I had to act against my own financial interest. Mr. Jones regarded his psychological treatment as a 5-year sentence, regardless of his progress; therefore, he had little incentive to take his efforts in therapy seriously. If, however, he could pay increasingly less money for therapy based on his taking psychological risks, he would then have a clear and meaningful incentive for taking therapy seriously.

I also felt that it was crucial to bring Mrs. Jones back into the sessions. She would not return unless he articulated caring for her, so I said to Mr. Jones in a session, "It seems to me that you care for your wife but that you refuse to give her the satisfaction of letting her know that you do." He replied that while this might be true, he would not tell her that he cared because it wouldn't do him any good. She would continue to treat him unfairly.

I offered Mr. Jones what I referred to as a "no-financial-risk gamble." I told him, "You say that if you told your wife that you cared for her, she would ignore your statement and just treat you as badly as before you made the statement. What if you could gamble on your point of view and if you were wrong you would win some money? I say this because you have expressed to me the concern that coming to these sessions week after week is expensive. Therefore, I will charge you $1 less on your next session, provided you tell your wife that, after a discussion with me, you realized that you cared for her, and provided she responds favorably to your statement, contrary to how you believe she will respond. On the other hand, if she responds as you claim she will, the bill will stay the same for the next session, but you will have lost nothing."

The reader may be aware that I was employing a combination of behavioral and paradoxical models in my attempt to restore power to Mr. Jones by providing him with an opportunity for negotiating for more favorable conditions within our therapeutic relationship. Parenthetically, I am generally opposed to using behavioral approaches that "solve" patient "problems" (see Chapter 6). However, when the existential concerns in the relationship are elucidated, behavioral techniques are frequently efficacious in reciprocal exchanges between the therapeutic agents (see Chapter 8). Moreover, I have found paradoxical techniques to be rather useful in circumventing resistive characterological patterns. I utilize paradoxical techniques (Frankl, 1969) to enable clients to participate actively in situations they have heretofore felt compelled to avoid.

These techniques have an absurd aspect. Mr. Jones could reap a financial reward by demonstrating that his limited but entrenched view of his wife was invalid. In the past, his anger and withdrawal evoked a predictably unfavorable response from her. As a person with a strongly moralistic orientation, he was rewarded with moral indignation. The situation that I presented him with, on the other hand, provided him with an incentive for proving himself "wrong" for his lack of demonstrative caring. If Mr. Jones deviated from his characteristic withdrawal and his wife reciprocated with affection, *uncertainty* would be evoked in their normative system. If this uncertainty persisted for any period of time, each would be compelled to reexamine expectations of and from each other. This reexamination would be a reconsideration of the dysfunctional contractual relationship they were currently maintaining.

I was aware, nonetheless, that there were strong forces in their relationship for avoiding this reexamination. Mr. Jones's continuing willingness to take psychological risks could not be maintained only by my rewarding him. Mrs. Jones was simply too much more of a significant person for him than I was. Her power to punish him was considerably greater than my capacity to reward him. The principles of equity and balance required that Mrs. Jones reward him by returning to the sessions. This was easier said than done.

Mrs. Jones was caught up in a preoedipal struggle between her unregulated, impulsive demands and cruel, introjected authority figures. She experienced most demands upon her as unfair. She attempted to free herself of these demands by dysfunctionally childish mechanisms, saying in effect, "If my husband expects me to be at the sessions, then I won't attend even though I actually enjoy them!" Mrs. Jones avoided facing her internal conflicts and contradictions by externalizing them. She skillfully, but unwittingly, "encouraged" her husband's angry reactions. His reactions "justified" Mrs. Jones's not meeting her promises to him to attend sessions or to meet his emotional needs. As long as I or any other authority surrogate insisted that she attend sessions, she would rebel. She would only be able to get in touch with her internal contradictions at such time as she was confronted by the realization that rebellion against external objects did not rid her of her internal turmoil. Consequently, in a session that Mr. Jones attended alone, I told him that I would like him to tell his wife that she didn't have to attend sessions and she would understand why I said this. As soon as Mr. Jones gave my message to his wife, she was on the phone yelling at me, "I know I don't have to attend sessions. You don't have to tell me that!" I pointed out that that was why I had said to her husband that she would understand. I had, with my provocative statement, made explicit the conflictual contractual relationship between Mrs. Jones and me. I had indicated that she didn't need to rebel against her husband and me to prove that she was a voluntary participant and an adult. I went on to indicate the time of Mr. Jones's next session, adding that if she cared to, we would be glad to have her attend. She attended.

In working with the Joneses and with other clients who have considerable difficulty attempting new behavioral patterns and taking psychological risks, I have developed the following working model based upon the principles of equity and balance:

1.  A client will tend to experience as unfair any therapeutic task that requires him to significantly exceed previous performance.
2.  The client's self-esteem tends to be increased when he is expected to perform at a level that exceeds his previous performance.
3.  The more concordant his expected behavior is with known standards of conduct, the more equitable and comfortable he experiences the task as being.
4.  The more the client feels involved in setting standards for his own behavior or is aware of the consequences of his intended future behaviors, the more equitable and comfortable he experiences his behavior as being.
5.  These hypotheses taken together suggest that clients who are being asked to modify or replace value systems in seeking new behavioral modes feel uncertain as to how their intended behaviors will be judged and accepted. This suggests that a basic therapeutic task for client and therapist is to consciously evolve a normative belief system appropriate and favorable to the qualities and ways of being the client intends.

I will, in the remainder of this book, explore the development of this working model, but before doing this, it is necessary to examine some of the existential and societal barriers to meaningful therapeutic encounters.

# chapter 4

# Barriers to meaningful therapeutic encounter

Better the devil you know than the one you don't!
—Proverb

Few psychotherapists, I trust, would disagree with Sidney Jourard's (1964) eloquent statement about the I-thou relationship in psychotherapy: "No patient can be expected to drop all his defenses and reveal himself except in the presence of someone whom he believes *is for him,* and not for a theory, dogma, or technique" (p. 65). In curious contradiction, the preponderance of the training for mental health practitioners that I have found available over the last several years has been concerned with psychotherapeutic technique. This is particularly true of workshops held at professional psychotherapy conferences. These workshops emphasize the theoretical and methodological considerations in how to do therapy: considerations that are designed to help the practitioner work with certain types of difficult client populations; techniques that Gestalt practitioners, for example, claim have more impact than analytic techniques; techniques that psychodynamic practitioners believe to be better thought through than those of transactional analysis or psychodramatic methodologies.

*The practitioner's
existential concerns*

Instead of an operational orientation to psychotherapeutic training, I believe that there is a serious need for training in grappling with issues that go to the core of human existence and human purpose, as manifested in the psychotherapeutic situation. In my view, there is a need for training models that serve to underscore the practitioner's own values and also the effects of his conduct upon those with whom he is 63 involved in critical interpersonal encounters. I am concerned that training deal with such questions as Why are we involved with another in distress? What do we, as practitioners, wish to accomplish in our encounter with another person in distress? Do our goals for the client differ from his own? In short, what are the values and existential concerns that shape our stance with our clients? How far are we willing to go in "helping" our clients? Until practitioners address these concerns, they cannot meaningfully address the larger question of whether the various therapeutic situations clients and therapists find themselves in may more often than not prevent the practitioner and his clients from actualizing their intentionality—that which each seeks to become (Goldberg, 1976a). This is not an idle concern.

I do not deny that other practitioners have also seen the need for designing exercises and situations to accentuate crucial concerns that inevitably occur in a meaningful therapeutic endeavor. Encounter group leaders and Gestalt practitioners have been particularly fecund in this endeavor. From my view, however, the ethos of the encounter and Gestalt ontology emphasizes individual assertion in such a way as to regard inclination toward social responsibility as a neurotic manifestation. I will not attempt here to explore the therapeutic implications of this ethos. It seems sufficiently clear to me, however, that psychotherapeutic training that emphasizes individual assertion is neither a sufficient nor an effective training methodology for practitioners who are attempting to master skills with which to enable individuals in distress to come to terms with their human condition by means of an interpersonally cooperative endeavor. Psychotherapeutic training requires a rationale and a methodology based upon a realistic assessment of the ontological conditions in the therapeutic encounter. This methodology must enable the practitioner to get in touch with his own and his client's loneliness and despair and to address the conditions that present themselves in a therapeutic encounter in which therapist and client take each other seriously rather than regard concerns about one another as neurotic manifestations (Goldberg, 1976b).

Steinzor (1967), a practitioner who has written about the healing partnership, argues that the therapist must stand "apart from his 'system' because he can never separate himself from his own humanity, from his own experiences of grief and joy and searching which create a bond with his patient much firmer than intellectual loyalty to a concept could ever be. In short, the voices of his experience are more compelling than the tenets of his system" (p. vii). Bergin (1975) reports several studies that support Steinzor's contention. In one study, 86 adult males who had received treatment during childhood or adolescence were investigated. The researchers were able to confirm the existence of a "deterioration effect" in psychotherapy and to discern the influence of the therapist in causing this effect. Patients who were equally disturbed at the time of treatment had sharply different long-term results. Therapist A was strikingly more successful with the more disturbed cases than was therapist B. "Although both were psychoanalytically trained, A seemed less concerned about inner personality dynamics when he could achieve improvement by direct action. B was more fascinated with the details of case histories, the boys' fantasies and deep exploration of their personalities. When the boys had difficulty dredging up such material he felt frustrated" (Bergin, 1975).

*The practitioner's values*

As a practicing psychotherapist, an educator, and a supervisor of psychotherapists-in-training, I am constantly faced with issues and concerns in the conduct of psychotherapy for which there are neither ready answers nor proven methodology. I find most psychotherapists I know, regardless of their disciplines or their theoretical disposition, to be caring and socially concerned people. Nonetheless, I find many of them lack a clear idea of their own values and have only an inchoate awareness of the effect their conduct has on the persons with whom they are working. These practitioners appear best able to deal with specific clinical issues and problems as they are brought up in treatment, but demonstrate a befuddling myopia toward what objectives will result from working on these issues and problems with their clients. In their therapeutic encounters, there may be some expectation of what they would like for the clients, but these therapists, in my experience, have little or no awareness of what they expect of themselves (Goldberg, 1976a). Fenichel (1945), who has been regarded as the standard-bearer of psychotherapeutic technique, states: "Everything is permissible if only [the therapist] knows why" (p. 24). Fenichel's statement suggests that it is sufficient for the client that the practitioner simply "be there" in an enlightened, interpretative way. This raises the issue of whether the practitioner's values should be imposed in any form in his therapeutic work. The following case illustrates this concern.

A behaviorally oriented practitioner was consulted by a woman who was extremely anxious because her husband had been having a series of affairs. Hoping to preserve the marriage, the client asked the therapist to desensitize her to her husband's infidelities. The therapist perceived her request as asking to adjust to what he personally regarded as a basically unhealthy situation. Should he have refused to administer the requested treatment or would his personal values be an unwarranted intrusion in this case (Blatte, 1973)? I take issue with the neutral stance of the psychotherapist. It is not enough for the practitioner to simply "be there" for the client. The practitioner must have some accentuated awareness of how he wants to be there and how he is prepared to be there for the other. The therapist must stand for something; he must represent and embody some values. In doing so, the practitioner must disclose his presence. His presence must offer meaning to their encounter together, or else the other is left alone to find meaning in the presence of another who is denying his own values and struggles for meaning. To make informed choices, the person with whom I am working requires honest and relevant information about how I am experiencing him. It is not enough for me to "understand" and "care" for another in an encounter. A practitioner who knows what is going on with a client, psychodynamically, but is unable to foster a relationship with him, cannot meaningfully influence him. I must also express my concerns in a manner in which they can be clearly perceived and deeply felt.

*Therapeutic partnership*
*as a journey into self*

To offer to the client relevant information about how I experience him, I must allow myself to experience freely. When experiencing freely, I tend to experience the encounter situation more emotionally than when feeling comfortable. I experience choking up, giddiness, irritation, anxiety, sensuality, and other emotional reactions that are apperceptively filtered out by my more clinical and "professional" formulations and notions of certainty of what I should be attending to in a therapeutic encounter. It is only from an immediate and continuing commitment to the real possibility of a relationship with the person with whom I am involved in an encounter—a commitment that is not bracketed off by oaths of conduct, statements of clinical interest, and responsibility for the other rather than responsibility for my own intentionality—that I am aware of a deep sadness and personal loss from our separation in the world. The closer we come together, the more we are aware of our separation. The more we get in touch with that ultimate estrangement, the more we can appreciate that which we are currently sharing together and the preciousness of the present moment.

In the enduring of a risky ordeal experienced together, people come truly to know one another and develop, as a result, a genuine liking and respect for one another. At the moment at which we lose the sense of certainty and security provided by theoretical and clinical procedure, so that we can no longer predict the outcome of our being together, the possibility of a meaningful encounter lies before us. It is to the degree that the client senses (as their relationship manifests it) that the practitioner is willing and able to negotiate how the client is to be regarded and treated, that both agents within an encounter can cast aside reactive fears and the need for safety and can accommodate to each other. In so doing, each, in exploring their interpersonal situation, comes to experience himself and the other with increased meaningfulness.

The journey into self requires the presence of another. We come to know ourselves through the other. The journey in quest of meaning is, in my view, most productive in a setting in which each agent seeks an increased awareness of his own identity (Goldberg, 1976b). The habit of denying one's own values while functioning as a therapist becomes resistently entrenched in most practitioners. They have been led to believe, from their training and from reports in the literature of other practitioners, that the responsible practitioner should not want anything for himself other than to be fairly remunerated. He should only be there to deal with how the client wishes to be. For many, the exploration of the being-in-the-world of the practitioner within the encounter is an unconscionable endeavor, as if the practitioner were without existential anxiety and concern that might be decisively shaping the encounter. Practitioners often do quite some numbers on themselves and their clients in maintaining this duplicity, as may be suggested by a conversation Jane Howard, a journalist who experientially explored the encounter movement, had with Dr. Abraham Maslow, a founding father and philosopher-in-residence of the movement. Miss Howard reports Maslow telling her in a conversation: " 'Face-to-face therapy is a luxury. It's too slow and too expensive. It's not the right answer if you think as I shamelessly do, in terms of changing the whole world. We need more shortcuts. . . .' So saying, Dr. Maslow excused himself and left for an appointment with his regular Freudian analyst" (Howard, 1970, pp. 36–37).

Issues of existential concern are denied in a setting in which the therapist suppresses his own intentionality. I am in agreement with Mullan (1955) that therapists frequently impose ritualistic requirements—e.g., not speaking until the client has, answering a question with a question, leaving unclarified the statements the client makes about the "nontherapy-related" aspects of the practitioner's life—supposedly for the benefit of the client, to promote his "cure," but actually a means for the therapist to avoid his own anxiety about the common struggle he shares with his client in their mutual seeking of their own humanity. I will examine this common being-in-the-world, beginning with a parable.

Young Coyote left the reservation in search of meaning. A sense of meaning, he had been told by those older and wiser than he, was the measure by which all men need to live. Young Coyote stopped each traveler he chanced to meet upon his journey, inquiring, "I am young and ignorant, not knowing the ways of the world. I seek meaning. Have you seen it? Can you tell me where to find it?" The bewildered travelers fled from young Coyote's naive and intrusive request, regarding him as a madman. Young Coyote abandoned the day's barren promise, traveling furtively by night. He scoured the sky seeking the brightest star of all, hoping that within might lie meaning. Bright stars, he observed, faded with prolonged inspection. Young Coyote grew older and wearier in journey, but apparently not wiser. He obstinately continued his pilgrimage.

By chance, he wandered into a university city on a dry, dusty plain. Meeting a bright-eyed scholar, he again posed his query. To young Coyote's plea, the scholar replied, "Truth is that which has meaning. All else is ignorance. Truth is an ode to him who plagiarizes experience—stealing it from the world, ripping it out of context and putting it into books!" Not understanding the scholar's sage words, young Coyote continued his journey. He encountered a gray-haired theologian in silent meditation and recited his now familiar spiel. He was told with earnest conviction that that which is truly meaningful is the Eternal Hand clinging in unrest above the boiling sea of human chaos. Meaningful emotion is the everlasting Eye, lashing a Heavy Tear above the stagnant hearts of futility. Meaningful regard is the Heavenly Smile turning grotesque above the charred cities of unholiness. Being yet a simple man, young Coyote did not comprehend the theologian's reference to ultimate concern.

Pushing on, he stopped by a grove of graceful willow trees where by moonlight sat a young man with the look of unrequited love still burning in his eyes. The meaningful moment, the young lover told him, is when summer's palpitating passions turn to languish and the leaves begin to fall. Thoroughly confused, having never experienced the magic of love, young Coyote dizzily wandered through the streets in a delirium. Stumbling against an expensive imported car parked outside a professional building, young Coyote opened his weary eyes to encounter the bulky figure of a middle-aged gentleman garbed in modish clothes standing over him. The gentleman was trying to pry young Coyote's journey-soiled hands off the highly polished car. In a weak but persistent voice, young Coyote uttered once more his obsessive inquiry. "Son, I haven't time to spare, as there are others who need me, but this much I will tell you. What would be meaningful for me, would be to be there for you!" He was a psychotherapist, you see!

## The career
## of a psychotherapist

Who is young Coyote? I am young Coyote, of course! So, for that matter, are most of those with whom I work in psychotherapy! Each of us initially sought the meaning of his existence through identification with the complacency and quasisecurity of the values and proposed ways of being of the prefabricated world into which we were thrust. As we moved slowly and painfully into the world at large, we sought confirmation of these values in scholarship, religion, competition, love, and productivity. For many of us, none of these prescribed modes offered us a final or stable meaning for our being-in-the-world. We entered psychotherapy with considerable disillusionment, often as a last resort, to assume careers as patients and/or psychotherapy practitioners. As a result of psychotherapy being regarded as a last resort—the one short step before divorce, abandonment of family and family values, indeed for some, the pause prior to homicide or suicide—psychotherapy and its practitioners have obtained a unique place in modern society, rivaled only by priests and shamans of the ancient world. Yet, many claim that the practice of psychotherapy is a profitable business that is becoming ever more popular, while at the same time unverified as a productive method for promoting human happiness or alleviating personal suffering. Dr. Leon Eisenberg, a distinguished Harvard University professor of psychiatry, reported in an address to the University of Pittsburgh graduate school of public health that members of his profession have oversold the public on the accomplishments of psychiatry. According to Dr. Eisenberg, mental health statistics have been manipulated in the United States to give the impression of a high success rate in treatment. Psychiatry, he claims, has about as high a success rate among its followers as witchcraft and spiritual healing have among their believers. He reported that although psychiatrists indicate that more patients than ever are being discharged from mental hospitals, they fail to report that 30 percent to 50 percent will be readmitted within 1 year and 60 percent to 70 percent within 5 years.

Dr. Allen Bergin (1975), an eminent psychotherapy researcher, lends support for the need to question seriously the current practice of psychotherapy. He reports that evidence from personal reports of former patients, together with data from empirical studies, indicates that clients of poor therapists end up worse than those who have had no therapy. He concludes from his review of psychotherapy research "that some psychotherapists, like some drugs, should be dispensed only under the most careful controls."

Despite this criticism, it has been estimated that three-quarters of a million persons earn their livelihood by ministering to the emotionally troubled. A conservative estimate of the number of people they treat at any one time is more than 15 million people (Shepard, 1970). Private psychiatrists alone conduct about 21,120,000 psychiatric sessions a year (Sharfstein, Taube, & Goldberg, 1975). Few families in the United States have never had at least one member in some kind of psychological treatment. An estimated $1.5 billion is spent each year in this country on the services of private psychiatrists and psychologists (Trotter, 1975).

For the more seriously troubled who seek first-rate treatment, the cost is enormous. The basic hospitalization cost at Menninger Clinic in Topeka, Kansas, is $120 a day. Added to this are the initial clinical examinations, psychological testing, and neurological laboratory workshops, which cost from $800 to $1,000. Psychotherapy sessions are an additional expense; sessions cost $40 or more each and may be required four·or five times a week. The average stay at Menninger for patients with serious personality disorders is about 9 months. Other highly rated private psychiatric facilities, such as Shepard and Enoch Pratt Hospital (near Baltimore), Chestnut Lodge (near Washington, D.C.), the Institute for Living (Hartford, Conn.), and McLean Hospital (Boston), have comparable rates (Webster, 1976). These facilities have, of course, large operating costs.

A practitioner, however, can conduct a very profitable practice with very little overhead; just a room with two chairs is sufficient. He needs client referrals, of course; that is not too difficult! "In the past it seemed that one entered private practice only after a good deal of experience and if one's credentials were beyond reproach. Times have changed, and it seems that the availability of insurance money has led to the change" (Meltzer, 1975). In Washington, D.C., which probably has the highest concentration of mental health practitioners of all metropolitan areas in the country, young psychiatrists generally find that in 6 months beyond the completion of their residency in psychiatry they can fill up a private practice. Psychiatrists and clinical psychologists must, of course, first apprentice themselves for some rather extensive training, but practitioners without extensive formal training in mental health are ubiquitous these days, as well. These practitioners utilize sundry impressive titles such as "psychotherapist," "family counselor," "analyst," or "communication specialist." Of course some practitioners who employ these titles may be well-trained mental health practitioners or well-trained nonprofessionals, but it is just as likely that they have little or no training. As long as they do not employ the legally protected titles of "psychiatrist," "psychologist," or "certified social worker," there are no laws barring their practice.

One autumn Sunday I came across the following notice under the heading of "personal and business services" in The Washington Post: "Couple Counseling—Group or individual. An opportunity to explore your relationship in greater depth. Call John, Julie C . . . [a telephone number was listed]." I decided to find out what kind of counseling was available through a newspaper notice. When I called, Julie answered on the first ring. I told her that I had read the notice that morning and I was interested in knowing about their counseling services. Julie asked me to call back in a half-hour. I called back. Julie again answered the phone. She said that she would like me to talk with her husband, who was "better at explaining these things than I am." Julie, her husband told me, was getting her PhD in communications, with a specialty in interpersonal relations (believe it or not!). John told me that he had a master's degree in English and that he was competent to teach couples how to communicate better. Communication problems, he claimed, were the basis of most marital conflict. Consequently, he and his wife were qualified marital therapists.

Many critics of psychotherapy agree with John and Julie. Opponents of psychodynamic and humanistic therapies maintain that the new therapies are no better, no worse, than the old therapies. They are based on doing your own thing. "If anything you do helps you find out what your thing is, then it stands to reason that just about anyone can do it . . . [consequently] traditional training in psychotherapy is not necessarily prerequisite to the successful conduct of the new therapies" (London, 1974). In "specialized" therapies, which enjoy popular appeal, abuses are often difficult to discern because the standards of practice are generally loosely and inchoately defined. Of the 3,500 to 5,000 sex therapy clinics operating in the United States, Masters and Johnson contend that not 50 of them are conducted by therapists who are competently trained (Schief, 1975). Gestalt therapy is another therapy that enjoys a popular vogue. One practitioner, an ex-minister with training in organizational leadership and the most minimal clinical experience, sent out a mimeographed pamphlet to friends and colleagues informing them that he was interested in convening a Gestalt therapy group and he would appreciate private referrals. Other mimeographed notices for therapy and encounter groups are found on notice boards of every college campus across the nation. Similar notices are found in virtually every magazine and newspaper that carries classified advertisements.

With so much difficulty achieving appropriate criteria to evaluate the work of professional colleagues, the practitioner can hardly not expect his patients to search disconcertedly for standards to separate professional, competent treatment from incompetent treatment. In the first few months of my private practice, a couple referred to me did not return after their initial session. The lady was kind enough to write me a note, which she thought might be helpful since it was apparent that as a young doctor I must be beginning my practice. The major reason they would not return, she reported, was that I was not professional enough. My office furniture confirmed this. (I held my practice in my townhouse living room, beautifully decorated, or so my other clients reported.)

This client wrote that they had found a "real" professional at a local university (who happened to be an unlicensed psychologist). His furniture, she indicated, was leather and firm as it should be in a professional office.

## The spreading influence
of psychotherapy

At one time, psychotherapy was a specialized medical technique for only a narrow and circumscribed patient population; it is now considered to be the sine qua non application in all matters in which human suffering is involved (Small, 1971). The craft of psychotherapy is now expected to provide answers to questions about "malfunctions" in all areas of human endeavor. The twentieth century has awakened to a fervent exploration of man's psyche in all of its irrational depths. The reader need only glance at current periodicals or view cinema or television dramas to appreciate readily that most complex human problems and concerns are typically reduced to the level of psychological explanation. The ideas of Freud and his followers, though they may seem somewhat less impressive than they did two decades ago, nevertheless remain as influential in modern thought and living as the ideas of any personalities who have lived in the last century. The questions are, of course, Is this influence justified? and What are the implications of psychological reductionism and explanation?

As irresistible as the lure of being a recipient of psychotherapeutic healing for persons who have been struggling desperately for meaning in their lives, is the lure of being a psychotherapist for others who are engaged in the same struggles. Far too many people who in no other way could gain the power and influence that would be magically bestowed upon them as practitioners are drawn to the practice of psychotherapy. Many of them are rather passive and introspective people who experience no sense of real power outside the therapeutic enterprise. Therapists tend to be thinkers, not doers. They are rarely those who lead armies, build bridges, or stop riots, although they have vast quantities of information and elaborate theoretical explanations as to why others do. Unwittingly and too frequently, therapists gain a sense of personal power and achievement through identification with the exciting and sometimes bizarre activities of clients. A New York psychiatrist recently wrote a book about his seven-year treatment of a social worker.

The book, reportedly, reveals the most intimate details of the client's life, her fantasies, innermost thoughts, and sexual activities. The client sought an injunction against the distribution of the book. The therapist claimed that the book had scientific justification.

Within the therapeutic enterprise, there are manifold illusory powers that come to the therapist by virtue of his clients' transference distortions and magical hopes. For the client, the therapist becomes the most significant and powerful figure in his life; the embodiment of every person he has ever known, cared for, feared, or hoped to encounter. To one who is uncomfortable with real power, the illusory power bestowed upon him by his clients is ideal. He can choose to nurture their sentiments as genuine when they are ego-syntonic or, on the other hand, to interpret and disarm them when he becomes threatened by the client's wish to act upon these sentiments in ways uncomfortable to the therapist.

## Cultism
## in psychotherapy

"Senate investigations have discovered that the Defense Department is paying for treatment of emotionally disturbed children of military personnel that includes beatings, burying children in shallow graves and injecting them with their own urine," reported *The Washington Post* recently.

In recent years these heinous excuses for psychological treatment and countless other manifestly less rank abuses have resulted in considerable criticism and dissatisfaction directed against the practice of psychotherapy. Increasingly, the psychotherapy establishment has been questioned sharply about lapses in intellectual, moral, and scientific integrity. Perry London (1964) has stated the issue rather clearly: "A detailed examination of the surfeit of schools and theories, of practices and practitioners that compete with each other conceptually and economically, shows vagaries which, taken all at once, make unclear what it is that psychotherapists do, or to whom, or why" (p. v).

Common sense dictates that psychotherapy requires the highest degree of flexibility of approaches. The practice of cultism and psychological witch-hunting in psychotherapy that I will describe in the following pages strongly militate against intellectual and therapeutic flexibility. I am concerned that there are practitioners who utilize a limited repertoire of methodologies and who are intellectually and emotionally limited in their appreciation of the diverse treatment philosophies available, yet willingly accept any one who requests treatment from them.

Unlike professional disciplines that treat circumscribed areas of human functioning, psychotherapy treats the whole man. To encompass the whole of human functioning in all its complexities would require an encyclopedic knowledge and a vast diversity of skills few persons could ever achieve. The psychotherapist, therefore, must simplify his complex task by reducing all of a man's concerns to the level of psychological functioning viewed in terms of a belief system the therapist has found to provide a plausible explanation for human behavior. Such a belief system is not objectively arrived at nor impersonally maintained. In his attachment to his professional belief system, the psychotherapist stands in sharp contrast to other helping professionals. The physician's hallmark is his proficiency in acquiring technical skill in diagnosing and treating organ dysfunction. Rarely do physicians develop an emotional attachment to their professional technology as do psychotherapists. Similarly, whereas attorneys may develop a rather pronounced social and legal philosophy, unless they become active politically (which is, of course, outside their professional roles as attorneys), they are not generally known to become emotionally imbued disciples of a legal mentor. The practice of psychotherapy issues more from the personality and temperament of the practitioner than from a body of ideas or technical procedures. In this respect, then, the psychotherapist's practice is radically different from that of medical healing (Szasz, 1969) or legal counseling.

Among the helping professionals, only the clergyman parallels the psychotherapist in an attempt to treat the whole man. Both identify emotionally with a body of professional aims and beliefs in such a way as to perpetuate a cult or a religion. In an address at the American Psychiatric Association conference in Dallas, Texas, May 2, 1972, Dr. Fuller Torrey pointed out:

> Over the past twenty-five years the number of primary mental health personnel . . . has increased from 14,000 to 100,000. Simultaneously, the number of ministers and priests has decreased from 250,000 to 200,000. Three examples of previous functions of organized religion that are now being assumed by organized mental health are: (1) explanation of the unknown, such as the behavior of strange persons; (2) ritual and

social function—instead of going to church, people go to their weekly groups; (3) the definition of values—who defines what is right and wrong.

In short, whereas religious teachings, and rituals formerly were employed to set standards of socially acceptable behavior, now what are regarded as "psychologically healthy" attitudes and practices have been substituted.

There are a number of significant ways in which therapeutic cultism shapes the practice of psychotherapy. The reader might think it strange for one attorney to discourage a client from consulting with a second attorney because the second attorney belonged to a particular school of legal philosophy. He would expect the first attorney to be more likely to base his advice on the other counselor's intelligence, legal ability, experience, or ethical reputation, in conjunction with his availability and fee. Yet in the practice of psychotherapy, intense personal arguments among psychotherapists have, as London (1964) indicates: "given rise historically to a large number of schools, some of which feel so strongly about their differences that they avoid contact or interaction with members of rival camps" (p. 44). London cites an example of a Freudian-oriented practitioner telling a client to prevent his wife from conferring with a Jungian analyst because "we can't have two kinds of therapy going on in the same family" (p. 44). Several years ago I treated a clinical psychology graduate student whose father-in-law was a well-known Baltimore training analyst. She described him as existing in a psychoanalytic ghetto. He analyzed the same seven or eight patients five or six times a week for several years. All of his "patients" were psychiatrists who were candidates at the analytic institute at which he taught. His social and personal life was also insulated from the nonanalytic world. At the theatre or opera he was always in the company of other analysts and their wives. This analytic ensemble would sit together, oblivious to what was going on around them.

Cultism among psychotherapists and psychological reductionism and explanation are closely related. For every disturbing societal event the psychologist can offer a psychological cause and a plausible explanation. The man in the street has become increasingly attracted to these explanations. They offer him some semblance of order and meaning in an otherwise inexplicable world. In the past, the man in the street was offered theological and, later, natural-science explanations of his human condition.

It may be useful to give some attention to the emerging importance of psychological theory and explanation. It is generally agreed that psychological theory rose to prominence in the second half of the nineteenth century. The view that prevailed in the nineteenth century prior to Freud was that the criminal and the mentally ill possessed a malignant, inscrutable disease that prevented them from behaving as rational human beings. This ontological view stemmed from a world sobered by scientific nihilism based on unswaying determinism, reinforced by witness to revolutionary and universally devastating war. Theological and scientific explanations had failed to offer resolute life strategies for dealing with personal dissatisfaction. They were equally unsuccessful in resolving societal conflict.

Psychoanalysis was a double protest against the prevailing concept of the nature of man. Freud rejected the view that mental disturbance was due to disease or to the genetic makeup of the individual. He protested no less vehemently against the doctrine of free will that held that a man can make conscious choices between good and evil in selecting a course of action. The idea of free will persisted in the theology and in much of the philosophy of Freud's day despite the nihilism of science. Freud thought behavior was determined by unconscious strivings. The mentally disturbed adult behaves irrationally because of childhood experiences that operate unconsciously upon him. Freud claimed a clinician is able to understand a disturbed person's actions by being able to discern the unconscious forces behind his behavior. More important, if the clinician is able to induce the patient to bring his childhood experiences and fantasies into consciousness, insight the patient gains into his own disturbances makes it possible for him to deal rationally with his situation. Hence, in Freud's view, mental illness was determined, comprehensible, and subject to therapeutic correction.

The psychological revolution was the third of four world ideological revolutions. The First World War ended for all practical purposes the rule of monarchial government by the will of God and Church. The Second World War demonstrated the inability of the scientific knowledge of industrial nations to control each other's destructive power. The Vietnam War was for the United States a fourth revolution. It was an individualistic and existential struggle in the sense that the collective beliefs in patriotism and governmental authority gradually eroded during the dragged-out course of the war. Citizens increasingly held their leaders personally accountable for their behavior, while at the same time demanding a shared responsibility for the conduct of government. Young people in large numbers altered their lifestyles, many gave up their citizenship, in a desperate striving for an authenticity of purpose and a personal commitment to try to live harmoniously with others.

The striving for authenticity has had a pervasive influence on the current practice of psychotherapy. The search for authenticity has become, for increasing numbers of practitioners, the purpose of their professional and personal endeavors. In reaction to the overemphasis on reason in the past, there is today a fervent concern with authenticity and personal commitment in the field of psychotherapy. This is not to suggest that the therapeutic stances formulated in one era are necessarily obsolete in the next. Many of the basic concerns therapists and patients are struggling with have plagued the therapeutic relationship since the dawn of therapeutic practice. Nonetheless, how these concerns are expressed and dealt with is determined by the particular resources and conditions in any particular period in history (Goldberg, 1975b). Schools of psychotherapy are products of cultural and historical periods. Many contemporary practitioners view the therapies of yesteryear and the psychological vehicles they offer for self-actualization as too limited and inefficacious for the conditions of contemporary society. These practitioners have come to band together in various schools of psychotherapy to offer their clients and society, in general, what they regard as more appropriate and efficacious explanations and modes of amelioration of personal and societal ills (see Chapter 11 for more detail).

In recent years, these rival camps of psychotherapy have switched from promoting clearly articulated belief systems (see Chapter 11) to promoting provocative techniques and psychological games, which are given ad hoc explanations and justifications. Conditions in the field of psychotherapy are fertile for this practice. Bergin (1975) points out, "Nothing prevents a licensed practitioner [or an unlicensed practitioner, for that matter] from discovering a new technique, making great claims for its curative powers, and using it indiscriminatingly on his clients." These new techniques and their belief systems, together with the message that they are superior to the techniques and beliefs of other schools of psychotherapy, are indoctrinated in students and trainees in the various psychotherapy institutes, professional workshops, conferences, and lectures. The battlegrounds for confirming the superiority of these rival psychotherapies are the various clinical settings in which clients are captive subjects. One practitioner in a public mental health clinic in which I worked agreed to treat only patients who would agree to primal scream therapy.

*Psychological*
*witch-hunting*

Not only do practitioners become promoters of their own psychotherapeutic dogma, but unfortunately, they sometimes become self-appointed psychological witch-hunters who, in identifying with conventional practices in the field, defend and guard these practices from the encroachment of other ideas, methodologies, and professional styles. Admittedly, psychological witch-hunters occasionally render the general public a service by exposing and dramatizing the practice of quacks, exploiters, and charlatans, but more frequently they do their colleagues and the general public a disservice. Their overly moralistic and judgmental attitudes cause them to view all professional practices as either strictly proper or strictly improper. Intelligent and productive dialogue among practitioners of varying persuasions is aborted by psychological witch-hunting. For those who are searching for skills to deal openly with their own and their clients' concerns, the psychological witch-hunter serves as an aversive role model who diverts self-doubts by projection and externalization.

Several years ago, my wife and I were asked to conduct a professional workshop for mental health practitioners in a university community in the Northeast. The chairman of the psychology department of the medical school in the area was aware that several of his former students and present colleagues had received training from us. His orientation to psychotherapy and psychotherapy education was rather divergent from ours. Since he had received extremely favorable reactions to our work from his students and colleagues, this distinguished psychologist apparently believed that we had beguiled them in some manner. He endeavored to uncover our fraud. He signed up for our workshop and brought with him several colleagues of his own persuasion. He spent most of his time in the workshop arguing and trying to discredit our work. Although his efforts were actually rather pathetic, so much time and energy was spent with him and with the belligerent colleagues he brought with him that the other participants were deprived of a productive workshop. They were furious at him. We were told later that he frequently does this sort of thing. His colleagues have come to expect it of him. But what of the impact this witch-hunter has as a role model of the psychotherapy enterprise upon the scores of students, trainees, and other professionals who encounter him each year?

Some years ago, I had another experience with a psychological witch-hunter. I was a guest lecturer on the S.S. *France,* and was asked to conduct a lecture-demonstration on the new group therapies that were in vogue at the time. Because I was not then an enthusiastic proponent of encounter therapies, I carefully explored what I regarded as the limitations and dangers in the movement as well as the options it offered to conventional psychotherapy. I was asked by members of the audience for an opportunity to experience sensitivity training exercises. Before moving into a demonstration, I expressed my contract with the participants at the lecture: The demonstration would not be therapy, a substitute for therapy, or even a demonstration of psychotherapy. Rather, I would be demonstrating a few nonstressful interpersonal exercises with those participants who wished to try them in order to explore various ways of communicating with other participants. These exercises would require minimal self-disclosure.

A heavy-jowled, stocky, middle-aged man stood up in back of the room, waving a pen and a writing pad in a menacing gesture. He identified himself as a member of a Midwest psychoanalytic society, but refused to give me his name or profession. He reported that the society he claimed to represent was "concerned about 'groups' like this" (implying that I was conducting a group). He predicted that several dangerous (but unspecified) events would occur in the "group." He was promptly and angrily dismissed by the participants. He sat down, apparently annoyed at not being taken seriously by the audience, but undaunted, jumped to his feet again and announced that he would be "taking notes for the ethics committee." He refused to specify to which ethics committee he was referring. I, with unquestionably mixed emotions, indicated to the participants that while I was sorely annoyed at the manner in which he chose to interact in the "group" and at the arbitrary, paternalistic, and authoritarian manner he was assuming, the participants should consider his cautions. Several people in the audience indicated that they considered themselves sensible, mature adults, intelligent enough not to participate in anything that would be dangerous to them. An older lady said that what I was doing (so far the participants were only talking) was not dangerous but complete nonsense and she would have no part of it. However, she remained to observe. I completed the demonstration and discussion with the witch-hunter sitting in back of the room taking copious notes. I never heard from him or from any ethics committee.

I have always wondered how such representatives of the psychotherapy profession as this witch-hunter and others like him serve the lay public that observes their strange behavior. I cannot help believing that, for the prospective therapy client, the witch-hunter casts the therapist as a soldier of the faith who utilizes his clients as a means to reaffirm his faith in a holy war. His demeanor, at any rate, contradicts the sentiments of choice and open dialogue most practitioners profess to promulgate.

Witch-hunting, moreover, enables adherents of conventional practices to avoid the demands of their clients to address limitations in their methodologies and belief systems. It allows them to remain who and what they believe themselves to be. In this posture they are able to rationalize whatever failures their clients experience in therapy as failures in their clients' character and motivation.

Implicit in our discussion of cultism and witch-hunting are the dimensions of influence and power in the practice of psychotherapy.

## The unspoken dimension of power in psychotherapy

If there is a single characteristic common to all who seek psychotherapy, it is the sense of loss or absence of personal power, with the concomitant sense of lost adequacy. Psychotherapists appear to agree that despite the diversity of symptoms and complaints clients present upon entering treatment, the common feeling is one of self-denigration. The psychotherapeutic experience is designed to supplement the client's natural group associations where they have failed to meet his needs adequately (see Chapter 11). Psychotherapy is devised precisely to resist rules and directives that have frustrated the client's previous attempts at a consistent and gratifying conceptualization of self. This section is intended to give the reader a greater appreciation of the significance therapist-patient power struggles have in the course of psychotherapy.

It is the nature of human interaction that people try to influence one another. Many of these endeavors are conducted in such a way that people can choose whether or not they will be influenced. In many other situations, however, people have little or no choice about the nature and the impact of how others will try to influence them. In which category is psychotherapy? As an influence process, is psychotherapy a democratic or equalitarian endeavor, as many of its practitioners claim? Are therapist-client struggles for control, therefore, essentially attributable to transference and countertransference distortions? Or are these struggles more frequently the sine qua non of interpersonal relations, without which psychotherapy would represent a pale imitation of social reality?

Power dynamics should be a basic concern in the conduct of psychotherapy. Power in psychotherapy refers to the awesome capability the therapist is given by the client (reinforced by societal sanctions) to affect his life and the lives of others who, though not clients of the therapist, live within the societal system of the client who is being treated (Gelb, 1972). In my view, neither theorists nor practitioners of psychotherapy have given sufficient attention to the issue of power in psychotherapy; for the most part, it remains an unacknowledged dimension.

Three analysts (Gadpaille, 1972; Gelb, 1972; Enelow, 1972) who have concerned themselves with the denial of power in the conduct of psychotherapy argue that an important reason for failures in psychoanalytic therapy has to do with the analyst ignoring the patient's distorted and often exploitative interpersonal relationships with people in his social system. Because of the focus on the patient's internal psychological processes, the mainfestation of the patient's conflictual interpersonal relations may be less appreciated in an analytic situation than it can be in a psychotherapy in which interactions are encouraged. In this chapter, I will limit my discussion of power relations to the denial of power struggles within the therapist-client relationship. I believe that this denial supports a basic dishonesty that contradicts the ideals of autonomy, informed choice, and psychological freedom that psychotherapy as an enterprise manifestly purports to engender.

In New York City, a few years ago, I was a participant in a workshop for experienced group psychotherapists. The workshop dealt with the rationale and technique of group supervision. The workshop leader was a renowned and rather strong-willed female analyst. Several other participants and I were disconcerted by the direction the workshop had taken. The workshop leader had told us that the workshop was ours (the participants'). It was all right with her, she said, to discuss whatever topic we wished and to explore these topics in any way we wanted. Nonetheless, it appeared rather difficult if not impossible to launch into issues that some of the participants wanted to explore. Toward questions of procedural direction raised by the participants, the workshop leader offered psychodynamic explanations categorically supporting or denying the usefulness of our comments for the consideration of what was transpiring in the workshop.

The most salient issue that was shaping the covert tensions and the direction the workshop had taken, it seemed to me, was the workshop leader's use of power. When I pointed this out to her, she became rather annoyed. She indicated that "power has no importance in psychotherapy. Psychotherapy is an almost democratic process. We must always deal fairly with our patients—otherwise it is a counter-transference problem. It needs to be worked out in the therapist's own analysis. But I don't want to talk any more about power. It is not important. Let us talk about other things!" The concept of power seemed repugnant to her. The struggle for power was essentially the client's problem, not that of the therapist.

Was the workshop leader correct in describing psychotherapy as an almost democratic enterprise? I was struck by the modifier "almost." To me the term "almost democratic" conceded a threat, a fear, and a cover-up by the analyst and the therapeutic orientation that she represented. This orientation suggested to me that the therapist and clients are equal, but like some of the creatures in Orwell's *Animal Farm,* the therapist is just a little more equal and just a little more knowledgeable about the direction the therapeutic relationship should take than are his clients. It is this inherent imbalance that gives the therapist the right to be less than equitable with his clients. If my inference is valid, then it seems to me that the psychotherapist, operating from this orientation, is espousing a hypocritical status denial. The psychotherapist says implicitly to his clients, "We are all in this situation together—to learn and grow. Just because you people pay a fee and I collect it, doesn't necessarily mean that I am different or better than you. You must realize that I, like you, need to eat and provide for myself. You experience yourself as not being able to deal with your condition because you essentially feel powerless. But, then, I don't feel that way about myself. I don't feel powerless as long as you believe and act upon the notion that I am worthy of being paid and continue to look to me for help. I guess, then, maybe we're not alike after all!"

The clinical conferences I attended as a clinical psychology intern at a large, psychoanalytically oriented New York City hospital had the fascination of a political trial following the French Revolution. The patient who was the subject of the conference was regarded as not quite human—something alien, someone to intellectually trap and observe. There was an aura of the patient having done something dastardly. Each of the clinicians present seemed eager to dissect these forbidden deeds in terms of theoretical concepts and dynamic explanations. A subdued but persistent animosity was directed not only at the patient but toward one another, as well. At times, there was a rather vitriolic intellectual sparring among the clinicians for the most cogent explanations of the patient's illness. Unfortunately, so much time and energy were devoted to diagnosing and tracing the patient's presenting problem back to his developmental history that treatment plans were only cursorily touched upon. I felt like the only person in the room who was concerned with the question, Given what we know about this person, how are we going to help him? Peter Marin (1975) has indicated in an insightful article about the current psychotherapy fads that "we [therapists] struggle mightily to convince ourselves that our privilege is earned or deserved, rather than [as we must often wonder whether our therapies are at times] a form of murder or theft. Our therapies [have] become a way of hiding from the world, a way of easing our troubled conscience."

A renowned, existentially oriented psychiatrist who supervised some of my clinical work while I was in training told patients in their first interview that if they terminated treatment before he thought they were ready, he would not allow them to return to work with him. As a supervisor, he insisted that the supervisee conduct psychotherapy in keeping with his rather specific ideas about how treatment should be conducted. Ironically, this same practitioner wrote extensively indicting the medical model for assuming responsibility for the patient, and he also popularized the concept of status denial in psychiatry. Obviously, this psychiatrist was more power-oriented than he let on.

Jay Haley is notable as one of the few psychotherapists who has publicly spoken out against the generally implicit and complex use and abuse of power in psychotherapy. According to Haley (1969), the traditional psychotherapeutic situation is designed to render the superior position of the therapist virtually invincible to the stratagems of the client. In many instances, the therapeutic situation is even designed to prevent clients from using effective interpersonal strategies in the therapeutic relationship in order to establish an equitable and balanced relationship with their therapist. A client I worked with after he had spent over half of his 30 years in various Southern prisons and forensic hospital units told me that he gained his release by submitting to weekly electric shock therapy sessions. By no stretch of anyone's theoretical position was this "McMurphy"[1] client a candidate for such treatments. *The Washington Post* reported the case of an employee of the federal government who refused her supervisor's order that she see her agency's psychiatrist. The psychiatrist concluded, without ever having seen her, that her refusal to consult him was a symptom of paranoid schizophrenia. She was fired immediately without a hearing.

Much therapeutic and clinical data provide abundant evidence that therapists and their clients are frequently, if not inevitably, involved in point-counterpoint power maneuvers with one another. In this process, the psychotherapist may become threatened by the client's manipulations. In turn, as Haley has forcefully described in his 1969 book, the therapist may revert to reactive manipulation of the patient and his situation in order to regain control over the therapeutic enterprise and thus diminish the threat to his reputation and to his sense of adequacy as a therapist. Occasionally a therapist becomes so frightened, angry, and vindictive that he is unwilling or unable to examine critically the irrational, reactive posture he has assumed toward his client's power ploys.

One of the most potent and frightening power tactics employed by clients is the threat of suicide. Psychotherapists often experience their reputations, self-esteem, and sense of adequacy as integrally linked to their effectiveness in checkmating the client's suicide threat. At least one well-known psychotherapist prefers to regard his manipulative therapeutic strategies as intentional, clinically indicated techniques rather than as emotional reactions to his clients' power ploys. This therapist, who undoubtedly represents countless other therapists who have the need to deny their own emotional reaction to client power, says, "Humanitarian fervor aside, it's the therapist's job to take power over the patient, push ahead with solving the problem, then convince the patient he or she is better, even if it means being devious. He can develop ploys beyond the wildest dream of a car salesman. One is to

---

[1] McMurphy is the protagonist in the book and the movie *One Flew Over the Cuckoo's Nest.*

make patients work or suffer to get into therapy and so increase their belief in its value" (Gillis, 1974).

The following are just three provocative examples of the checkmates that therapists with a manipulative orientation employ to invalidate a client's suicidal power ploy: A client calls his therapist late one night and tells him that he is seriously contemplating suicide. The therapist tells him to come to his office the next morning and not to take any action until he sees him. As the client enters the office, the therapist greets him with: "You are going right into the hospital and you are not coming out until I have some assurance that you have stopped acting like a child!" Or, he may say: "Threaten me with suicide, you bastard, I'll make you a promise, if you succeed and kill yourself, I'll go over to your grave and piss on it. Just keep that in mind." Or, the therapist may say: "Look, friend, my practice is confined to patients who want to work on their problems. I won't stand for your wasting my time nor with threatening me with suicide. If you are to continue to work with me, I will insist that you secure a life insurance policy that names me the beneficiary." These ploys have been used by several experienced psychotherapists of my acquaintance. The first of them is so ubiquitously employed by therapists that the strategy has long since attained the stature of a clinically indicated technique, which, nonetheless, doesn't alter the fact that it is a very powerful and often devastating checkmate.

There are those practitioners who not only refuse to give in to their clients' power ploys, but actually seem to enjoy the challenge of a client's suicide threat. One such practitioner refers to himself as a humanistic guru. One of his clients called me not long ago. The client was a psychotherapist himself, and had worked with me as a colleague a number of years before. He told me in a rather agitated conversation that he had been seeing this guru psychologist for a couple of years. In the past year or so he had become increasingly more depressed and suicidal. He had even bought a second-hand pistol. He told his therapist that he felt so worthless and confused that he had been seriously considering going out into the woods and putting the pistol to his head and blowing his brains out. His guru reacted with a barrage of abusive and denigrating statements, telling him that he was clearly a coward and probably a fag as well. Indeed, the therapist emphasized, this opportunity might be the client's moment of truth—a test to see if he had any guts. The client faced his moment of truth. He fulfilled his fantasy and put the gun to his head and pulled the trigger. Apparently the gun was in poor condition; fortunately, it didn't fire. Was this moment of truth a productive growth experience for the client? He didn't think so. He hadn't resolved the issues for which he came into therapy, and now he had to struggle with additional rage, confusion, and fright about the power he had given the therapist over his life. Those who deny that power is a significant unspoken issue in psychotherapy would undoubtedly write off the above illustration as the flare-up in the guru of serious and unresolved feelings of counter-transference. Whether or not the issue is simply one of countertransference, innumerable cases I can cite suggest that the use and potential abuse of power is central to the therapeutic relationship and frequently lies at the heart of the covert tensions.

Many therapists are anxious to avoid employing checkmating power strategies that divest the client of his power and his sense of adequacy. They realize that a therapist cannot be a useful agent for his client if he cares too much whether or not the client succeeds. If the therapist cares too much—indeed cares more than the client cares for himself—the client can manipulate the therapist's caring in order to retain neurotic and psychopathic patterns. This creates a situation in which the therapist is the center of the therapeutic process and the one who determines therapeutic success. The psychotherapy is based upon the therapist's choices and their consequences rather than upon those of the client.

Adding to the problem of power is the fact that, whereas a practitioner may be anxious to avoid abusing his power in a therapeutic relationship, the clients frequently wish to divest themselves of power and adequacy in dealing with their life situation, leaving themselves incapable of taking care of themselves. The following case accords with Thibaut and Kelley's (1959) concept of *dyadic connection*, indicating that in a stressful interpersonal situation in which a client experiences himself as having no direct control over his own outcomes, he can use his ability to act in a dysfunctional manner to control the other's outcome so as to influence his own payoffs, i.e., have the other take care of him. In psychodynamic terms, this is referred to as *secondary gain*. The psychotherapist is placed in the bind of having to choose whether to take care of the client—in many instances, as in the following case, with personal loss to himself—or to withhold from the client the psychological attention he acutely requires.

A hippish-sounding 25-year-old woman telephoned a therapist, whose name she had gotten from a hot line referral service. The woman stated that she had been in treatment for over 2 years with a rather passive female social worker who simply interpreted her behavior and at the same time let her avoid issues with which the client felt she needed to deal actively. The client claimed that she needed a confrontive therapist. However, she was not currently working and could not afford the therapist's full fee, though she expected to get a job and health insurance shortly. The therapist agreed to see her at a reduced fee set during the initial interview. There were three sessions. They agreed that the client would pay at the time of each session because the client had difficulty budgeting her money. At the third session, the client reported that she had forgotten to bring a check. The therapist indicated that according to their agreement he would need to receive a check before he would schedule another session. She agreed to mail him a check that day. A week later no check had arrived. The client called and said that she had been raped that week and needed to see the therapist. The therapist agreed to see her but sheepishly pointed out that she had not complied with her agreement. The client angrily indicated that she had lost her job and wouldn't be able to pay for that session either, and she reproached the therapist for his materialistic attitude. The client did not show up for the scheduled appointment. She called later that day, saying that she had been detained at the police station concerning the rape. She asked not to be charged for the session since she couldn't afford the money and she especially needed help then.

It is my impression that what traditionally has been regarded as unethical therapist behavior frequently occurs at this kind of juncture in the therapist-client relationship in which a client fails to keep payment aspects of the contract. The therapist, feeling exploited and used, may ask implicitly or explicitly to be repaid in love for his caring and taking care of the client. In this way the therapist tries to regain equity and balance for himself. I am speaking here of *love treatment,* whether it involves sexual intimacy or not. Love treatment refers to potentially very potent abuses of the therapist's power. People who can in perhaps no other way gain the power, influence, and love they can as therapists are drawn to the field of psychotherapy. To avoid slipping into the exchange of love for caring, there is a need for clarity about the specific goals therapist and client have for being in a therapeutic encounter.

The exchange of a fee for a service, as materialistic as it may appear, serves to reinforce the essential notion that psychotherapy is an exchange that benefits both agents. Without a clear reciprocal consequence for the practitioner's involvement, there is often confusion about why the agents are involved in an encounter, and a firm understanding about fees can help to avoid this.

The following case raises further questions about the soundness of clinical and ethical considerations from which mental health workers operate and the difficulties involved in ascertaining these frames of reference. The case may appear unusual, but probably is not unique.

A rather attractive, slim, and demure 24-year-old woman, with long blonde hair worn loosely, walked anxiously into a county mental health clinic in Maryland. She reported to the intake worker at the clinic that she had a rather embarrassing concern about which she needed some information. After considerable probing, the intake worker was able to ascertain that the young woman had been receiving premarital counseling without fee from a young minister in the community. She felt rather upset and confused about the direction the counseling sessions had taken. Not having had any counseling or psychotherapy before this, she did not know what was expected and proper in such sessions. The minister had told her only that she might discuss whatever she liked. Apparently, by means of subtle and effective persuasion, the minister had convinced her to doff her clothes. The minister had claimed that an authentic and meaningful dialogue could best be developed by setting aside superficial barriers. The last two sessions were conducted in the nude.

Are there clear, ethical guidelines governing the case cited above? What are the responsibilities of the clinic to which the young woman went for help? The minister was not a licensed psychotherapist. Was his behavior illegal, immoral, or even ineffectual psychotherapy? A number of claims have been made for the effectiveness of nude encounters in psychotherapy (Bindram, 1968). Even well-known practitioners with all the proper degrees and professional qualifications have been known to require that female clients strip and walk around the room nude before being accepted as clients. Professional colleagues who have been clients of such therapists claim that they do competent therapeutic work. One psychiatrist tried to persuade his more attractive female patients that a sexual relationship would intensify their transference relationship and make progress in psychotherapy speedier.

On the other hand, at least as many claims have been made for the dangers and ineffectiveness of nude encounters. Should the director of the mental health clinic to whose attention this matter was brought have assessed the minister's conduct in terms of professional ethics (despite the fact that he was not a professional therapist), or should he have reported him to some authority (who?), or for that matter, did the staff at the clinic have a right to tell the young woman that she should stop seeing her minister? The answers to these questions on the use of power and influence are not obvious. Perhaps the most crucial question that these cases raise is also reflected in Hans Huessy's statement about ethical concerns in the conduct of psychotherapy:

> I suspect that instead of finding too many kinds of gross abuses, the more difficult problem that [needs to be addressed] is how is the decision made as to what kinds of therapy are used for what kinds of patients. The caricature of American psychiatry and psychology is that the treatment is not determined by the patient's ailment but by the therapist's predilection. (personal communication)

For the therapist whose sense of personal adequacy is well integrated, the transference phenomena reflected in the cases I have cited serve as a useful therapeutic dimension. For the therapist who doubts his own adequacy and avoids critically assessing his illusory powers, however, the potential for abuse is serious and manifold. He is apt to feel, "Maybe I am lovable and desirable after all. Maybe it is not the patient's distortion, but that *he knows something others cannot or will not see. I must hold on to him because he makes me feel powerful and adequate!*"

# chapter 5

# Restoring power
# to the client

The patient should be educated to liberate and
fulfill his own nature, not to resemble ourselves.

— Sigmund Freud

Near Union Station in the District of Columbia in 1973, a young,
upper-middle-class, college-educated woman who had had several
psychiatric hospitalizations was found brutally raped and murdered.
The previous day a concerned reporter from a local newspaper had
found her wandering along the streets in a dazed and confused state. He
drove her to Saint Elizabeth's Hospital, hoping that someone there
would commit her to the hospital and give her appropriate psychiatric
care. A federal court had, shortly prior to this incident, rendered some
strongly worded decisions on involuntary psychiatric commitment; the
staff of Saint Elizabeth's Hospital was commanded by the court not to
commit unwilling patients to the hospital unless the admitting physician could discern psychiatric evidence that the patient to be admitted
was a clear danger to his or herself and/or others. Although the admitting psychiatrist recognized that the woman was suffering from severe
psychiatric problems, he evidently did not detect evidence that she was
a clear danger to herself or to the community, so he tried to persuade her
to sign in as a voluntary patient. She refused. The physician, reluctantly, permitted her to leave the hospital.

Undoubtedly, some readers may claim that the psychiatrist was
abdicating his professional responsibility in not taking the woman into
psychiatric custody. A considerable number of lawyers and mental
health workers who have identified themselves with the movement for
the civil rights of psychiatric patients have argued that, while this case is
an unfortunate tragedy, the psychiatrist was actually highly responsible
in safeguarding the rights of thousands of other patients who, while   91

suffering from psychiatric problems, will never prove themselves a danger to others or be murdered. Bared to its core, the crucial issue posed by this case and scores of others raised earlier is: How far should we go in trying to help others? And what are our obligations and the limits of our obligations?

*The power*
*of the client*

Too many people enter psychotherapy without giving sufficient consideration to the complex and risky nature of psychotherapeutic experience. Practitioners are vastly different in style, training, and competence. On the other hand, there are few reliable guidelines prospective clients have available to assess the appropriateness of therapeutic programs. It is for these reasons that I have developed a guide for clients in selecting a therapist and formulating a therapeutic contract (see Appendix A). It is hoped that this rationale will restore the client's power in exploring therapeutic options. In this section I will present several significant problems that are incurred when a therapeutic partnership is absent from a therapeutic relationship.

I am concerned with my power, real and illusory, in the therapeutic situation and with its potential for abuse and for amelioration. In developing guidelines to evaluate the conduct of psychotherapy, peer review committees should be obliged to consider seriously and come to understand the dimension of power in the therapeutic relationship. To do this, we must first realize that the power in the therapeutic relationship essentially rests with the client. It is the client who gave the therapist his illusory power.

In discussing the power of the client, we must keep in mind the circumstances that bring client and therapist together. A person in the throes of confused agitation, who has been thwarted in seeking help, experiences himself as having little or no personal power or adequacy. His attempts at providing himself with solace and understanding have been repeatedly rebuked by friends and relatives. How he decides to seek psychotherapy and how he is treated in the search are crucial to the course of psychotherapy that follows. Any exploration of psychotherapy as an endeavor to increase the individual's capacity to choose must deal with the problem of how the client selects a psychotherapy practitioner with whom he can work efficaciously. This selection can be rather difficult for the prospective therapy client. In his search for psychological assistance, he may feel like a ship in a storm.

The plight of Joan, an airline stewardess who works for a transatlantic airline, illustrates the difficulties of some quests for a competent practitioner. Joan was told by the first psychiatrist she phoned that she could not be seen for an appointment for at least several weeks. Various mental health clinics she contacted referred her to residents, interns, and trainees who, she perceived, knew as little about what was going on with her as she did herself. She then consulted a Reichian practitioner who put her in an orgone box and furnished her with a pillow, into which she was requested to scream. Joan next sought out a Rolfist therapist who forcefully massaged her stomach, pressing out what he referred to as the "negative energy" in her muscles. She then conferred with an Eastern swami who advised her that sexual relations are unhealthy and that she should practice celibacy and turn her mind to meditation. Failing to experience help from all these people who purported to practice psychological healing, Joan tried acupuncture, also without discernible success (Morgan, 1974).

Although Joan felt neglected, disregarded, and powerless to get competent psychological assistance, the experienced practitioner knows that the client, though he doesn't realize it, holds a potent power over the therapist. He may never share this knowledge with the client, which is rather unfortunate. The client's inherent power threatens the therapist's status, reputation, and financial livelihood because, without clients, psychotherapists would have to find other sources for these commodities.

Naturally, there is a direct relationship in how the therapist employs his therapeutic role and the degree of power and freedom the client experiences in negotiating his own role in the therapeutic relationship. Agel (1971) has drawn an important distinction between therapeutic *skill* and therapeutic *role*. Therapeutic skills are useful in making available to the client an understanding of his behavior; the therapeutic role contributes to the privileged and nonaccountable status of the therapist, enhances the mystique of the therapeutic relationship, and prevents the client from effectively utilizing his personal power. This effect on the client's use of power is perhaps seen most clearly in the interactions between client and therapist of different socioeconomic backgrounds, but it is inherent in most therapeutic encounters (even when there are similarities in socioeconomic status). The verbal symbols the practitioner employs may serve to put the client on guard rather than help to establish a meaningful human encounter because the practitioner's symbols often imply, to the client, diagnosis and evaluation. It is difficult for a client to maintain a balanced relationship with a therapist when he feels that his behavior is regularly regarded as inappropriate. Because the therapist "knows" what is appropriate and the client doesn't, the client's feelings of self-denigration and impotence are exacerbated (Goldberg & Kane, 1974b).

People differ in their abilities; psychotherapy will not make them equal. Psychotherapeutic experience should, however, promote a fuller realization of how each person uses, and tries to deny the use of, his own power. Due to the unwillingness of professional psychotherapists to explore openly the dimension of power in their dealings with clients, a number of laymen (e.g., Ringer, 1975; Korda, 1975) and a pair of psychologists (Alberti & Emmons, 1975) have published books that purport to offer training in assertiveness and adequate use of power. Many female clients, believing that they, even more than male clients, are deprived of their power by male therapists, have turned to consciousness-raising groups, conducted by female leaders for female participants only.

The client's power, if realized and utilized, could transform the practice of psychotherapy—now characterized by generally unimpressive rates of success—into a more meaningful, equitable, and viable endeavor. From an idealized, ethical point of view, the client, as a purchaser, has the inherent right, or power, to define what he requires from a therapeutic relationship. In reality, though, the client's desperate hope that the magic of the therapist will make things right again usually subverts the rational use of the client's power. He opts to barter his rationality and his power in exchange for the innocence of the child and the protection of a powerful ally, the therapist. The following therapeutic situation is a good example.

After 5 years of 5-times-a-week treatment, a middle-aged woman consulted a second analyst. She told him that she was more depressed than when she first consulted her analyst. After 2 or 3 years in analysis, she had a rather serious back operation and was bedridden for 3 months. Her analyst continued to charge her $55 an hour for each of her 5 weekly sessions for the entire period during which she could not attend them. Her physician-husband paid the bill without question. The second analyst recommended that she consider changing therapists.

She wrote back that she was going back to the first analyst in order to work out her "negative transference" and her analyst's anger at her. He was quite offended that she had sought a consultation.

In order to establish guidelines for the practice of psychotherapy, practitioners need to develop models that recognize the tendency to distort human relationships (Mullan, 1955) yet take a positive approach to the therapeutic relationship by delineating how client and therapist can openly and rationally negotiate for the use and restriction of their personal power. Whereas I agree with Gillis (1974) that "all modern psychotherapists, whether they know it or not, engage in maneuvers and manipulations that add to their power over the patient," I don't believe that we should smugly view this inequitable relationship as desirable or even inevitable, as Gillis and other therapists apparently do. Practitioners need to learn how to deal with power in psychotherapy as in other interpersonal situations. The power base inherent in therapist and client roles must be understood so that the therapist may be free to exercise his considerable influence with the client in an open, informed, and negotiable manner.

In the following example, the therapist and the therapeutic group exemplify what I regard as "power-adequacy" in enabling a client with a long history of psychiatric hospitalization to recover his lost power. *Power adequacy* will be defined operationally in its relationship to the therapeutic situation as: the inner experience of being aware of one's personal needs; knowing that the resources to satisfy them are available; and realizing that, to utilize one's power, one needs the ability and permission to obtain these resources. The therapist enables the person with whom he is working to obtain power adequacy by affording the client the opportunity to experience him as a *role model*. The example also shows the part played by the therapist-as-role-model in returning power to the client. (See Chapter 9 for a full discussion of role modeling.)

Mr. Loschile had a history of drug abuse, alcoholism, serious suicidal attempts, and assaults on psychiatric hospital staff and fellow patients. He bemoaned the fact that he could not attain the musical career he yearned for and for which he had seemed destined in his youth. Mr. Loschile blamed his assaultive behavior on his being forced to live with anti-Semitic, illiterate blacks who, he claimed, were envious of his intelligence and talent. His strategies in therapy were directed toward having the therapist figure out why he was a "misfit" and why his plans never worked out. Loschile strenuously avoided exploring what he could do about his adverse condition in the present.

In a group session on his psychiatric ward, Loschile became furious at the therapist when he was told that he was once again behaving as he had in the last session: as if he felt very sorry for himself. Loschile leaped out of his chair, ran over to the therapist and hovered over him, threatening to slug him. The therapist told him to sit down or he couldn't continue in the group. Other patients pointed out to Loschile that the group contract, agreed upon by all, precluded acts of violence. Loschile picked up an ashtray, left the group circle, and flung the ashtray against the wall. He returned and sat down. He said to the therapist, "You lying bastard, are you going to tell me that I am not a man?" He was told by the group that he was certainly not acting like a man at the moment; he was behaving like a child who would not take responsibility for his own actions.

Someone in the group rather wisely asked Loschile on what basis they were to judge him if not on the basis of his actual behavior? This seemed to reach Loschile. He pleaded that he really wanted to be a man and wanted to assume adult responsibility. The therapist gave him this opportunity by indicating that since he was rather upset, he had the personal responsibility to decide for himself whether he was able to continue the session in a rational manner or preferred to leave the group then. He was told that he could return when he felt he could handle critical assessment of his behavior. He chose to leave, but he left without sulking or impotent rage. He returned the next day appreciative that the group had not permitted him to get away with acting like a spoiled child.

Loschile lacked a sense of adequacy. As the reader will remember, my definition of power adequacy supposes the need for *permission* to get in touch with and satisfy needs. Loschile's unhappy childhood as an unwanted adopted child was pervaded by contradictory and confusing attitudes from his adopted parents about what he was expected and allowed to do. In the situation recounted above, the therapist and group gave him the permission to get in touch with his needs and meet them in a socially acceptable manner. Two psychoanalytic notions are relevant here. One is that it is generally the parent of the opposite sex who gives the child permission to evince certain attitudes and behaviors and the parent of the same sex who teaches the child how to express these attitudes and perform these behaviors by role-modeling their expression. The second psychoanalytic notion is that the therapeutic group is responded to by each of the patients as if it were a *homogenized mother*, that is, the embodiment of the combined unconscious feelings of all the group members about desires for and fears of nurturing and care. The group, as a mother surrogate, had told Loschile, in effect, "No, you don't have permission to assault others in order to try to gain a sense of power from the therapist-as-father-surrogate, who you feel has emasculated you. But you do have permission to become more adequate by learning to live and act responsibly among us." The therapist-as-father-surrogate role-modeled handling anger as a potential threat to the therapist's own personal power and adequacy. He said, in effect, "I value myself too much to permit you to physically attack me. We have agreed as a group—so that none of us gets exploited and so that we can learn more effective ways to handle potent feelings—to deal with our interactions in particular ways. In this process I get a feeling of power and adequacy from helping us maintain an agreement (contract) we all realize is beneficial to each of us."

Insofar as psychotherapy inevitably is involved with the use of power, the therapist must teach the client how to rationally use his power or how to regain his lost power. The therapist, having gained an unfair advantage of power over the client due to the client's self-denigration, must become the client's advocate by not permitting the client's shame and guilt to deprive him of his inherent powers and rights within the therapeutic relationship. Psychotherapy, to the extent that it is taken seriously by its practitioners, must be characterized by personal involvement in the existential concerns of the client, by the abandonment of the role and status of a superior, and by the emphasis on a working contract (see Chapter 3). The working or *therapeutic contract* is intended to protect each agent from the abusive power of the other; it is an agreement on how each agent will use, or restrict his use of, power.

In essence, the contractual model for psychotherapy is an egalitarian partnership model predicated on the following orientation. The therapist enables the client to become that which he intends to be (i.e., self-actualized) by respecting his potential for autonomy and self-development. He does so by not trying to protect the other from having to make choices. Szasz (1969) points out that the common element in all so-called psychiatric symptoms "is the expression of loss of control or freedom. Each symptom is experienced or defined by the patient as something he cannot help doing or feeling or something he must do.

. . . [Because] the patient experiences [these symptoms as] involuntary occurrences, . . . he usually claims that he ought not to be responsible for [his action] and its consequences" (pp. 14-15). The question this raises is how a client can be taught responsibility. The therapist encourages this learning by being careful not to force the client to desist from dysfunctional behavior or to prefer growth to outmoded defenses. Freud (1919) long ago argued that "the patient should be educated to liberate and fulfill his own nature, not to resemble ourselves."

The therapist represents his point of view as his own. He enters into the therapeutic relationship with the intention neither of persuading the other nor of accepting the other's behavior uncritically. He treats the other as he expects to be treated—openly and directly. He presents himself as an autonomous person with the aura of potency that comes from being autonomous. He proposes by his own behavior that personal exchanges be made by negotiation rather than by use of threat, manipulation, or authority. He acts responsibly, accepting his behavior as being of his own choosing. He deals openly with the consequences of his choices. He protects his own integrity and also that of the therapeutic relationship.

The integrity of the therapeutic relationship depends upon the therapeutic agents relating to each other in accordance with their explicit agreements. In contractual psychotherapy, the therapist agrees to help the client but not to take care of him. The client agrees to assume personal responsibility for how he experiences himself in the world and how he deals with his experiences. If he is unwilling to comply with the contract within the therapeutic relationship, he and the therapist must sever the relationship, but without anger or condemnation. The therapist explains precisely the reasons for his decision. He points out that it is his responsibility to himself and his work not to be exploited and manipulated by the other. Szasz (1969) has expressed this attitude clearly and succinctly. "The analyst tries to help his client, he does not 'take care of him.' The patient takes care of himself" (p.24). For the client to become a more responsible and effective person, he needs to be given responsibility for collaborating in his own emotional development. As I have argued, this endeavor requires a partnership between therapist and client, one in which the practitioner serves as a role-model of acting as a responsible agent in their encounters.

## My *personal contract*
## *in psychotherapy*

I have come to realize that I am most uncomfortable with those clients who assume helpless and passively or aggressively dependent roles because they progressively increase the time I must spend within the therapist aspect of myself. I also realize that seeing clients over a long time is no real difficulty for me; I have worked comfortably with individuals, couples, and groups for 4 years or more. What causes me discomfort is not duration of therapy, but how much it encroaches on my nontherapy time and involves me in a client's demands for me to take up functions that significant others in his life have been or should be carrying out. To become more comfortable in such a relationship, I must enable the client to take responsibility for his life more immediately than other therapists might feel the need of doing. Accordingly, I have selected the concept of *personal strategies* as the unit of analysis in my ameliorative work, not only because it meets the criteria of economy of explanation and logical and consistent ordering of experience, but also because it meets my own existential needs.

The concept of personal strategies is based upon a view in which the individual is seen as responsible and accountable for his transactions with others (Goldberg, 1973). Accepting behavior as governed by personal strategies, psychotherapy may be conducted in egalitarian and transactional terms in which each seeks to explore and come to understand the intentionality of the other. The therapist in this model "functions primarily as a guide, not as an arbitrator of the client's consciousness" (Clark, 1975, p. 91). The client is not relegated to the role of a victim of his inscrutable nature and circumstance who needs to be taken care of by the therapist. The therapist's function in this orientation is not to change the client, and certainly not to take care of him, but to help him discover his intentionality so that he may have more conscious choice about his behavior. Psychotherapy conducted in an egalitarian context asserts minimal control on either client or therapist.

*The egalitarian model*
*in contrast to the medical model*

The work of many practitioners suffers from what Schaffer (1974) has called "an insufficiency of speaking personally to the patient." These practitioners paternally protect their clients from the full realization of their condition because they believe that "full and conscious participation in the process of existence is not desirable for those persons in whom it arouses intolerable impulses and anxieties" (Spotnitz, 1972, p. 20). In so doing, they have ignored Laing's (1965) fervent argument that "psychotic" and disturbed behavior is a symptom of the condition of human existence, rather than an individual's private illness. "Crazy" behavior is the patient's way of trying to preserve the centrality of his personality within a dehumanizing and depersonalizing world. Such individuals have the need to come out of their centeredness to participate and become involved with others (May, et al., 1958). This leaving one's centeredness always involves a risk. An individual may return to his centeredness and experience his core self as too confining and inadequate to incorporate the vista he brings back with him, resulting in a serious psychotic depression. Conventional psychotherapy, as Spotnitz suggests, attempts to avoid this risk by keeping the patient with a tenuous sense of reality within the confines of his centeredness. This requires the conventional practitioner to take responsibility for his client and to treat him as if he is incapable of exercising reasonable choices.

This model, whether practiced by a physician or a nonmedical therapist, has a long tradition based upon a medical-model prototype. Advocates of this prototype claim that the psychotherapeutic relationship based upon the medical model "is the only system which is humane, decent and most apt to help sick people" (Hoffer, 1972). I, of course, take strong issue with this point of view. I ask how the medical model can be humane when it regards psychiatric patients as mindless, irresponsible, childlike objects, depriving them of their liberty, civil rights, and privacy. The treatment offered by the medical-model practitioner consists of heavy doses of psychotropic drugs, electroshock, and custodialism, together with a paternalistic attitude that conveys the impression: I am the doctor; I am well. You are the patient; you are sick. Those who have witnessed, as I have, patients medicated against their will, forced to adhere to orders by burly attendants, or screaming in sheer terror in anticipation of having their brain cells reassembled, have to take strong issue with the statement that the medical model is humane (Goldberg, 1972b).

The question, however, is not whether the medical model offers humane treatment, but whether the medical model, by describing emotional disturbance as an illness, offers an accurate explanation of disordered behavior and a viable model for its treatment. I maintain that if emotional disturbance is an illness, it is unlike other illnesses treated and regarded as within the expertise of physicians, namely physical illnesses. A physical illness is an affliction of a bodily organ. What organ(s) would the medical-model practitioner suggest promotes "mental illness"? As Szasz (1961) has persuasively demonstrated, mental illness is a myth. It is a myth created for a variety of purposes and resulting in a variety of payoffs as beneficial to the practitioner as they are detrimental to the psychiatric patient.

There appear to me to be three reasons why psychiatrists in particular perpetuate the myth of mental illness:

1. Emotional disorders are mysterious and puzzling disabilities. After centuries of study, observation, and treatment attempts, we know little more about schizophrenia and other "psychotic" reactions than did the ancient Greeks, who explained aberrant behavior on the basis of a diseased liver (bad bile), possession by demons, or freely chosen iniquity. Schatzman (1971) has stated it succinctly: "All that is certain about 'mental illness' is that some people assert that other people have it. Epistemologically, 'mental illness' has the status of an explanatory concept or a working hypothesis. No one has proven it to exist as a thing, nor has anyone described its attributes with scientific precision and reliability." By making an analogy between something that is mysterious (i.e., emotional disturbance) and something that he is familiar with (i.e., physical illness), the psychiatrist seeks to demonstrate that he understands emotional disorders. For anyone but a psychiatrist, this sort of absurd reasoning would constitute magical thinking.

2. Given a lack of understanding of emotional disorders, it is difficult to know who should render treatment and how. Borrowing the medical model and calling emotional disorders illness, we create clear role allocations in terms of the study, treatment, and professional responsi-

bility for patients. This process places the psychiatrist, by virtue of his training in dealing with illness, highest in the status hierarchy.

3. By calling emotional disorders illness, which only he is trained to treat, the psychiatrist justifies receiving the highest fees. Moreover, by assuming administrative responsibility, he places himself in a position in which he controls the livelihood of other mental health workers. On the other hand, were the mental health professions to discard the medical model and explain disturbed behavior in some other way, for example, as a learned behavior, as an interpersonal communication disturbance, or as poor cognitive habits—types of problems for which the psychiatrist has only rudimentary training—the services of the psychiatrist would be unsubstantial, if required at all.

What implications does the medical model have for the treatment of emotional distress? Unlike the diagnosis for physical disorders, being labeled "mentally ill" in no way facilitates appropriate treatment. Indeed, the label of "mental illness" impedes treatment. For example, a patient in a therapy group for alcoholics told the other group members that he had stayed in treatment for many months with a private psychiatrist who was not helping him. Asked why he did so, he said, "Because by telling me that I was sick, he helped me keep drinking. Why shouldn't I drink! I have an emotional problem!" Physical illness (with the exception of venereal disease) rarely carries a moral stigma. It never carries a lifetime judgment of disapproval. Unfortunately, diagnosis is not objectively derived in psychiatry as in physical medicine. The practitioner in psychiatry views the patient he is attempting to understand in terms of his own belief systems, rather than in terms of a "neutral" disease process as in physical medicine. The practitioner, as a representative of his own culture, is caught up in the attitudes of society at large. Society has always required scapegoats on which to displace its dark mood and malevolent intentions. The "mentally ill" conveniently serve this function.

In addition to its intrapsychic implications, emotional disturbance reflects strain within a social system. Treating the patient in isolation colludes with the pathological forces in that social system, confirming the patient's lurking fear that no one wants him, that he is expected to suffer alone. In actuality, every member of his social system in some way shares, participates in, contributes to, or supports the patient's disturbance. Jan Foudraine, a psychiatrist working in a highly regarded psychiatric facility, tells us in his book Not Made of Wood (1974) that patients who were declared to be "sick" by their psychiatrists in the hospital in which he worked were given by their doctors no notion or understanding of how to transcend their "sickness" role. Their stay at the fashionable psychiatric facility simply perpetuated their emotional infantilism that had begun with their own families. Patients who attempted to overcome their helplessness and dependency by seeking responsibility evoked considerable anxiety in the psychiatric staff. According to Foudraine, the professional identities of the psychiatric staff were defined in accordance with their ministrations to the emotionally ill.

We need to recognize that those to whom we assign the title "mentally ill" are acting upon and possessing feelings and moods that are inherent in any human who is in touch with the frailties, paradoxes, and absurdities of the human situation. We are all participants in a human society that systematically drives people out of their minds (Laing, 1965). The "mentally ill" differ from other people in two essential respects: They are more masochistic, and they have not learned to play society's games as well as the rest of us. Why else would they subject themselves to the physical and emotional abuse we render them, when similar feelings and moods enable other men to become captains of industry, generals of armies, and leaders of nations (Goldberg, 1972b)?

## Contractual
## psychotherapy model

Rather than the therapist defining what is "healthy" and what is "ill," the client must do this for himself. A *life contract* is a means of enabling a client to define for himself his own latitudes of health and disease. The idea of a life contract was suggested to me by a young premed student with whom I worked. He entered therapy to deal with his sexual identity confusion, which caused him to switch back and forth between tender heterosexual relationships and masochistic homosexual contacts. In a tumultuous 3-week period, he seriously considered severing all his friendships and committing suicide, and closeted himself with an older woman whose husband was threatening to shoot on sight anyone with whom he might find her. His relationship with the woman served as a life raft that temporarily saved him from destructive self-doubts. In his desperation to hold on to the life raft, he was willing to give up medical school and other future plans for which he had arduously worked and sacrificed. The client realized that the life raft wouldn't keep him afloat forever. He said that he was tired of continually having to discourage himself from suicide and other forms of nonbeing. He indicated to me that he had never made a decision to live. He asked me to help him make a contract with himself to fulfill important goals in his life. We explored those conditions that would enable him to fulfill his life contract and those conditions that would subvert the contract. (Several techniques for working on life contracts are discussed in Chapter 3.)

A contractual model in psychotherapy requires that each agent negotiate with the other without resorting to abuse of power, tactics of coercion, or manipulation. Therapists are more likely to resort to power strategies at those junctures in the therapeutic process in which they regard the client as "resisting" treatment. Too often, in his experiences outside of therapy, the client has become overwhelmed with his inability to express disagreements with others, and as a result, he has chosen to cherish his differences with others as too sacred to question. In his previous interpersonal encounters, therefore, he has refused to examine his images of himself and others in an open and negotiable manner. He brings the same resistance into the therapeutic relationship. The occurrence of resistance in psychotherapy indicates that the client and the therapist have reached a crucial point in their interpersonal encounter. The therapist must help the client to experience his difficulties with external intrusion and learn to handle them in a constructive manner. Concurrently, the client must alert the therapist that he is experiencing a personal difference with him and wishes assistance in dealing with his feelings.

The therapist who is able to help the client tolerate the experience of opposition to others does so by personally demonstrating that the occurrence of opposition will not cast the client adrift from human company. I agree with Schaffer (1974) that *speaking personally* rather than "objectively" and "clinically" with a client is the preferred mode of dialogue in a therapeutic encounter. The power of the psychotherapist to help the client stems from the relationship; human power has very little meaning outside the context of a relationship. The practitioner's progressive and spontaneous personal declaration of his understanding of where he is in relation to the person with whom he is in encounter confirms that there is meaning and purpose in the client's being-in-the-world, and that the difficulties he experiences in pursuing his humanity may be dealt with by means within his own power and capabilities. When a client experiences his behavior being responded to in terms of explicitly negotiated roles and responsibilities, he experiences the relationship as incomparably fairer than a relationship based upon implicitly set rules he had no part in establishing. In the former type of relationship, he experiences himself as having permission to utilize his own personal power in meeting his needs. By freely negotiating the terms of their relationship, the therapist supports the client's prerogative to seek whatever he wishes to be, because, although therapist and client may be interrelated in a caring relationship, they are ultimately and ideally separate and autonomous persons.

Even the best intentions and practices, however, will not prevent the therapist's values from shaping his stance toward the client. At some point, ignorance, insensitivity, or a momentary slip will cause one of the agents to interact with the other in disregard to the latter's established way of interacting. The inevitable clash of values has, of course, serious consequences for the therapeutic relationship. The therapist, by dealing immediately and directly with his own reactions to behavior about which he himself has strong feelings and convictions, conveys to the client that the client's concerns are not his alone to solve. Problems, tensions, and strains in the therapeutic relationship are issues that can be openly and mutually dealt with. Strains within the therapeutic relationship involve both client and therapist, deeply and personally. Such conflicts in therapy are not procedural issues that require merely technical manipulation. Having encountered a resistance, the therapist and client together explore ways of discovering the source, be it in the therapist or in the client or, more likely, in the condition of their interrelationship (Goldberg, 1973).

# chapter 6

# Existentially oriented training for the mental health practitioner

We know the truth, not only by reason,
but by the heart.

— Blaise Pascal

At a faculty meeting of a well-known postgraduate institute for psychotherapy training, the faculty discussed whether to drop from their group psychotherapy program a candidate whose supervisors thought that he used supervision poorly and conducted himself rather dogmatically with his patients. The candidate in question was a physician who had completed his residency in psychiatry prior to entering the institute. The chairman of the program pointed out that as a licensed physician this young psychiatrist could continue to practice virtually as he liked. The chairman contended that if the candidate was kept in the program there was a greater likelihood for his being constructively influenced than if he was dropped. One faculty member pointed out that such latitude was not accorded to nonphysician candidates who were viewed as not meeting the program's standards. To permit the candidate to graduate with a certificate would be an affirmation of competence from the institute. From the discussion that followed, it was apparent that the faculty, physicians and nonphysicians alike, approved of keeping psychiatrists in the program at all costs; they decided not to drop the candidate. Apparently the candidate had more respect for himself than his mentors did for their professional integrity because, shortly after this, he withdrew from the program. This incident naturally raises serious questions both about the integrity and the quality of training of the people who deal with human suffering.

It is the hope of layman and practitioner alike that the practice of    107 psychotherapy will eventually become a legitimate scientific endeavor, with a verified body of principles, techniques, and methodologies. Under these conditions, we might be able to predict with perhaps statistical significance those students, trainees, and candidates who would become successful practitioners and to know what training they would require. At that time, standards of conduct might be sufficiently developed to insure the integrity of effective therapeutic work. But psychotherapy today is more of an intuitive art than a science (Goldberg, 1973). Yet to be defined are those personal qualifications of the psychotherapist that may be more influential in the outcome of his therapeutic work than are the quality and precision of his methodology (Powermaker & Frank, 1953).

Not only is current psychotherapy not a valid science; its practitioners are not members of a single profession. Practitioners of psychotherapy come from many different professional disciplines, such as medicine, psychology, social work, nursing, and the ministry. Depending upon how psychotherapy is defined or, more properly perhaps, how its practitioners define it, a large number of nonprofessionals—some with and many more without academic degrees, or with degrees in fields not generally regarded as directly relevant to the practice of psychotherapy—regard and hold themselves out to the public as psychotherapists. The problem of promulgating standards of ethical conduct is difficult or impossible under these conditions. Professional ethical behavior implies, by strict definition, behavior conforming to the standards of conduct of a given profession.

Having been originally trained as a psychologist, I am aware that the ethical standards of my profession are not predicated on the specific complexities and dilemmas of the practice of psychotherapy. Authors of all major national health insurance bills in Congress have, according to Zimet (1974), omitted psychologists from their bills because a psychologist "is not necessarily a health service provider and there is no easy way to determine who the psychologists are that are qualified to provide a health service." In May, 1968, *The Washington Post* reported on a case in which the defendant's sanity was in question. The article reported that "two doctors appeared for the defense yesterday, but the two-judge panel hearing the case blocked one, a psychologist, from testifying whether [the defendant] was legally sane. 'That,' said Judge Ralph W. Powers, 'is the area for a qualified expert in psychiatry.' " Private insurance companies have traditionally made similar arguments. The ethics of conduct for psychologists are addressed to the professional behavior of all psychologists, including those who do laboratory experiments on mice and other nontherapeutic professional work. This is more or less true of the ethical standards of the other mental health professions.

Even more difficult to come to terms with are the diametrically opposed views of human nature and the different views of the right to alter and change the personality of designated patients held by a number of behavioral therapists, psychosurgeons, and medical model clinicians on the one hand and by humanistic, existential, and psychodynamic practitioners on the other. A rather typical reaction of the psychotherapy establishment to this complex issue has been a massive denial of the problem.

There is considerable question as to whether there is a single best type of therapist. Of course, the personality of the therapist is of immense importance. His personality and character must be such that he can be personally and intimately committed as a therapist. In general, he must be able to be open with others and capable of engendering mutual trust. Nevertheless, very different kinds of personalities exhibit such qualities and may be equally suited as therapists. (Foulkes & Anthony, 1957). Furthermore, whereas it may be possible to select the very gifted and the poorly qualified, it is often rather difficult, indeed, to differentiate simply adequate therapists from mediocre practitioners, and it may be misleading and fatuous to try. We have come to realize that no one kind of ameliorative approach is effective with all clients or even consistently successful with the same individual. Correspondingly, every therapist is not equally comfortable and successful with each of the therapeutic tools at his disposal. The therapist's work needs to be a creative endeavor in which his style and the techniques he employs fit congruently with his own personality and temperament and with the demands of the therapeutic situation (Foulkes & Anthony, 1957). The question, What is the best therapeutic approach? becomes What is the best therapeutic approach for whom and by whom?

How important is formal training in the practice of psychotherapy? There are professional and nonprofessional practitioners who argue rather persuasively that an effective practitioner heals less by utilization of a proven technique than by bringing into play his own life experiences in such a way as to offer his clients increased behavioral options. Having said this, it still seems evident to me that in most instances a trained practitioner is a more effective therapist than is a practitioner without supervised training. It is my contention that, in addition to didactic education, supervision, and personal psychotherapy, a competent practitioner requires *experiential training*, and this is the area of education in which many conventionally trained practitioners are poorly prepared.

I believe in this need for experiential training because as a therapist I encounter myself in every client with whom I work. I come to understand him from the reverberation of his struggles in my own experiences. Simply knowing about human behavior and interpersonal dynamics does not sufficiently enable me to appreciate what my clients are experiencing. In responding to the pressing concerns of a client, I must concurrently respond to my own internal reactions to my involvement in the therapeutic encounter. Therefore, my most pressing concern is What am I all about as a person in a therapeutic encounter with another?

For many practitioners, psychotherapy is a relationship that emanates from the depths of their being as a desire to share and participate with an accentuated sense of relatedness to the kindled struggles of the other. The skills of the psychotherapy practitioner are more closely related to his own intrapsychic and interpersonal development, therefore, than are the skills of other professional disciplines. The therapist must acquire a fund of existential knowledge and skill that differs from the "factual" orientation of the behavioral scientist. His work with relationships between people requires its own ontological orientation and its own program of training and apprenticeship. For all these reasons, in my view, current methods for training practitioners to work meaningfully with others need to be recast. In this chapter, I will discuss experiential training for practitioners focused upon basic existential concerns shared by therapist and client, concerns frequently neglected, I have found, in current psychotherapy education.

They have been neglected in existing programs of psychotherapy education because of the naive and fallacious notion that the therapist's values interfere rather than abet the client's struggles with coming to terms with the meaning of his existence. For example, psychoanalytically oriented practitioners have traditionally claimed that they are able to provide self-knowledge without at the same time prescribing values for clients. Erik Erikson tells us in *Life History and the Historical Movement* (1975) that he has come to regard this claim as an illusion. Erikson argues that the analyst routinely intervenes in the process by which clients create their values. Sometimes this is done by adjusting an individual to society's expectations, sometimes by discouraging destructive, "unrepressed" behavior. In still other instances, values are conveyed by the conditions under which the patient is treated. Quite often it is not simply the seriousness of the client's condition that relegates him to inferior and institutionalized treatment, but also the implied "moral" nature of his problem (see Chapter 4). No less eminent a practitioner than Karl Menninger indicated (to a law enforcement audience) that he would be unwilling to treat a patient on an outpatient basis who had given in to homosexual seduction, just as he would refuse to treat an unincarcerated arsonist or murderer.

There are several basic existential concerns that underlie the therapeutic encounter: the meanings of *time, purpose,* and *existential guilt* in human experience. The training program presented here focuses upon how mental health practitioners struggle with, or fail to struggle with, these concerns. Albert Camus (1955), in a penetrating statement of the human condition, indicated that the first question the individual must answer for himself is whether or not he will commit suicide. All other questions are contingent on this fundamental concern. However, until one's existence is terminated, the question of suicide is never resolved. At each crossroad of his life, the question of suicide is raised again for the individual. The importance of temporal structuring in human existence is thus realized by the continuity of the individual's choice of whether to continue his existence (Goldberg, 1976a).

Let us look for a moment at the therapeutic situation in which the client who has attempted suicide requests psychotherapy. Exploring the practitioner's own anxieties about his role in the patient's struggle with his being-in-the-world will highlight the concerns to which I am alluding. Is the practitioner's contract to help the client decide whether or not he wishes to take his life, though leaving the decision up to the client, or is it to find ways of preventing the client from acting on his suicidal urges, the responsibility resting with the therapist? Although these contracts are not mutually exclusive, the roles and responsibilities are distinct. The practitioner, upon hearing the client request the former contract, may, because he is unaware of his own anxiety about the position he is placed in, subvert the contract. That is, he may adopt the latter contract, because he is more comfortable with it, without attempting to explore his anxiety with the client. Unless both agents in a therapeutic encounter struggle with the meaning of their existence, the therapeutic encounter rarely transcends that of problem solving and symptom removal. With this consideration in mind, I have developed a rationale and a methodology for exploring the ontological conditions present in a therapeutic encounter. This methodology is intended to teach practitioners definitive skills that will enable them to minister to their own and their clients' loneliness and despair and to address the alienation and existential exhaustion suffered by a great many twentieth-century men and women. Definitive skills for dealing with existential concerns are essential for a practitioner to foster a meaningful therapeutic partnership with his clients.

*Time, immediacy, and guilt*
*in psychotherapy*

Each of us, quite habitually, tends to deny to himself the reality of time in his own existence. Nonetheless, our time is limited; the past cannot be held onto without cost to our present and our future. As clinicians, we undoubtedly observe that the most disturbing psychological experiences are those that threaten the individual's relation to time. In the throes of emotional distress, "the most painful aspect of the sufferer's predicament" is experienced as his inability "to imagine a future moment in time when he will be out of [his] anxiety or [his] depression" (May, et al., 1958, p. 68). These experiences have been described as so vividly "immediate" that they break through the usual steady progression of time (May, et al., 1958).

The philosopher Henri Bergson has pointed out that "time is the heart of existence." I, too, am struck by the observation that our most profound human experiences, our joys and depressions, our ecstasies and our fears, occur more in relation to time than to the dimension of space. Accordingly, our reactions to deeply experienced events generally fall somewhere in the continuum of "I wish this experience would go on forever!" to "I cannot stand another moment of this!" Insofar as temporality is the essence of existence, it can be posited that an individual's purpose and meaning are essentially predicated upon his use and structuring of time (Goldberg, 1973). Without recognizing the reality of time, existence, human purpose, and meaning are not possible. Put another way, human purpose is only meaningful to an *existent*—someone who is finite and will someday cease to be. An individual gains purpose by seriously grappling with his finiteness and his mortality (Goldberg, 1973).

The crux of our existential dilemma is that whereas the use and structuring of time is essential in seeking meaning in human existence, the fear of contaminating and dissipating our precious time by probing the dimensions of temporality has led to our pervasive disuse and denial of time. The acquisition of the sense of real (i.e., objective) time is imbued with the symbols, fantasies, and experiences of the past. "We destroy time the moment we begin to use it . . . for in living our time we die of it"; if one could eliminate the sense of real time, one could also "avoid the ultimate separation that time brings—death" (Bonaparte, 1940). The sense of timelessness, therefore, "is the fantasy in which mother and child are endlessly united. The calendar is the ultimate materialization of separation anxiety" (Bergler & Roheim, 1946). The link, then, "between time and reality is so involved we can divorce ourselves from time only by undoing reality, or from reality only by undoing the sense of time" (Bonaparte, 1940).

Despite its critical nature, time is a relatively unexplored human dimension. The dearth of interest in the meaning of time in human experience is particularly acute in the training of mental health prac- titioners. Only quite recently have such topics as suicide and thanatos, inseparably adjoined to the meaning of time and purpose in human experience, been forced upon the attention of the mental health prac- titioner. Concerns about suicide, death, and nonbeing reveal quite baldly the irreducible conditions of human existence that therapist and client share in common. Psychotherapeutic training that focuses on theory and methodology tends to obscure and deny dilemmas of being- in-the-world common to therapist and client.

In my opinion, what is currently required is a methodology and accompanying rationale that gives practitioners and their clients the opportunity to indulge themselves in the *immediacy* of their existence. Without appreciating the meaning of time in human existence, the practitioner's attempts at a meaningful definition of himself and his clients as finite, purpose-seeking beings are doomed to futility. To ignore the individual's phenomenological experience of time, that is, how he uses and structures his existence, is to deal with artifacts of human experience oblique to the mercurial uncertainty of "lived" existence (Goldberg, 1976a; Goldberg, 1976b).

I first became interested in the meaning of time in psychotherapy a couple of years ago when I was asked to present my views on extended group psychotherapy sessions on a panel at The Washington School of Psychiatry. To my surprise and dismay, the other panelists (all heavily involved in private practice) chose to address only the financial aspects of the extended group session. It continues to be my observation that practitioners are making radical changes in the temporal structuring of psychotherapy with little or no regard for the philosophical issues that differentiate psychotherapy from other life experiences in which their clients are involved. I am speaking not only of the duration of treatment, but also of the increasing number of sessions a client is seen and of the frequent use of extended group sessions (Goldberg, 1970a). An extension of psychotherapy, per se, is no real issue in itself. The 50-minute hour, the hour-and-a-half group session, and the twice-a-week number of sessions are arbitrary limits, designed largely for the convenience of the therapist. Time, then, is one of the few dimensions in therapy over which the therapist has some control, for it is a dimension that both therapist and client share in common.

The real issue, however, is not of real time, but of subjective time[1], that is, the progressive encroachment of therapy time into what was previously nontherapy time. In extending therapy time, therapist and client alike slip too easily into a role relationship in which the therapist, and in the case of group treatment, the other group members, progressively take on the functions and responsibilities that the client and the significant others in his daily world have been assuming or should be assuming (Goldberg, 1975c). This subjective time encroachment relates to a number of fundamental ethical questions raised earlier in this book, such as: How far are we willing to go in order to help our clients? and Do the therapeutic situations we promote more often than not prevent us and our clients from actualizing our intentionality?

These questions, I maintain, can best be understood from an existential perspective, from which the unique characteristic of psychotherapy is that it is a process of *termination* from its onset. In this sense, termination in psychotherapy, as in life, is a pseudo issue. The client is beginning to terminate from the onset of treatment just as the infant is beginning to die as soon as he is conceived. Some may regard this as a

---

[1] Categorical, objective, or real time is measured by clocks. Phenomenological, existential, or subjective time is that which is lived, rather than observed (Bonaparte, 1940).

depressing view of life, yet ongoing termination is an existential reality. It is with existential realities that the practitioner must deal in psychotherapy if therapy is to deal with the meaning of the client's existence. The real issue is not when to terminate treatment but, indeed, whether or not the client ever begins treatment.

Most daily roles and relationships generally involve proliferating and consolidating time and interpersonal functioning. Through diverse forms of object fusion, daily relationships deny and buffer people from their aloneness and their dread of nonbeing. The collusive denial of a person's existential fate occurs in countless ways—in fusion with human and inanimate objects, or through identification with superordinate human enterprises (Goldberg, 1975c). A client of mine who owned a small computer firm could not bear to leave the care of his computer to another person. While the machine was being repaired, he sat with it for several nights as another person might with a sick friend. Still another client, the son of the president of the firm for which he worked, transferred his conflictual feelings about his bright, popular, and ac-complished older sister on to the computer of which he was in charge. The computer, like his sister, operated too rapidly for him to catch up. He spent hours brooding about how unfairly the computer was treating him.

Psychotherapy stands in contrast to the relationships of daily life and to the fused object world of these clients in that it is a process of enabling an individual to separate himself from nuclear masses and become a differentiated individual. The authenticity of psychotherapy is derived from its similarity with the natural life cycle, which is also a process of separating. Remove this unique feature from psychotherapy and it becomes artificial. Unfortunately, practitioners all know of too many instances in which clients come alive only in analysis or relate well only with their fellow group members. The reader may also be aware of the encounter group hoppers, persons who only feel vibrant during a marathon. The rest of their existence is spent biding time until the next group. For all of these people, therapy is subverted because the separa-tion process is not functioning.

Interminable psychotherapy renders psychotherapy a substitute for life. It is not the time in itself, but the trend away from nontherapy time and the consequent proliferation and consolidation of relationships within therapy, that has the proclivity for making therapy time more important than nontherapy time. Regardless of the therapeutic indications for it, an increase in treatment, or therapy in which time is not consciously dealt with, is existentially an overevaluation of treatment.

Karen Horney has made a distinction between love and the neurotic need for affection that can be extrapolated usefully to the issue of overevaluating psychotherapy. Horney indicated that the "difference between love and the neurotic need for affection lies in the fact that in love the feeling of affection is primary, whereas in the case of the neurotic, the primary feeling is the need for reassurance and the illusion of loving is only secondary" (Horney, 1937, p. 109). Similarly, in the trend toward encroachment of therapy time and relationship into nontherapy life, the provision of security is primary and the quest for autonomous living is secondary. A message and an attitude too easily accepted by therapist and client is that the full experience of living is possible only within a setting in which relationships are consolidated and time spent together proliferated. This attitude is inconsistent with the process of life, because life, as I have suggested, is a process of separating. For psychotherapy to enable an individual to come to terms with the meaning of his existence, he must come to grips with the reality of nonexistence. Psychotherapy is true to this quest insofar as it is a process of termination rather than a process of consolidation of relationship and proliferation of time (Goldberg, 1975c).

This leads us to the existential sources of guilt about which many conventional practitioners are frequently unconcerned or unaware. These practitioners reduce all of the client's guilt symptoms to his experiental residual of forbidden thoughts and urges. Far more frequently in my own experience I find my clients' senses of guilt related to their failures to find meaning. They sense their inability to live up to their own potentialities. Their encapsulated immobilization is a reflection of their unwillingness to continue "failing" while at the same time having no sense of what they are actually trying to succeed at. A viable therapeutic endeavor must take into account the existential sources of guilt that hold fast to the client's inability to recognize his own intentionality (Goldberg, 1977). An individual's experiences of meaning and purpose are predicated upon his use and structure of time. Therapist and client need to keep clearly in mind that meaningful relationships are not derived from exclusive relationships with one's therapist or with fellow group members; meaningful interpersonal relationships are found within the community to the extent that "patient" roles are not evoked to provide false safety from the individual's existential dread—his fear of nonbeing (Goldberg, 1975b).

## A structured
## existential workshop

Owing to the difficulty I had in finding psychotherapy training that explores and deals with the existential dilemmas in psychotherapy, I decided to design and conduct workshops for mental health practitioners that would focus on the meaning of time in human existence. I have conducted these workshops for the past couple of years at the annual conferences of the American Group Psychotherapy Association, as well as in a number of other settings such as departments of psychiatry in medical schools. In these workshops I address myself to how the participants experience, structure, and utilize phenomenological time, and I do this by focusing on their immediate here-and-now concerns. These workshops are not designed for conducting group therapy, nor should they be regarded as a substitute for psychotherapy by those participating in them. However, the exercises and situations used in the workshop may be used in ongoing psychotherapy and are particularly helpful in situations in which therapist and client have been avoiding dealing with such existential issues as separation, loss, aloneness, termination, death, and the avoidance of here-and-now concerns. I myself have employed each of the exercises described in this chapter with ongoing therapy groups and in dyadic sessions. These simulated situations also are applicable to psychosocial education for nonclinical populations and nonprofessional mental health practitioners (Goldberg, 1976a; Goldberg, 1976b).

When I have used the existential workshop as a structured modality for professional training, I have generally conducted it within 2½ hours, according to the following approximate time schedule:

Orientation (5 minutes)
Lifeboat situation (45 minutes)
Epitaph exercise (25 minutes)
Except for. . . . exercise (25 minutes)
Potlatch exercise (optional)

Discussion about focus on immediacy of experience (20 minutes)
Discussion of time, purpose, and psychotherapy (20 minutes)
Summary discussion of workshop (10 minutes)

*Orientation.* I have come to recognize that however a therapist behaves in therapy, his behavior is directed toward dealing with his own
anxiety, and there is not necessarily anything inappropriate about this.
The important thing is not that the therapist is trying to avert his own
anxiety, but that he realize that it is he who is uneasy and that it is he
who strives to become more comfortable (Goldberg, 1973). In keeping
with contemporary orientations to the therapist's role in a group, to
enable the participants to become personally involved in the workshop,
I, too, must become ego-involved and model the process that I am
intending to induce.

During the workshop I try to get in touch with and articulate the
personal meaning of time within my own work. In the orientation, I
discuss my own involvement in time-binding collusion with clients.
Unless I avoid colluding with my client in guaranteeing him a future as a
patient, therapy will never begin, because both of us will become fused
by the magical notion that that which is not born cannot die. I explain
that I must also realize that my own levels of comfort and anxiety as a
therapist determine, in large part, whether or not treatment ever begins
as an existential reality. Hence, I must not overlook or deny my own
needs in deciding how to conduct therapy. Instead, I must use them
purposefully as indications of my own intentionality, of that which is
uniquely me (Goldberg, 1973).

I discuss how I encounter my own intentionality in psychotherapy. I
think it can be agreed that that which a therapist enacts in his encounter with another who identifies himself as a patient is not simply a
professional role that he can conveniently turn on and off. Rather, that
aspect of the therapist's being that is enacted in his encounter with
another in distress is an integral part of his personality, one that is *time
limited.* I personally cannot maintain the requirements of the role of the
facilitator for long and highly concentrated periods of time; perhaps
other therapists can. Perhaps there are therapists who can be therapeutic 24 hours a day. Because I cannot, time has meaning for me in
psychotherapy by making my own finiteness startlingly immediate.
Time forces me to maintain an aspect of my personality that causes me
strain and tension. The therapeutic situation forces me to extend the

boundaries of my ego, often past the point at which I remain comfortable. Time, therefore, vexes my narcissistic and irrational conceptions of myself, forcing me to feel my finitude (Goldberg, 1975c).

*The lifeboat situation.* To accentuate the phenomenological sense of time, I ask the participants to remove their watches and other objective standards of movement (e.g., physician's message beeper). I darken the room and I speak the instructions for the exercise in a slow cadence. The participants are randomly assigned to small groups of no more than six or seven persons. Whenever possible, these groups are assigned separate rooms or locations within a single large room where they will be least distracted by the other groups.

Before the participants move into their groups, I tell them: "In keeping with the notion that only the present is immediate and real, I would like each of you as best you can to consider as immediate and real the following situation: You and the people in your group are in a lifeboat in the middle of the Atlantic Ocean, far off from the shore and any real hope for immediate rescue. You find that the boat is springing water. There is too much weight in the boat. Someone has to be dropped overboard. There is no way to avoid this problem, so please don't spend your time planning ways to avert this dilemma! You have 30 minutes to handle this immediate situation."

I move from group to group trying to discourage any "solutions" that avoid or deny the "reality" of the lifeboat situation. Invariably, the participants first view the lifeboat situation with amusement and intellectual excitement. Inevitably, they spend the first moments in the situation planning ways to avoid having to consciously struggle with what their life means to them and whether or not they wish to fight for or justify their existence in the presence of other persons also struggling with the meaning of their existence. Each person, in his own way, tries to escape the awesome responsibility of his creative and destructive powers (Goldberg, 1973). Once intellectual solutions have failed or been discouraged, the feelings in each of the groups become emotionally heavy, similar in some respects to a long-term psychotherapy group at work. (The benefits for training are obvious: The trainee is provided with the opportunity to experience a salient psychotherapeutic situation that would require a long development to evolve in actual psychotherapy.)

Near the end of the 30 minutes the participants were given for their task, I say to each of the groups, separately: "Apparently a serious error has been made! The boat is taking in water at a rapid rate. It appears that only *one* person in the lifeboat can be saved. You have 15 minutes to handle this situation."

At the end of the 15 minutes, I move the participants out of the lifeboat situation and encourage a discussion in terms of the following questions:

1. Were any of you actually able to get yourself into the situation and experience it as immediate and real?
2. What was the situation like for you?
3. How did you experience yourself?
4. What did you learn about yourself?
5. What values and meanings did you get in touch with in this experience?

The lifeboat situation reveals that human meaning and purpose cannot be separated from interpersonal encounter. "The search for interpersonal encounter is a central human quest. Perhaps the most pressing existential crisis of our age is the pervasive sense of aloneness which so many of us feel so much of the time" (Haigh, 1967). Man's ontological responsibility, although born in aloneness, does not require separation from others. Indeed, separation from human company makes man's ontological responsibility more difficult as a process, unrewarding as an experience, and meaningless as an exercise in ethical concern. A man's separatedness from his fellows makes the ethical concerns of his life unknowable to others. Man may best choose that which he intends to be by making himself known to others. Several decades ago, G. H. Meade (1934) brilliantly described man's need for the mediation of another's perspective in order to participate consciously in his own choice. Disclosing is vital for a man because, in the act of disclosing himself to another, he makes his intentions known to himself as well. In contrast, a man permits himself to become that which he does not intend to be through passive collusion with others (Goldberg, 1973).

During one application of the lifeboat situation in a professional workshop for group psychotherapists, considerable shouting and arguing came from one of the groups. One of the participants was angrily complaining to his group about another of the participants seated across from him: "Goddamn it! Why are you always putting yourself down! If you want to sacrifice yourself and make it easy for the rest of us, big deal! But in every [professional] meeting I see you, you're doing the same thing—making yourself out to be worthless. Don't you have any ego at all! Don't you have any self-esteem!"

During the general discussion that followed, the participant who was being shouted at, a psychologist with a distinctive German accent, explained with considerable animation, surprise, and emotion that until he found himself in the lifeboat situation he had completely repressed the memory that a favorite uncle of his had, just prior to the Second World War, given up his place in a lifeboat to a woman in the water, after their ocean liner had sunk on the crossing from Europe. Without realizing it, he was colluding with a family role, to his own detriment. When a man withholds himself from others, they, in experiencing him and trying to make meaning of their experience, define him as they will, rather than as he seeks to be known. Man is defined by his own actions; to the extent that he remains passive and undisclosed, he is defined by others (Goldberg, 1973).

On the other hand, people permit others to remain undisclosed in order to deny their own fears. A highly respected psychiatrist and educator was rapidly losing his eyesight. In the lifeboat situation, his colleagues spoke of their admiration for him, while at the same time avoiding a discussion of his value to them in the lifeboat situation. He responded by speaking poignantly of his sense of increased distance and aloneness from his colleagues. Others in the lifeboat talked about the loss of eyesight as the slow but steady approach of death and nonbeing in their own fears.

*The epitaph exercise.* To know a person, we need to appreciate not only what he experiences but, more important, what he has done to make his life more congruent with his intentionality (Goldberg, 1973). In this exercise, I tell the participants: "I would like each of you to sum up the essence of your life. This is more frequently done by others. It is usually someone else who writes an epitaph for one whose existence has terminated. I would like each of you in turn to make a terse statement or two in which you summarize your life as if your existence were now terminated."

In one of my long-term therapy groups, after the epitaph exercise, a 27-year-old woman, who had come to the group passively angry and guilty for her inability to select and maintain a career, became aware that she had written off her life as having terminated with graduation from a small-town Southern high school. In high school she had been the brightest and most attractive student. Although this "interpretation" had been offered to her in various ways before in the group, it was the finality of her "epitaph" that evoked an active display of anger and a willingness to confront her narcissistic stubbornness, which she had previously regarded as simple laziness. The epitaph exercise gives the participants an opportunity to review their values and intentions and the extent to which they have actualized them. The next exercise in the workshop is integrally linked to this review.

*The except for . . . exercise.* In this exercise, I tell the participants: "I would like us now to go around the circle and for each of you to get in touch with what has been and is still missing in your existence. You can do this in the following form: 'I would have *done* _____; I would have *felt* _____; I would have *cared* _____; *except for* _____!' "

Following this exercise, I lead the participants into a discussion of the same sort of questions used after the lifeboat situation.

It is rarely the environment or other people that prevent an individual from becoming that which he intends to be. An individual lacks the ability to actualize himself to the extent that he is unwilling to accept himself as authentic and worthwhile and, as such, capable of shaping environmental conditions for his intentions. That which a person intends to become is accessible to realistic endeavor at the moment when the person regards his intentions as a legitimate possibility. Stunted ambition, failure to actualize, dysfunctional behavior all stem from a compromise with oneself as an authentic person. Revealed are subjugating feelings that one is neither capable nor deserving of what one seeks (Goldberg, 1973). The epitaph and the except for . . . exercises are both intended to enable the participant to get in touch with the compromises he has made with himself.

A few years ago I conducted a 30-hour marathon encounter group in a mountain lodge in rural Virginia. The group was composed of extremely bright and well-educated people in their thirties and forties, all of whom had been in psychotherapy for a number of years and were now at a therapeutic impasse. One of the brightest of these was a supergrade executive in the federal government. In the opinions of all but himself, he had reached outstanding social and career success at a relatively young age. During the except for . . . exercise he became aware that he had made a half-conscious decision while a senior in high school that had thereafter cloaked him with depression and unhappiness and that was still negating his achievements 15 years later. He had impregnated his high school girl friend. An early and unwanted marriage posed a serious threat to his "unlimited" potential for career success. He persuaded her to have an abortion. To assuage his guilt, he made a half-conscious decision to remain unappreciative of the events he was experiencing. Not appreciating what he was experiencing resulted in his remaining numb and depressed. He tried to ignore his numbness by becoming involved in work projects, but to the extent that he would not permit himself to experience what was happening inside himself, his sense of continuity and inner direction was denied. He was left with a dull sense that he did not know who he was or where he was going.

If we assume that a behavioral act is chosen, then we must also assume that this act is preferable to other states of action. It is chosen because the conditions of the situation—the perceived demands upon the acting agent—dictate certain rules and rewards for that course of action. The except for . . . exercise helps enable the participant to spell out explicitly those situational demands to which he has tacitly responded over such a long period of time that they have become entrenched attitudinal stances toward himself and the external world.

*The potlatch exercise.* This is an optional exercise because there often isn't sufficient time to employ it within a 2½ hour workshop. I first developed this exercise with group therapy patients in response to the paradox that clients frequently come to treatment to further develop and strengthen areas of personal and social functioning in which they are already competent or, at least, comfortable, yet shy away from areas of real concern, keeping them well-disguised until the therapist, client, and other group members have concurred that the client is ready to terminate treatment.

Briefly, the potlatch exercise is derived from a tribal ceremony conducted by the Kwakiutl Indians of northwestern North America during which every member of the tribe casts into a large bonfire his most valuable material possessions. For purposes of an existential workshop, the potlatch ceremony has intriguing possibilities. I ask each of the participants to think about his personality, to select that aspect of himself—that trait or feature—that other people admire most about him, and then symbolically to toss that aspect into an imaginary bonfire in the middle of the group. For purposes of the exercise, the participant

symbolically "disowns" this attribute and its implications for his behavior. Then I ask each of the participants to describe how he feels
about himself now that he has cast aside what may be regarded as a vital
component of his personal functioning. (When I use the potlatch
exercise with therapeutic groups, I suggest that they continue this "as if"
stance outside the group and report the results back to the group.)

In a professional training institute for group therapists, a timid young
social worker, who had been struggling for 2 days to get in touch with
deep-seated resentment and anger, asked the two group leaders and the
other participants in the group for permission to be assertive. She asked
the group for help in disowning her cooperative and placating demeanor. One of the leaders and the other participants readily agreed.
The other leader, instead of agreeing, suggested that the social worker
go around the group and ask each participant directly for his permission
to be assertive. Each again readily agreed. She smiled, assuming that she
was again successful in avoiding conflict in "becoming more aggressive"
and casting aside her cooperative manner. When she came to the
second leader, he said, "You don't need my permission to be either
assertive or angry, but if you're asking for my permission, you can be
angry with anyone you want to in the group, but not with me. You don't
have my permission to be angry with me!" The group leader had
imposed a paradoxical dilemma on the participant along the lines of a
potlatch exercise. The social worker was forced then and there to face
squarely the fact that she was asking for the appearance but not the
substance of responsibility as an autonomous adult. Here, as in other
instances in her life, she required the protective goodwill of others,
purchased with her cooperative and placating personality, so as not to
have to experience directly her aloneness and separation from others.

All systems of psychotherapy and psychosocial education seem to
have in common the aim of increasing the participant's choices in the
conduct of his life. Each person has a choice of how much of himself he
is willing to experience deeply. Experiencing the deeper recesses of
one's self is frequently painful because it reveals the unbuttressed loneliness and dread that the individual's ontological responsibility in a
world of uncertainty evokes. The defenses people erect, which may be
perceived as admirable personality traits by themselves and/or others,
provide a respite from pain by averting the probing of their deeper
concerns. *Man's basic choice is the choosing of how he wishes to experience
life* (Goldberg, 1973). The potlatch exercise is designed to uncover the

individual's basic choice: how he has chosen to experience himself-in-the-world.

## An *unstructured*
## *existential workshop*

I have conducted professional workshops that focus on the immediacy of the participants' experience without utilizing structured exercises. For this kind of existential workshop, I have used the Tavistock Study Group as a process model (see Goldberg, 1970a for a detailed description).

I start the workshop by saying to the participants: "Each of us quite habitually tends to deny to himself the reality of time in his own existence. Nonetheless, our time is limited: The past cannot be held onto without cost to our present and our future. We tell ourselves, notwithstanding, that the present is not ripe or opportune—we are not presently ready to live fully or openly. Tomorrow, instead, there will be plenty of time. Some of us may even say that our opportunities for happiness and fulfillment are already gone. In more critical moments we are faced with the realization that only the present is immediate and real. If we question our right to utilize and live fully in the present, for even an instant, that moment—and its potentialities and opportunities— are lost forever. Today, I would like you to indulge in the present. The next 2½ hours is all the time you have. Unfinished business, hopes, and fears are to be addressed now or forever denied. If you have unfinished concerns about yourself and others, now is the time to address them."

During the experience, I notice how each of the participants uses or avoids himself and others in facing up to the immediacy of his situation. I make comments, interventions, and interpretations to share my observations with the group.

## *Requirements for*
## *workshop leader*

The skills required of a leader of an existential workshop such as those described in this chapter are similar to those of the group psychotherapist. He needs skill and experience in group dynamics along with experience and training in psychotherapy. He also needs, of course, an existential orientation to ameliorative endeavors. An existential orientation focuses on concerns in living rather than on problems to be solved. The existential workshop leader asks the participants to speak and think in a language different from that of the society at large, whose language uses terms of problems, solutions, and cures. The existentially oriented practitioner, when his clients present problems for which they expect solutions, asks them to reexperience themselves at a more fearful level than that of solution seeking. He asks them to orient themselves to the language of insoluble concerns. Every person goes through life with some apprehension. For some it is an overwhelming sense of foreboding and doom. Those who enter psychotherapy ask for reassurance that they need not feel so afraid. Many therapists readily offer this assurance. An existentially oriented practitioner may be identified by his attitude that if he readily reassures his client about events over which he has no control, he may not get beyond the immediate crisis that brought the client into treatment.

To appreciate fully what is required of existentially oriented workshop leaders, it is useful to consider the contrasting orientation of the practitioner who regards the concerns his clients bring him as problems to solve, cure, or be reassuring about. The latter orientation is best exemplified by the behaviorist or the medical-model practitioner. It seems to me that operating from a behaviorist or medical-model position, the practitioner takes a rather straightforward, practical, and single-minded approach to the client's concerns. Both medical and behavioral practitioners posit that there is a specifiable goal that the client wants achieved. The therapist, unless he regards the client's stated goal as personally objectionable, goes about finding the simplest, most expedient, and most effective method for reaching that goal. (Health insurance would appear to be "appropriate" for medical-model and behaviorally oriented psychotherapy, but not for existentially oriented psychotherapy. When a practitioner claims that emotional distress is not an illness—thereby negating the medical model as inappropriate—he cannot logically or even reasonably justify the payment of third-party insurance. It is a medical model that third-party insurance serves and upon which the subscriber contracts to pay his claims.)

The medical model tacitly assumes that the human organism should function without distress and pain and with the capability of performing physical and social activities in keeping with its development, training, and energy intake. Any sign of distress, pain, or incapacity not in keeping with its normal development is regarded as unhealthy or sick.

Such signs require special attention from persons trained to diagnose the cause of the sign or symptom. Symptoms are eliminated by medication, change in diet or activity, exercise, or advice leading to change in unhealthy attitudes. The medical model recognizes that the needs of the human organism are such that it requires some interaction with others and that these interactions have some impact upon the organism's development. Consequently, the medical practitioner may utilize persons who interact significantly with the patient to favorably influence the patient.

The behavioral therapist is a pragmatic problem-solver. He views life as composed of everyday problems requiring solutions. His task is not to question why these problems occur or to seek the meaning of their presence, but to accept them at face value and to shape the external environment of the client in such a way that the problem is solved. The behavioral therapist takes the lion's share of responsibility for finding solutions to problems. Success is determined by the elimination of the problem.

This point of view is well presented in the writing of Perry London (1974), who has on a number of occasions sharply criticized psychodynamic practitioners for lapses in intellectual, moral, and scientific integrity. London calls psychodynamic psychotherapy a game. He implies that any attempt to seek the meaning of despair and boredom is an ineffectual pastime. London suggests that, whereas psychoanalysis was a salve for people who felt guilty for seeking their own satisfaction, the new therapies are a pastime for hedonistically oriented and bored people. The moralist in London objects to this enterprise; he tells us that "the meaning of personal fulfillment has shifted, to become *self*-fulfillment in very 'selfish' ways—that is, with primary reference to one's own needs and pleasures, and with less concern for other people or society." London seems to be implying that psychotherapy, which aims at exploring meaning, is a palliative for self-centered people who, if more involved in and caring about other people, would be less bored and experience more meaning in their lives.

The psychodynamic practitioner cringes and laughs sadly at the "convincing" experimental evidence that behavioral therapists offer to demonstrate that symptom removal in treatment is a sufficient goal merely because it does not lead to symptom substitution. Concerns in living are both inevitable and ongoing. Furthermore, it doesn't happen that they occur only once in life and then are either cured or remain chronic. Whereas the behaviorist speaks factually, the psychodynamic psychotherapist speaks metaphorically. He asks, "How do you prove to a robot that he is not alive? It is far easier to prove to a man that he is beginning to die!" If a client is concerned with finding solutions to the problems of today, a behavioral approach is a more expedient and effective technique because it is concerned with straightforward solutions. But I feel that we must also look behind the solution. Two examples will illustrate what I mean. Several behavioral psychologists reported to the Association for the Advancement of Behavioral Therapy at their annual conference in San Francisco a few years back that they had had success in bribing children to shut up with monetary rewards. A behavioral therapist acquaintance of mine reported to me his great satisfaction in resolving his nightly hassles with his 15-year-old son over responsibilities in the home. He pays him 25 to 50 cents each evening and the chores are carried out without fail. But what is the cost of these solutions? For my acquaintance, the meanings of responsibility, the father-son relationship, and anger need not be discussed and struggled with because the problem has been already "solved." There is no longer a problem or crisis to deal with or to be bothered by.

If a patient wishes to deal with the concerns of living, behavioral therapy will not meet his needs. To ask if psychotherapy cures or achieves lasting solutions is a pseudo question in psychodynamic psychotherapy. Psychotherapy, as I have defined it in Chapter 1, is an endeavor that aims to broaden the client's willingness and ability to make informed choices in the conduct of his life. As long as a person breathes and is aware of himself, he is caught up in the conditions, dilemmas, and concerns of living. There is no living solution to this condition. In his indignation against psychosurgery, Breggin (1973) has spoken cogently to the issue of treating problems as opposed to involvement with concerns in living.

> If life is to have any moral meaning, man must be treated as if he has free will. The problems of life can then often be examined and understood as reflecting the anxiety generated by free will, the agony of choice, the despair of failure to choose and to act. What is man without this capacity? When we partially destroy the individual's brain [or condition him to respond to his ontological condition in the world without anxiety and concern] we bring him and those around him some measure of peace, but at the price of his irrevocable and inescapable enslavement to a permanently defective mind [or in terms of behavioral therapy, a defective ability to exercise his will].

The task, then, of the existentially oriented workshop leader is not to make the participants comfortable, to enable the participants as a group to make a decision, or to minimize conflict and tension. Participants in the workshop require some appreciation of the uncertainty, frustration, anger, alienation, anxiety, and other intrapsychic discomforts they experience in the workshop and of the roles, attitudes, and defenses they evince in reaction to these feelings. It should be obvious that without the opportunity to deal with their existential dilemmas, the participants will be unable to maximize their skills and personal willingness to handle similar situations with their clients (Goldberg, 1972b).

In summary, then, existential training in psychotherapy is designed to enable practitioners and their clients to get in touch with the immediacy of their lived existence by helping them with the following questions:

1. What am I actually experiencing?
2. What does the experience mean in terms of the person I intend to become, that is, what is the relation of my experience to my own core values?
3. What fears and conditions are interfering with my experiencing my existence directly?
4. How can I reexperience my experience, bringing my experiences into fuller awareness, that is, what experiments, exercises, and ways of being will help me complete my experiences?
5. Having reexperienced and completed my experience, I should have a more lucid conception of who I am. How do I put these values into action?

# chapter 7

# Interpersonal partnership through the development of emotional communication

To make anything a habit do it;
to not make it a habit, do not do it;
to unmake a habit, do something else
in place of it.

— Epictetus

In previous chapters, I have been concerned with psychotherapy as personal mastery. In this chapter, I am concerned with interpersonal competence in psychotherapy. There is abundant data to show the importance of educating the client in how to work effectively in psychotherapy. Nonetheless, preparation of clients for therapy is still predominantly indirect, careless, and frequently conducted by psychological upmanship. The practitioner often waits the situation out until the client figures out what he is supposed to be doing in his therapeutic encounter. Meanwhile, the practitioner interprets the client's difficulty as resistance and intervenes accordingly, rather than trying to foster dialogue in which therapeutic responsibility can be realized. For too long, psychotherapy has been treated like a dark secret with clients kept mystified, not told what the therapist knows (Agel, 1971).

Schaffer (1974), an analyst, argues that an indirect orientation to therapeutic preparation results from an inexact understanding of psychoanalytic work:

> Talking to patients is a resource that, in my observation, the psychoanalytically-oriented psychotherapist neither draws on as often nor employs as masterfully as he should—the psychotherapist has uncritically fashioned his therapeutic activity in terms of the so-called

psychoanalytic model. According to this model, the psychoanalyst limits himself to making interpretations; otherwise, he remains as nondirective as possible. He neither instructs nor speaks personally because he believes that instructing his patient will intensify her resistance by encouraging her to intellectualize and that speaking personally or emotionally will contaminate the analysis of the transference.

This statement, of course, can also apply to practitioners who practice from orientations other than that of psychoanalysis.

In my view, psychotherapy is currently in need of a conceptual frame of reference and treatment methodology based upon contemporary understanding of human relations. People today have a greater appreciation of their psychological impact upon one another than they have had in the past. Contemporary psychotherapy must develop a methodology to take the most advantage of its transactional arena. This methodology must teach clients definitive interactional skills for obtaining equity and balance in their relationships; this will enable them to minister to their own and significant others' loneliness and despair, to address the problems of alienation and existential exhaustion of which contemporary man has become so acutely aware (Goldberg, 1973). Psychotherapy practitioners must stop operating from negative (sickness) models and adopt instead a set of concepts that explains both malfunction in human relations and functional, positively adaptive, and gratifying behavior in terms of *interpersonal units.* I stress interpersonal concepts not only because of the increased awareness today of personality as an interpersonal process but, equally important, because the therapeutic situation requires a model for inducing collaborative interpersonal endeavor.

A question that has been asked by many practitioners is whether the existing models of psychological assistance should be revised or whether, indeed, the practice of psychotherapy should be entirely discarded. Carl Rogers, as long ago as 1951, indicated in his book, *Client-Centered Therapy,* that books, friends, and many other life enterprises may provide therapy for some people. A number of practitioners today believe that it is time to bury conventional psychotherapy and turn to teaching as the preferred mode of psychological assistance. Carkhuff and Berenson (1976) present this point of view well. They argue that human needs are expanding at a geometric rate so that society can no longer afford the luxury of the traditional modes of psychotherapy and counseling, which, in their view, have not delivered anyway. They claim that the emphasis should not be on changing the psychodynamics and the character structure of a client, but on teaching clients to use therapeutic, psychological, and educational concepts and principles to influence their daily human relations.

Gendlin (1974) claims that if a practitioner knows anything at all, it is probably not what a client is experiencing or what he should be experiencing but how to make something happen. In this view, psychotherapy has an action orientation. Practitioners need to make available to their clients (and to others concerned with their psychological growth and development) schemes and strategies that have been found useful by others in addressing their psychological concerns. I will refer to this concept of psychological endeavor as "psychosocial training or education."

Implicit in the psychosocial orientation is the axiom that psychological distress must be addressed with action. This axiom in no sense repudiates the importance of exploring psychological distress in depth in order to understand its meaning for the client's being-in-the-world. It is a rejection, however, of the cautionary procedure of first "treating" a client before any action is taken. Understanding is an active process. In the past, practitioners generally utilized a motivational approach to deal with psychological concern. In this endeavor they searched for the whys of the client's behavior while asking him to inhibit exploratory attempts to master his concern until he fully understood how he experienced himself in the world. In recent years, many practitioners have come to appreciate that although a motivational approach has general merit it suffers from being too slow and far too speculative and indirect. Moreover, though some clients act too impulsively for their well-being, far more suffer from the lack of courage of their convictions and a reluctance to stand up for what they deserve. A motivational approach that restrains the activity of the client stifles what little spontaneity these clients permit themselves. In short, many practitioners have learned that waiting for the whys of behavior colludes with the entrenched passivity and dependency of their clients.

Steinzor (1967) maintains that continually asking clients "to think before [they act,] to know [themselves] before [they engage themselves] with another," indicates that practitioners regard their clients and those with whom they engage as "weaklings in danger of collapse at the first display of intense feelings, be they of pleasure or anger." Steinzor believes that "even the most disturbed person can take an honest expression of thought and that his disturbance or withdrawal are the consequence of being treated like a coward and driven into isolation" (p. 10).

Active approaches to psychotherapy enable the client to experience himself in various stances and thus give him an experiential appreciation of how he finds himself in the world and how he and significant others in his life treat his condition. The experiential mode provides the client with an interpersonal laboratory for exploring improved modes of psychosocial functioning. Psychosocial skills are most effectively engendered if people who are in significant relationships (spouses, family members, etc.) come to sessions or workshops together to work on these issues. Practitioners of rather diverse theoretical persuasions have found that some clinical problems that have been most complex and resistant in dyadic psychotherapy, often requiring years of individual treatment and even then not yielding outstanding success, have been rapidly mastered in conjoint sessions. For example, one of the most difficult treatment problems has been primary sexual dysfunction. Direct behavior training together with exploration of the client's and his partner's relationship and communication system in conjoint sessions has had impressive results (Kaplan, 1974).

*Emotional dialogue*
*as an existential concern*

In his *Politics* centuries ago, Aristotle argued that man by nature cannot be purely egocentric. Since man lives in the community of other men and achieves his greatest satisfaction in their company, his highest aim is found in friendship. Friendship creates common bonds with one's fellows, fulfilling the social requirements of personality. From this, it follows that the nature of man can never be understood properly without consideration of how men relate to their fellows. People cannot appreciate or understand others unless they can communicate emotionally and meaningfully with them. The principles of equity, balance, and contract negotiation play an important part in developing a meaningful emotional communication between persons involved in a significant relationship.

"In 1921, Rome was introduced to what G. B. Shaw called the most original play ever written. The clash of the Pirandellians and anti-Pirandellians at the first performance of *Six Characters in Search of an*

*Author* almost caused a riot" (Irmscher & Hagemann, 1963). Luigi Pirandello's provocative drama is useful for the exploration of communication in human relations because of its vicious attack on the validity of language. This attack is most clearly expressed by the major character, the Father:

> But don't you see that the whole trouble lies here. In words, words. Each of us has within him a whole world of things, each man of us his own special world. And how can we even come to an understanding if I put into the words I utter the sense and the value of things as I see them; while you who listen to me must inevitably translate them according to the conception of things each one of you has within himself. We think we understand each other, but we never do. Look here! This woman [his wife] takes all my pity for her as a specially ferious form of cruelty. (p. 224)

The characters in the play, like psychotherapy clients, claim that they have no reality unless their suffering is understood by others. Initially, the characters burst upon the scene in search of an author who they claim has created them and then thrust them into the world inadequate to deal with their human condition. They soon realize that their creator has discarded them as misshapen creations:

> The author who created us alive no longer wished, or was no longer able materially to put us into a work of art. . . . (p. 218)

They desperately turn to the director of a troupe and his actors as surrogate family. They request that the stage manager, as surrogate parent, recast them, giving them solace from their anguish. Nonetheless, similar to many patients, they refuse to abide by the director's clear but rather simple-minded notions of what they must do to effect mastery over their dysfunctional behavior. Pirandello's characters, not unlike many psychotherapy clients, insist that they cannot change their unknown and inscrutable author's script. They claim that they are fated to repeat the behavioral enactment of their script over and over again:

> We act that role for which we have been cast, that role which we are given in life. . . . (p. 235)

They then turn on the director and his actors, justifying their attempts to take over control of the stage production on the director's lack of appreciation of their dilemma. This misunderstanding quite naturally focuses on the use of language.

Language has evoked man's awareness of his existential being. Verbal and kinetic language has forced us to experience our psychic pain and anguish. We detect our own lurking terrors and silent longings from the reverberation of these sentiments in others. It is not, however, only the experience of anguish but the prospect of interpersonal solace through encounter that human communication promises. Yet for most of us, meaningful human communication eludes us like the hellish grapes above Sisyphus's head. The anguish of knowing that our words bear false witness echoes in the Father's words, as he tries to express his remorse for hurting his wife:

> I don't know what to say to you. Already I begin to hear my words ring false, as if they had another sound. . . . (p. 243)

Rather than struggle with the elusive and complex nature of meaningful human communication, the characters settle for the illusory palliative of superficial discourse. This resolution is not entirely self-illusory; the Father cynically comments on human encounter:

> Phrases! Isn't everyone consoled when faced with a trouble or fact he doesn't understand, by a word, some simple word, which tells us nothing and yet calms us? (p. 222)

There are some, however, who will not settle for the palliative of empty words. Psychotherapy, as perhaps no other human endeavor, investigates the intricacies of human meaning and purpose through the expression of emotional communication. Psychotherapy "is more permissive than most forms of playacting in which a prepared script is adhered to. [Clients] are encouraged by the preparation of the situation to be spontaneous . . ." (Abse, 1974, p. 116). Nevertheless, the modality of psychotherapy sets certain limits on the particular expression of human language. Communication in most therapeutic encounters is limited to the parameters of vocal and nonactive tactile language. Sensual and active tactile expression is generally explicitly prohibited or anxiously avoided by therapist and client.

Restriction in the expression of emotion crystallizes the underlying conflict existent in every therapeutic encounter between therapist and client as to how each shall address his personal concerns to the other. Conflict between therapist and client is the focal issue in psychotherapy; awareness of this prevents the therapist from managing the lives of his clients and moving them to a logical conclusion that may contradict the existential conditions of the client's existence. In Pirandello's play, the director finds this conflict unmanageable. He maintains that the six characters' expression of their human condition won't fit neatly into a theatrical production. He asks the characters to refine and control their disturbance so that their personal sagas can be theatrically directed.

Each therapeutic system may, therefore, do violence to the client's existential needs. This is reflected in an exchange between the Father and the director. The director points out:

A bit discursive this, you know!

The Father exclaims:

. . . This is life, this is passion!

The director retorts:

It may be, but it won't act.

The practitioner's therapeutic system is based on his value orientations. These values determine how the practitioner will involve himself in the client's attempts to deal with his human condition. For a therapeutic relationship to become a partnership rather than a constant struggle of wills and moral persuasion, therapists are obliged to inform their clients of their value orientations. I will discuss my value orientations in terms of my model for interpersonal partnerships.

*Interpersonal
partnership*

Crucial to the model of interpersonal partnership that I have been exploring in this book is the goal of enabling each of the partners to retain his or her own individuality as a partner in a functioning, interrelated unit. I have described this individuality as "personal responsibility" in my book *The Human Circle* (1973). To be personally responsible, an individual must accept accountability for his own thoughts, feelings, and actions. He does not consider his actions to be determined by what others expect of him or by forces beyond his control, but by his own choices. He must therefore be willing to take the consequences of these actions. He is not compelled to act; he behaves in ways that he regards as being in his own best interest. Accepting responsibility for his behavior does not mean that he accepts blame for his actions. It means, rather, that he seeks to find out why he acts at times in ways not in his best interest and that he then strives to redirect these tendencies by coming to understand himself. Other people are not expected to change for him because he is unhappy, feels in need, or is distressed; it is he who must do something to change these conditions. These attitudes, taken together, I refer to as *constructive selfishness*. [1] They serve as an ego ideal for both therapist and clients in their partnership in my contractual model. In the co-therapy model I will propose in Chapter 9, they are acquired by observing and participating with therapists operating from this stance. They may also be accrued by acquiring specific psychosocial skills from performing specific psychosocial tasks. Though an eclectic canvassing of psychosocial approaches to psychotherapy could fill an entire book, I am limited here to a discussion of just one of the specific approaches I have found useful in supplementing and redirecting my psychotherapy practice when dealing with clients deficient in communication skills. One of these psychosocial tasks, *basic emotional communication*, I will describe here. This approach to teaching these skills is most efficacious with two clients who are involved in a significant relationship and come into therapy together, but I have also employed it with single participants in human relations workshops and with ongoing heterogeneous therapy groups.

*Basic emotional
communication*

Basic emotional communication (BEC) consists of a dialogue occurring between two or more individuals involved in a significant relationship in which the needs of each are both heard and responded to, emotionally as well as cognitively. The aim of this task is to keep the momentum going in a relationship. A useful analogy to the process would be to keep a Ping-Pong ball in motion on a table through the continual strokes of

[1] There are two classes of selfishness. *Destructive selfishness* rewards weakness and failure. The person who is overweight and claims he wishes to diet may, for example, reward (console) himself for the emptiness of his life by consuming rich foods. He, in short, eats to celebrate the inability to feel good about himself. *Constructive selfishness* rewards (celebrates) work and success. The person with an alcohol problem no longer has a drinking problem when he only celebrates accomplishments that make him feel good about himself. In short, he celebrates his ability to feel good about himself.

each of the two players. Such an exchange requires that neither player try to move the ball out of the reach of the other in order to win a point; otherwise the ball would hit the floor and cease to be in motion.

BEC is built upon the guidelines of dialectic process and as such has a temporal structure. The partners:

> alternate in their presentations, and each successive statement has to reflect at least the one immediately preceding. Incorporating only the preceding statements represents, of course, a minimum requirement for a dialogue. A maximum is attained if each utterance reflects all of the earlier statements. Strictly speaking, one never enters the same dialogue twice. Each utterance must be consistent with the [other's] own views and must represent equally consistent or systematically modified reactions to all statements made by the [other]. (Riegel, 1976)

Moreover, each alternating statement must reflect the basic theme the speaker has presupposed and until that moment not consciously realized. If a reflective coordination is not built into the dialectic process:

> the dialogue would degenerate into alternating monologues in which each [partner] would merely follow up on his or her earlier statements without reacting to the [other's] elaborations. The [other's] statements would appear as distractive interruptions, and the only remaining dialogic feature would consist of the alternations between the [partners]. (Riegel, 1976)

BEC is still in the process of refinement. At present, it consists of the following 20 instructions based on the concepts of equity and balance and on the existential principles already discussed:

1. *Speak directly and personally to the other.* Assume that the other has no previous information about you, that the other will know you entirely on the basis of what you are willing to reveal in this specific encounter.

2. *Make "I" statements rather than "you" statements.* Take ownership of your statements. This will move both partners away from blaming, dependent, object-fused stances and toward positive, direct statements of want and desire.

3. *Make statements out of your questions.* This keeps the momentum going in a dialogue by moving the exchange away from excessive reflection, intellectualization, and hence, hesitation.

4. *Make statements of your present feelings rather than of your thoughts or past feelings.* This moves the exchange onto an emotional experiential

plane in which the wants and desires of both partners are open to sharing, exploring, and negotiation rather than one in which demands are presented as concluded (fixed) and closed (nonnegotiable). Emotions are facts not limited to any single means of expression. Using a constructively selfish approach, ask directly for what you want and do not "protect" the other from "selfishness" (i.e., your wants). Regard the other as capable of responsible and rational agreement or disagreement with your requests.

5. *Make statements of your desired expectations rather than of what you hope to avoid.* This enables each of the partners to become aware of what is gratifying to the other rather than only of what the other wants to avoid. Psychologically, it is easier to initiate new behaviors than it is to terminate old ones. To do this, each of the partners must avoid apologizing for his feelings and his needs.

6. *Specify exactly what is wanted.* It is important to be exact about what you are asking for in an exchange (e.g., time, place) rather than simply to speak of wanting behaviors initiated or terminated. This is because, psychologically, an individual can best adjust his behaviors in a situation in which he knows specifically when these behaviors are most crucial to the partner as opposed to a situation in which he experiences himself as being expected completely to adapt or drop behaviors.

7. *Keep your statements brief.* Clear and terse statements make it easy for the other to respond immediately. Elaborate and tangential statements are apt to cause the partner to lose the essence of the communicative intent.

8. *Give feedback for clarity.* Periodically summarize (play back) what you have heard as objectively as you can. This provides a mirror for you to use to reflect upon what you are presenting to your partner.

9. *When examining conflict in the relationship, avoid interpretations and value judgments.* Employing interpretations and value judgments effects an imbalance in the relationship by informing the partner that his behavior needs to be morally restructured according to your system of equity rather than according to explicitly negotiated norms established by both partners.

10. *Keep the momentum going in the exchange.* A relationship feeds on the balance of energies contributed by the external system (i.e., the two partners). You cannot, therefore, allow yourself to let the exchange abort by becoming upset or angry and tuning out.

11. *Move from a statement of needs to a statement of preference.* Necessity and preference are often confused. Most people can meet their basic needs in order to survive, but they do not experience the "permission" (i.e., power adequacy) to want more than to meet these basic needs. Consequently, many people force themselves into positions of isolation, desperation, depression, and despair simply in order to secure some human contact. You don't have to need a response from your partner to ask for it.

12. *Be aware that your interpersonal involvement in a dialogue is dependent on your interpersonal risks.* The cautious, introspective person becomes isolated and detached in an exchange because he feels a need to express only statements of which he feels certain. This stance erodes the dialogue until it loses its momentum. The exchange is intended to be an opportunity for you to explore uncertain, uncomfortable, and threatening aspects of yourself with another person.

13. *Say "no" but never say "never"!* View the dialogue as an experiential laboratory for searching for a greater awareness of yourself and your partner rather than as a situation in which personal limitations are to be judged. Let your partner know where you are at the moment, but leave the possibility of modification open for the future.

14. *View strong feelings in an exchange as mediators of intentionality.* If in an exchange you feel bored, misunderstood, or unloved, you are required to act. Interpret states of feeling not as calls to remain passive and deprived but as calls on you to enact the state of being you feel is lacking.

15. *Act with the other as if the other partner is the person with whom you would like to be involved and as if you are the person you intend yourself to be.* I view personality as a process rather than a fixed entity. A person becomes that which he seeks to be through action and intent rather than through passive induction of intrapsychic arousal and stimulation. A person is shaped toward being the kind of person another seeks him to be when he is treated as if he were that person. A person's intent, therefore, serves to role-model desired attributes he seeks in another.

16. *When you experience unfulfilled gratification from the partner, initiate the gratifying behavior toward your partner.* If you feel unloved, it is likely that you are treating yourself as unlovable. Acting as if you are lovable, you are lovable. In an exchange, partners often become hung up on justification of their behavior by expecting and demanding reciprocal behaviors by their partner. One acts lovable toward another

not only to evoke desired responses from the other, but to evoke desired responses in oneself.

17. *Realize that you and your partner are not responsible in the dialogue to any outside agent.* In dysfunctional relationships, each of the agents attempts to manipulate the other into assuming his own idiosyncratic system of equity in exchanges. More functional relationships result from realizing that neither partner is responsible to any outside agent or system of conduct in his interactions with the other.

18. *Explicitly review norms, standards of conduct, and other values brought in from society-at-large in preparation for negotiating them within the relationship.* Because you view your partner's contributions to the dialogue in the context of these values and sentiments, you need to decide how they function within this particular relationship, which, because it represents a contractual arrangement between just the two of you, is open to renegotiation to improve functioning.

19. *Avoid giving or asking for declarations of essence.* Many of the depressed and passive-resistant clients I see in psychotherapy are caught in the tragically "romantic" trap of saying, "I don't really care how he (or she) treats me as long as he (or she) says 'I love you'!" and "I don't care whether the relationship ends or not as long as I feel that he (or she) loved me!" Love, or any other emotional condition, is not a single entity; it is a series of specific ways of relating to another person. The individual who refuses to ask directly for equitable and meaningful specific responses from his partners is left with an empty declaration.

20. *Ask for compensation to restore equity and power.* A societally sanctioned manner for canceling out acts of inequity, insensitivity, and mistreatment is saying, "I am sorry," but this too-often-perfunctory statement does not usually assuage aversive feelings. I have found that when you ask for compensation for inequitable treatment, balance is restored to the relationship, which helps dissipate aversive feelings toward the partner.

I am proposing the utilization of basic emotional communication for several purposes. First, as a means for persons involved in intimate and significant relationships to explore their relationship; second, as a model for resolving conflict and moving beyond impasse in the therapist-client relationship; third, as a model for transactions at all three levels of a co-therapy (or at the two levels of an individually led therapy) system, to be discussed in Chapter 9. In my experience, equity and balance are maintained or reestablished when exchanges are based on the procedures of basic emotional communication.

# chapter 8

# Contract negotiation
# in marital psychotherapy

The world is hard to love, though we must love it
because we have no other, and to fail to love it is
not to exist at all.

—Mark Van Doren

How can psychosocial and contract negotiation skills be employed in
relationships with significant others? As an example, in this chapter I
will present a contract negotiation approach I call "exploring the
couples' courtship contract" (Goldberg, 1975a).

   In marital therapy the most "influential hypothesis and near-theory is
that marital conflict is based on the neurotic interaction of the partners.
In this formulation . . . the problem of marital conflicts is seen as a
product of psychopathology in one or both marital partners: disturbance
occurs as a result of the development of mutually antagonistic need
systems" (Manus, 1966). If Manus's observation is still valid, and I
believe it is, then marital therapy methodology is essentially confined to
a psychodynamic formulation of marital conflict: to the extrapolation of
the intrapsychic dynamics of each of the partners to a two-person
marital system. Combining the knowledge about each individual's
psychodynamics, however, does not explain the subtle, elusive, and
complex interactions of systematic events within a marital relationship.[1] A marital system, as any other social system, is a product of an
established set of rules, roles, and sanctions. It is my thesis that resistance to therapeutic movement in dealing conjointly with marital
partners is due in large part to the therapist neglecting or being unaware
of the normative structure that frames and shapes the events within a
marital system.

[1] The term *marital relationship* in this chapter can be taken to stand as well for
living-together relationships; the courtship contract approach to be described
has obvious relevance for nonmarried couples as well as those legally joined.   143

*The courtship*
*contract*

To understand the normative system governing a marital relationship, the therapist must direct his attention to the courtship period, because it was then that the partners began to establish normative attitudes in regard to each other. The courtship period is generally that time in the life of each partner in a marital dyad in which some of the strongest romantic, idealistic, and intimate feelings are experienced toward each other and oneself. The courtship period is also that situation in the life of each spouse-to-be in which fused past objects and ego-ideal sentiments become matched to a specific real object (the spouse-to-be). Each spouse-to-be, therefore, anticipates, at varying levels of awareness, marital union as the embodiment of continued past satisfactions and the fulfillment of yet unattained yearnings and desires. Each partner harbors, therefore, a host of explicit assumptions about marriage and even more implicit expectations and demands he or she anticipates marriage will fulfill and grant (Goldberg, 1975a). However, the qualities and meanings partners look for in a relationship seldom are clearly articulated. During the romantic phase of the relationship, the courters communicate with phrases and declarations frequently lifted almost directly from overly idealized films, novels, and television dramas. The partners rarely communicate precisely what they expect from each other until they are thrown into a crisis or serious dilemma, and sometimes not even then.

In crisis situations, as in the normal course of their relationship, couples find themselves ill prepared to work together as partners (Goldberg, 1968). They berate each other for their inadequacies, declaring that they are furious that the other has not measured up to their standards, standards, of course, that were never clearly communicated. A magical fear militates against open communication of needs with many of the couples with whom I have worked. The fear is that by directly communicating needs to one's spouse, one gives the spouse not only the opportunity to give gratification, but also the permission to hurt one where one is vulnerable. They fail to realize that if one communicates indirectly, one's spouse may find one's vulnerability by inference and violate it without permission as the justification. So frequently after the breakup of a marriage, one spouse exclaims to the other, "I never knew what you wanted of me!"

A *courtship contract* is a device designed to serve as a conceptual frame of reference for assessing both the normative structure and the psychodynamic components of marital systems that are suffering from conflict and distress. A courtship contract may be defined as the responsibilities, behaviors, and states of being each partner assumes the other spouse has agreed to carry out in meeting the former's expectations and demands and, reciprocally, what the former understands that he or she has agreed to fulfill in regard to what he or she interprets as the partner's needs and desires. Of course, quite naturally, the courtship contract is modified and revised throughout the course of marriage (or at least it is in a flexible marriage).

*A technique for reviewing*
*courtship contracts*

A major task in marital treatment, as Chapter 7 suggests, is to move the partners away from predominately abstract and arbitrary standards of conduct toward more functional standards so that they can develop their own explicitly negotiated standards. To do this, practitioners must teach the partners interpersonal skills with which to minister to their spouses' needs and in return have their own needs met by their partners. In my work with couples, I have found that I can help the partners become aware of the expectations and demands they are imposing upon each other by getting them to review their courtship period. To expedite the courtship exploration, my wife and I have developed an inquiry that helps marital partners get in touch with what each expects to give and to receive from his spouse and with the factors and conditions that impede and facilitate this exchange. The courtship inquiry consists of the following steps:

1. I ask the couple when they last touched one another affectionately. A brief follow-up to this question brings out the current state of the couples' affections. Unless there is a clear indication not to, I ask the couple to hold hands and inquire how this makes each feel. The following dialogue is excerpted from a session with a couple who requested treatment for alleviation of conflicts over marital infidelity and abandonment:

THERAPIST  When was the last time you touched each other? Do you remember?

| | |
|---|---|
| WIFE | This morning . . . this morning we did. |
| HUSBAND | This morning. |
| THERAPIST | Affectionately? Or just accidentally? |
| WIFE | Affectionately. |
| THERAPIST | When did you hold hands last?<br>(*Both shrug their shoulders and look questioningly at each other.*) Do you think you could do that now? |
| WIFE | Sure (*laughingly*). |
| HUSBAND | Sure. |
| THERAPIST | How does it now feel to hold hands? |
| WIFE | Okay, I guess. |
| HUSBAND | Just fine. |

2. Next, I ask the couple to close their eyes and fantasize about what their courtship was like. For partners who experience blocking in recalling these memories, I ask specifically about when they met, where they met, what the other was wearing, what the circumstances were, whether there were any unusual circumstances in the situation, what their first impressions of the other were, and how the spouses-to-be resembled partners in earlier relationships. After the partners have had some time to get into their fantasy memories, I ask them to share the fantasy with me.

| | |
|---|---|
| THERAPIST | Do you remember back when you were courting? |
| HUSBAND | Yes. |
| THERAPIST | That was more than six years ago. (*They had been married six years.*) |
| WIFE | Nine years ago! |
| THERAPIST | Nine years ago! It was a long courtship, was it? |
| WIFE | Yes, it was. |
| THERAPIST | What was it like? Where did you meet each other? |
| HUSBAND | We had known each other for a long time. I guess the first time I saw her she had this sexy hat . . . at a party I think her sister was giving . . . and she smiled sort of warm and I saw her again at a dance in the country. I can remember the first time I kissed her.<br>(*The husband went on to describe this event in some detail.*) |

First and early impressions of character traits of the spouse-to-be are rather significant indicators of qualities important to the spouse who reports these traits.

THERAPIST   What did you think of Nancy *(his wife)* the first time you kissed her?

HUSBAND   *(Long pause)* I saw her as someone who was full of life . . . just who was a very enjoyable person . . . just someone who I could relate to . . . attractive and vivacious and outgoing.

The spouse-to-be often perceives in the other traits that may prove useful in complementing character traits of his own about which he does not feel comfortable. He expects assistance from the spouse in either developing qualities similar to hers or learning to deal with his own.

THERAPIST   How did this compare to your own personality at the time? Were you as active as Nancy . . . were you as full of life?

HUSBAND   I think I was. I was a little more guarded. I sort of hold my feelings inside, which I am trying to get out of because I've been looking back recently . . . I held back a lot of things which were bothering me . . . which popped out the last two months.

The husband is vaguely alluding to his implicit expectations of Nancy. The therapist would take note of this for exploration later on in the interview.

THERAPIST   How did you see Ernie *(the husband)* at that time at the fair? Do you remember?

WIFE   Yeah, I remember that . . . I saw him as a real nice looking, sophisticated . . . he knew a lot more things than I knew . . . he had a lot more experiences than I.

THERAPIST   He was a lot more sophisticated and assured than you were?

WIFE   Yes.

THERAPIST   This was something rather important to you?

WIFE   Yes . . . ah, . . . yeah, it was . . . he had, I felt, he had . . . a lot of strength of character . . . which I did not have at the time. *(This issue was explored in some detail.)*

Frequently, I inquire specifically about their first date, asking how each saw the other at the time and why each decided to date the other again. I examine with each of them the attributes of the other that were most attractive and have them explore together what "happened" to these qualities.

3. My next step is to inquire on what basis each decided to marry the other. I follow up with the questions, Who did each first tell about their decision? and How did this person react? I then ask about specific thoughts and feelings each spouse had about himself and his spouse-to-be at the moment he or she decided to marry the other. Specifically, what did each spouse hope would happen for himself as a result of being married to his partner? What would his spouse be like in 5 years? (Or whatever number of years the couple have been married at the time they are being seen in treatment.) What would each do for the other in fulfilling their marital life?

THERAPIST  Nancy, you have just told me how you re-met Ernie after you were separated from your first husband. I wonder what thoughts and feelings you had about Ernie the moment you decided to marry him. What, for example, did you imagine marriage with Ernie would be like? What would happen as a result of being married to him?

WIFE  Yeah, I was just very young . . . not knowing what I wanted of life. I was living with my parents . . . which was a total drag. I had a whole lot of frustrations. At that age the way I got rid of them was to dance, to get drunk and just sort of release things in that way. That is pretty much what we did for a pretty long time. Then we settled down and got more serious about things. Because Janie, who is our little girl, was very hard to raise.

THERAPIST  Janie was a child of your first husband?

WIFE  Yeah. (*Wife went on to explain that at the time she re-met Ernie she was not prepared to raise Janie. An important reason for living with her parents was their taking responsibility for the child. This resulted in feelings of inadequacy and guilt. She perceived Ernie as someone who could help her mature, rendering her able to care for the child and leave her parents.*)

THERAPIST  (*To Ernie*) At the time you asked Nancy to marry you, what did you imagine marriage to Nancy would be like, say, 6 years from that moment?

HUSBAND    I had to do something fast. *(Husband explains that he was in the Army at the time. He came home to see Nancy and found out that she was involved with another man. He experienced feelings of loss and rejection—a reexperience of what he felt two years previously when he found out that she was living with another man and had had a child by him. Rather than having had any clear notion of what he expected or wanted their life together to be like, he frantically acted to prevent her from leaving him. He married her to hold on to her without any clear notion of what he wanted from her. Further exploration revealed that her dependency on what she perceived as his maturity and sophistication was extremely gratifying to him. Her attempts at autonomy – going to college and taking a position working with unwed mothers – were experienced as a threat to his symbiotic hold on her.)*

4.  At this juncture, I ask for shared reactions and fantasies about what the marriage is actually like at the present time. This is the point at which many marital therapists begin their interview of the couple in distress. A major difficulty in beginning at this stage is that the content and the expression of material is extremely conflict laden, confused, contradictory, and hostile. The therapist, therefore, frequently finds himself either having to act as a referee to calm down the spouses in order to elicit relevant material or simply trying to weather it out. Starting with the courtship period—because it helps the spouses get in touch with many of the constructive, pleasant, and gratifying elements experienced in their relationship, or at the very least at positive things they had hoped for—creates a climate more conducive to constructive marital treatment. Moreover, by the time the therapist asks the spouses to discuss their present situation, he has a welter of clinically and socially relevant information to help the couple sort out their conflictual issues.

5.  Finally, I ask the couple to synthesize what they have been reexperiencing and discussing in the interview(s) in order to ascertain what seems to be missing in the marriage, that is, what implicit, as well as explicit, expectations have not been fulfilled for each of them in the

marriage to date. The discrepancy between what each partner expected to achieve and what, indeed, each has achieved in the marriage becomes the objective to be worked on and negotiated for in subsequent sessions and, of course, in working on their relationship at home. Together, we draw up a verbal treatment, or working plan, in which priorities are enumerated by each of the partners, both in terms of those behaviors each most desires to change in the other and in terms of those behaviors each requires help from the other in improving and feeling better about in himself. I stress that these behaviors must be those that reasonably can be addressed by the other partner given his psychological resources, skills, and awareness at that time. No less important to the realization of these behavior changes is the attitude of the spouse who desires them; each spouse must be willing and able appropriately to reward the other for addressing these needs (Sager, et al., 1972). It is also important to make the behaviors to be changed as specific as possible in terms of the times and situations in which they occur or have failed to occur and to be precise about how these behaviors are to be modified.

The review of the courtship contract reveals the hopes and desires of each spouse and the conditions that hinder as well as those that facilitate the gratifying of these hopes and desires. The courtship contract review technique provides a foundation for goal-oriented marital psychotherapy, appropriate for either behavioral or psychodynamic orientations.

# chapter 9

# Therapist partnership
# in co-therapy

Certainly we should be able to describe clearly and
simply the game rules that govern the conduct of
the analytic players. Yet this has never been done.
Usually a few things are said about what is expected
of the patient, but not of the therapist.

— Thomas Szasz

Outside private practice, the preponderance of therapeutic situations
involve more than one practitioner, albeit frequently indirectly
through supervision and consultation. Moreover, co-therapy or multiple therapy (and various other appellations for psychotherapy conducted by two or more therapists with one or more clients) is hardly a
rare occurrence in private practice either. Nonetheless, there is a dearth
of literature on models for working with one's co-therapist.

*Review of*
*the literature*

Unfortunately, the literature on multiple and co-therapy does not
provide practitioners with ready models of interpersonal partnership.
The various reports on co-therapy in the literature deal essentially with
the special types of transference and countertransference that lend
themselves to treatment in co-led groups.

    Co-therapy originally came into being as a shortcut for the training of
group therapists (Gans, 1962). The child guidance clinics that Alfred
Adler and his co-workers established in Vienna in the 1920s provided
not only group therapy but co-therapy as well (Dreikurs, 1950). The
similarity of the multiple therapy situation to that of the family group
soon became apparent, and this feature has remained central to the
co-therapy modality for the past half century. The principal value of
co-therapy, according to this school of thought, is in its ready applica-    151

bility to clients' oedipal and preoedipal problems (Minitz, 1963a) and to the resolution of special difficulties clients have in relating to either male or female authority figures. Clients who secure a warm, protective relationship with one therapist are enabled to venture forth and explore feelings toward the more-feared therapist (Minitz, 1963b; Loeffler & Weinstein, 1953–4). The therapists' stance recommended by this co-therapy model is that of neutral transference figures. This stance enables each of the therapists to provide objective and validated observations of the interplay of the different levels of transference present in the group (Demarest & Teicher, 1954).

There are several factors that investigators of the co-therapy relationship have postulated as being significant in a co-therapy working alliance. Bailis and Adler (1974) have found that the success of co-therapy is heightened by (1) a felt compatibility of the co-therapists, (2) a felt approval from each other, and (3) the presence of a postgroup discussion. Hellwig and Memmott (1974) indicate, as the reader might expect, that differences in orientation can become a source of antagonism between co-therapists if each does not accept the value of the other's knowledge. In another investigation, Solomon, Loeffler, and Frank (1953) showed that the activity level of each of the therapists may significantly affect compatibility between them. An active therapist, they recommend, must always be paired with a more passive therapist because two active therapists will compete with each other and two passive therapists can't support one another. Adler and Berman (1960) have suggested from their work with delinquent youngsters that one co-therapist should be aggressive and masculine and the other protective and feminine. In this way, one therapist will be reacted to with more or less fear and guilt, while the other will be perceived closer to the idealized image of the parent. This is in general agreement with Minitz's (1965) observation that one therapist should represent the reality principle for the client while the other therapist allows the client free play with fantasy.

What concerns me is not whether these recommendations are clinically valid, but that they are based on models that will lead to serious obstacles in the development of a growth-producing, collaborative, personal psychotherapy experience for each of the therapists. Because my own model for co-therapy, which I will go on to explain, emphasizes the importance of the therapists as role-models of interpersonal partnership, I believe that each therapist must feel free and willing, as the situation warrants, to move from a position of care-seeker to one of care-giver. Therapists who must assume fixed roles in therapy, in keeping with a transferential model, cannot be expected to be successful in pursuing their own growth in co-therapy. Negotiation between the co-therapists requires that they move out of fixed roles. Moreover, I would question whether what co-therapy investigators have regarded as complementary therapist styles may actually be therapeutically antagonistic orientations. The passive-nondirective therapist, for example, may find it difficult to maintain a positive relationship with a co-therapist who is active and directive, while the more active therapist might find the relationship unfulfilling, although the two therapists might be the best of friends (Paulson, et al., 1976). The usefulness of fixed roles pertains to sex roles, as well. Several writers have argued for male-female therapy pairs (for example, Minitz, 1963a and b). Rabin (1967), on the other hand, maintains that therapists of the same sex who are reasonably clear about their own sexual identities can successfully work together to enable clients to introject sexual self-acceptance.

*Advantages and limitations*
*of co-therapy*

Since each co-therapist is a finite being with his own skills, sensitivity, and experience, co-leaders who are complementary offer the client a wider array of responses and opportunities for exploration than a solitary therapist does. Moreover, two therapists give the client the opportunity to observe how responsibility can be shared in a working relationship. Each co-leader can take his turn initiating interactions and interventions, while the other serves as a participant-observer who conveys his personal reactions about what he experiences going on in the group. At various junctures, the observing co-leader may express puzzlement or disagreement with concomitant statements of data in support of his view (Goldberg & Goldberg, 1975).

An important function of a therapist in psychotherapy is to provide a client with the opportunity to experience the therapist as a role model. In brief, *role modeling* may be defined as a dimension enacted in psychotherapy in which the therapist presents himself in such a way as to convey effective and gratifying interpersonal strategies and problem-solving skills to the client. Indeed, whether or not the therapist intends to present himself as a model for emulation, he does so from his initial contact with the prospective client. In a co-led group, there are three interrelated, yet separate, interactive systems: the therapist-client system, the client-client system, and the therapist-therapist system. (These relational positions are more fully elaborated when there is an ongoing and intimate relationship between the therapists, such as spouses working as co-therapists.) In this situation, clients have the opportunity to observe and experience not only how each of the therapists relates to clients in the group, but also how each therapist relates to the other.

The therapists-as-partners, through their utilization of self-disclosure, congruence, and personal responsibility in pursuing their own growth, serve as expressive role models for the group members. Their goal setting, negotiation, and effective work attitudes serve as an instrumentally oriented role model, which renders interpersonal relations a therapeutic and enabling experience beyond its inherent influential, educative, and affective stimulating qualities (Polsky, Claster, & Goldberg, 1968; Polsky, Claster, & Goldberg, 1970).

Co-therapy thus offers each client in a therapeutic group an opportunity to observe and, if he chooses, to adopt interpersonal strategies demonstrated in the therapist-therapist system that differ from those he presently employs. Co-therapy also offers him an opportunity to work with two practitioners who effectively solve problems as partners through their competence in relating in terms of meaningful, basic emotional dialogue. No less important, the client occasionally sees, in the therapist-therapist system, struggles with the inability to be understood and nontherapeutic expressions of anger, annoyance, and other emotion; but at the same time, he sees the practitioners' refusal to deny or rationalize these states of being. It is as important for practitioners to acknowledge their imperfections as it is for them to demonstrate competence.

Despite the wide use and obvious advantages of co-therapy, some practitioners have reported deleterious experience with co-leadership work, and have formed cautious and restrictive attitudes toward the utilization of this form of therapy. These points of view should be taken into consideration in exploring the co-therapy model. A number of practitioners have indicated that in some respects the co-leadership model is more fraught with hazards than are groups that are individually conducted. In a co-led group the client is being confronted with a clinical situation more closely resembling the reality of his own conflicts than in a group with a single therapist. If the client senses a lack of respect, some disharmony, or infantile competitiveness between the therapists, similar to that which marked his earlier years, then the restorative functioning of psychotherapy may be not only subverted but, indeed, reversed, effecting additional psychological damage (Lundin & Aronov, 1952).

Other disadvantages may be stated as follows:

1. There is already a shortage of qualified psychotherapists. Co-therapy further limits the number of persons who may be treated at one time (Maclennan, 1965).

2. Interest in co-therapy work is often a manifestation of the beginning group therapist's anxiety about clinical responsibility and a need for support (Maclennan, 1965).

3. Co-therapists may act out their countertransferential distortions more than a single therapist will in a group (Solomon, et al., 1953).

4. Co-therapists as a team may be as vulnerable and limited as a single therapist (Maclennan, 1965).

5. When hostility is generated between the co-therapists, there often is a tendency for one of the therapists to give up attempts to work with the clients' concerns and to displace his aversive feelings onto the group (Solomon, et al., 1953).

6. Co-therapy may intensify already existing countertransferential reactions toward a client in such a way that the therapist himself feels threatened. He may then ally himself more strongly with the client in order to avoid dealing with these conflictual feelings (Solomon, et al., 1953).

7. More complex patterns of resistance may develop in a co-led group, given the more complex stimulus field, than in a single-led therapy group (Pine, Todd, & Boenheim, 1963).

8. In order to avoid dealing with their fear of one of the therapists, clients may attach themselves to the more benign co-therapist and develop an indifferent attitude toward the threatening co-therapist (Demarest & Teicher, 1954).

*A model*
*for co-therapy*

Protection, care, and socialization of the young have traditionally been the principal functions of the consanguine family system. Basic to group therapy is the concept of the designed group as a new family in which earlier, distressing life experiences can be examined, modified, and more satisfactorily reexperienced (Goldberg, 1973). My model for group therapy led by co-therapists goes beyond the repair-adjustment model of therapy; it focuses upon growth and active development in the new family group by affording considerable attention to the co-therapists' relationship. This model stems from the concept of interpersonal partnership discussed in Chapter 7, in which the major feature is individuality as a partner in a functioning, interrelating unit. Hence, my partnership model gives special attention to such issues as how the co-therapists work through their courtship contract with one another; how they communicate with one another; how they deal with systematic processes in their relationship, such as equity and balance; and how they negotiate with one another for the personal and professional growth each intends for himself. The fact of two therapists working on their relationship with each other can constructively modify the other relational systems in a therapy group (Goldberg, 1976c), but I wish to concentrate primarily on aspects of the co-therapists' partnership in this chapter.

To understand properly the transactions within a co-therapy relationship, knowledge about the co-therapists' personal history and psychodynamics is, by itself, insufficient. Also required is an awareness of the therapeutic situation as a normative system that is ordered by various structural and dynamic properties and shaped by principles of interpersonal functioning and by the assumptions of the agents involved in the system about the amelioration of psychological disturbance. As with any partnership, both practitioners who agree to work together bring to the situation an implicit set of fantasies, expectations, and demands about what will happen as a result of their joint encounter. These expectations and demands must be openly and explicitly communicated if they are to collaborate effectively. Frequently, however, these expectations remain hidden and unexpressed, resulting in an unproductive therapeutic impasse, if not in deleterious consequences for each of them and their clients. In my view, it is of utmost importance in a co-therapy relationship to avoid these problems by establishing at the beginning a contract binding the practitioners together as partners. To be viable, a working partnership must adhere to the principles of equity and balance (Goldberg, 1976c) by stating clearly and explicitly the expectations and demands of each of the partners involved in treatment; that is, what each has to offer and what each is to receive from the other in the therapeutic partnership (see Chapter 3).

The concept of a courtship period, described in Chapter 8, applies as well to the initial period of a working relationship. The courtship period in the life of a partnership is also characterized by intense, intimate, and idealized feelings about the prospect of a new relationship. Just as in the marital relationship, each working partner brings unresolved issues from past relationships and intense hopes and expectations for resolutions in the new relationship. The partners form a courtship contract (see page 145). To render a therapeutic relationship a viable working partnership, therapists must work together (and perhaps with a third colleague acting as a consultant) to transform their courtship contract into a *working contract*. To do this, each therapist's task is not to diagnose or collect data about his partner but to engage him in a meaningful dialogue at relevant moments in their work together in order to relay appropriate information and sentiments to him and receive these data in kind from him. In my model, the aim of each partner is to increase his own choices in the conduct of his own life, beginning with how he wishes to involve himself with his partner in a therapeutic endeavor. This requires the specification of the roles and the responsibilities of each partner in the relationship. My model proposes that the partners begin their work by asking themselves and each other the questions: Why are we here? What are our expectations of one another? What would we like to gain from this experience? and How can we, as collaborators, go about achieving these ends? (Goldberg, 1976c).

If a working contract is not clearly specified in co-therapy, certain problems will almost surely emerge throughout the course of the work that follows. First, without a clear set of objectives as to what constitutes *work* and *task* behavior in the therapeutic situation, there is nothing but subjective value judgments against which to measure interpretations or interventions by the other therapist. This applies to interactions between the co-therapists as well as to their interactions with clients with whom the partners are working. Second, goals and expectations that remain implicit and unexpressed are not likely to be satisfied by the other partner. Insightful critical evaluations and attempts to deal with dissatisfactions in a therapeutic partnership are not viable without clarity about what is being sought and how each partner conceptualizes the means for achieving these ends. In the absence of negotiation, what frequently arises is a battle of wills in which therapists and clients end up working at odds with each other, none realizing why this is happening. This may be seen in terms of the striving for increased intimacy between the partners. The openness between the therapists frequently creates anxiety for both therapists and group members because they are unsure of how to respond to new aspects of one another. Openness transforms the therapeutic relationship by requiring each partner to take a new stance toward the other (Goldberg, 1973). It is this ongoing transformation that keeps the momentum going in a relationship. However, when uncertainty results in excessive amounts of anxiety, it can break down the partner's ability and willingness to stay in emotional contact with the other. Then contractual considerations and basic emotional communication can be used to assuage the excessive anxiety and restore systematic balance and momentum for the free exploration of personal concerns in all three relational systems in a co-led therapeutic group.

It is my conviction that gratifying and enabling relationships develop when the partners grow together over time. For this to happen, a relationship must be enjoyed in its own right, regardless of its enduring quality. If asked for a description of the ethos toward which my model aims, I could not better than recall what D. H. Lawrence says in *Women in Love* of the ideal marriage: Each partner is like a separate star, brilliant in his or her own respect, but more brilliant for their coming together.

In many relationships this sense of autonomy is absent. To the extent that an individual does not permit himself the opportunity to enjoy the potency of his own autonomy, he becomes disturbed. This disturbance emanates from a feeling deep within himself that that which he seeks to become is being denied (Goldberg, 1973). To experience the potency of his own being, a person must first disengage from relationships in which his happiness and productivity are dependent upon the feelings and regard of another. Properly speaking, the co-therapists are not in the group to help or support each other; they are in the group to openly investigate their own condition in the group. Similarly, clients generally assume that their task in a therapeutic group is to be helpful to the other clients in the group; it is necessary to indicate that they are not there to help one another. The major requirement for all those participating in a therapeutic group is to explore their feelings about themselves and others in the group in such a way as to ascertain how these sentiments influence their behavior. It is the encouragement of open exploration of personal concerns that enables—gives permission to—clients and therapists in a group to take responsibility for themselves and enables them to permit others to take responsibility for themselves. Basic emotional communication (described in Chapter 7) can be applied in this model for co-therapy to help participants arrive at personal responsibility.

## Co-therapy as
## personal psychotherapy

An important aspect of co-therapy is its parallel function of providing personal psychotherapy for the therapists. Freud (1919) recommended analysis for the physician who practiced psychoanalysis. He was aware, however, that analysis would remain incomplete following formal therapy. He further recommended a continuing self-analysis. A therapist in a group is a participant as well as a facilitator. Hence, I periodically ask myself what I would like (what I need) from the experience in which I am participating. Co-leadership raises the question of whether the growth needs of the therapist and client are mutually exclusive. The advantages of co-therapy from the clients' point of view have already been discussed. Working with a co-therapist can provide an opportunity for continuing personal psychotherapy or, on the other hand, it can impede professional growth.

I have found that in working with a co-therapist who is more comfortable with particular responses to clients than I am, I tend to rely on my partner to tender these responses. I also tend as a co-therapist to be more of a specialist than I can afford to be as a solitary therapist. Clients who have observed me with and without a co-therapist tell me that I am more responsive when I work alone. Yet, working alone I lose the reactions to my work of a respected colleague. The solution for me is to work with a colleague who both differs from me and won't permit me to specialize in the group.

My goal for myself while working with a co-therapist is to retain my individuality while fully functioning as a member of an effective interpersonal partnership. I pursue my own growth as a therapist in a co-therapy partnership by concentrating on my own being-in-the-world. I consider the concerns and issues that I am currently working on in my own life. I explore how well I am doing with these issues in order to assess what my current pressing needs are and what the impediments are to making progress with these concerns. These subjective data inform me of what may interfere with my effectiveness as a facilitator for

others during therapeutic encounters. Following this reflection, I inter-
polate my personal concerns into my current concerns as a practitioner.
Then, to avoid being overly didactic and detached in the therapeutic
encounter, I cast aside for the time being what I have already figured out
about neurosis and human nature. I realize that my preconceived
formulations and firm convictions about my work will issue forth more
quickly than is necessary when I become uncomfortable during a
therapeutic encounter. To be most in touch with the struggles of the
people with whom I am working, I must stay as persistently as I can with
my own dissatisfactions and unfinished work. All through this process,
a trusted co-therapist who challenges my firm convictions and preconceived formulations enables me to continue my own growth as a
therapist and as a person.

My model for co-therapy, by enabling each of the therapists to retain
his or her individuality while functioning as a partner in an interrelating
unit, promotes continuing personal growth. This model is intended for
practitioners who agree with Warkentin and his associates (1951) that
psychotherapists enter their profession to find solutions to their own
personal conflicts. However, the co-therapists' work together is not to
be taken as a substitute for personal psychotherapy or for clinical
supervision. My model is intended as a preferred modality for ongoing
personal and professional growth, developed in a partnership with a
colleague, in which both practitioners have already had their own
personal psychotherapy and are well trained in the various therapeutic
modalities. It is intended for therapists who are prepared, at a gut level,
to achieve parity and share their deep fears and fantasies with their
co-therapists during their work together.

# chapter 10

# Group psychotherapy

In the heart of each man there is contrived, by
desperate devices, a magical island—we place it in
the past or future for safety, for we dare not locate it
in the present. . . . We call it memory or a vision to
lend it solidity, but it is neither, really: it is the
outcome of our sadness, and of our disgust with the
world that we have made.

— E. M. Forster

The increasing emphasis on working with family members conjointly
has greatly increased our understanding of therapeutic partnership. My
experience with groups has impressed me with the importance of regarding group treatment as a distinctly separate modality from dyadic treatment. Group psychotherapy's outstanding feature—the opportunity for
each "family" member to be facilitative in the growth and healing of the
other—needs to be more fully and intelligently exploited. Experience
in groups suggests that peer influence is best utilized when the focus is
contemporary. Magical and transference cures, which are common in
dyadic treatment, are related to the past. Interpersonal healing comes
from the immediate impact of others as they are actually behaving and as
they will behave in the future as a result of the client's continuing
interaction with them.

*Natural groups*

To understand the psychosocial processes I will be discussing in the next
chapter, it is necessary first to examine the development of the socializ-
ing process as it unfolds in its natural settings. A *natural group* is,
manifestly, a spontaneous group of peers who come together to serve
some personal or societal function. A rather fundamental principle of
both natural and social order is that of *functional solidarity*, the organic
principle that unites solitary elements into categorical or societal aggre-   161

gates: "Man, in common with many animals, has to cooperate with others of his own species for survival. He 'naturally' does things in groups, activities ranging from actively coping with a hostile animate environment to . . . gather[ing] in groups of his fellows to seek solace, obtain information, or take action" (Abrahams, 1947). Such groups are not organized by outsiders, nor are they seen by their constituents as intended to improve deficiencies in their members.

From very early in life most of our existence has revolved around group life. We have eaten our meals, carried out our chores and responsibilities, prepared our studies and stretched out our future plans, engaged in play and experimentation, and suffered our frustrations and limitations in the midst and as part of a social unit. Initially, we were part of the interrelation of family members one to another and later part of the relationship of fellow members in nonkinship groupings. With so much of our early experience spent with others and so many of our needs met by these same others, it is not surprising that each of us is drawn throughout life toward some rather closely knit group that is designed to meet our current pressing needs.

In directing itself to its members' needs, each group develops its own self-regulatory norms and places a premium on certain values. As the group becomes increasingly more structured, group values and the personal needs that the members bring to the group become translated into roles. *Roles* may be regarded as more or less coherent and unified systems of behavior (Slater, 1955) directed toward goals that both satisfy personal needs and maintain group values. The more functional certain roles are in meeting these needs and maintaining these values, the more crucial they are to the survival of the group and to the maintenance of its members. Therefore, roles that contribute to satisfying group life are not allocated without reference to the personal histories of the members. Role allocations develop day-by-day, as the group struggles to meet the needs of each member, to gain for him affection, approval, and the other qualities of living that the members value. To the degree that current groups do not fully meet an individual's needs (perhaps left unmet by still earlier groups), he seeks new groups in the hope of addressing this deficiency.

One of the most important personal needs the group addresses is the conceptualization of the individual's function in the world. In addressing this need, roles are developed and employed by the group to help define for the individual what life is, what man is, and who he is.

Natural groups may not answer these deep philosophical questions directly. Nonetheless, since roles within a social system are socially developed and socially sanctioned, they contribute toward a definition of what is "good" and what is "desirable," and they tend to set limits on the means of expressing these values, as viewed by the society in which we live and the groups toward which we have reference. In short, groups establish the parameters in which their members are expected to deal effectively with their fellows. The role structure of groups, as Bales (1950) has indicated, can be understood essentially as a *system of solutions* for the functional problems of interaction that becomes institutionalized in order to reduce the tensions growing out of the uncertainty and unpredictableness in the actions of others. In sum, roles are shaped by group values; they are an expression of expected standards of conduct and of the interest of the group members.

In the process of translating values into roles, personal interests and incentives are often sacrificed in favor of group needs. Individuals enter groups because groups can accomplish things that individuals cannot alone, so roles that sacrifice individual incentives are experienced as inadequate by those in a group to the extent that they fail to permit group members socially sanctioned access to personally desired goals. In terms of the individual's psychosocial development, roles are inadequate when they are allocated in such a way that the unique limitations and the unique abilities of the group members are not taken into consideration. This perspective may be applied to the role structure of natural groups. When a role fails to regard the uniqueness of the role incumbent, it fails to help the group member conceptualize who he is. The group member does not internalize such roles in his self-system, nor does he experience them as being useful to becoming the person he would like to be because he experiences them as failing to apply to him. Prolonged maintenance of inadequate roles leads to dysfunction and eventual disintegration of the group, and it may deleteriously affect the psychological integrity of its members.

If a group is to survive, it must be in dynamic equilibrium in order to adjust the needs of the members to the demands and opportunities of the social system in which the group is located. These group dynamics hold true for the small, closely knit family unit as well as for larger and more loosely connected informal friendship and vocational associations in which the individual holds membership.

Natural groups that adequately meet the psychosocial needs of the individual are, of course, preferable to designed groups. Designed psychosocial experience is called for only at such time as important psychosocial nurturing and interpersonal skills cannot be obtained readily by the individual in natural group life (Goldberg, 1973).

## Designed
## psychosocial experience

Designed psychosocial experience is devised to provide for the needs that the individual's natural groups have failed to satisfy adequately. As such, it is planned precisely to resist rules and directives that have frustrated the client's attempts at a consistent and gratifying conceptualization of self. Through designed therapeutic experience, the client comes to appreciate consciously the interrelationship between the uncertainty, frustration, anger, alienation, anxiety, or whatever intrapsychic discomfort he is experiencing in relating with others and the roles, defenses, and attitudes he evinces in reaction to these discomforts.

Cooley, Mead, and other important sociologists have impressed upon the social sciences that each person's self-concept is created from socialization. That is, an individual comes to form a conception of himself as an "I" from interaction with others, interaction that is decisively influenced by the language of the society in which he lives (Broom & Selznick, 1955, p. 88). This concept of self emerges from observing how others respond to him. The attitudes developed from interaction with others and incorporated into "the individual's self-concept are, for the most part, emotive; they are attitudes of approval and disapproval, acceptance or rejection, interest or indifference" (Broom & Selznick, 1955, p. 88). The judgments others make of the individual, as expressed in their attitudes toward him, become judgments the individual tends to make of himself. The cogency of the judgments of others for one's own self-concept is obvious in the view of self held by the person who has experienced situations of unmediated neglect, deprivation, and rejection and who, because he is neglected and receives inadequate care and concern from others, comes to think of himself as unworthy of fulfillment: "Because he is unloved he may think of himself as inherently unlovable" (Broom & Selznick, 1955, p. 88). In short, the treatment a person receives in one situation creates expectations of how he will be received and judged in other situations.

The individual uses these expectations to evaluate what is expected of him. These expectations are all-important in understanding aberrant and deviant behavior.

H. S. Sullivan, influenced by the social philosophies of Meyer, Cooley, and Mead, reported that patients who were labeled as "schizophrenic" by other clinicians did not behave schizophrenically when he interacted with them. Sullivan claimed that he refused to reinforce their pathological attitudes by regarding them as "mentally ill" or incurable as did other practitioners of his day. Instead, Sullivan initiated for these patients active group membership and participation in a wide variety of social activities (Rioch & Stanton, 1953). Under his guidance, group therapy techniques that had until then been restricted to psychoneurotics and persons with character problems were employed with hospitalized schizophrenics. Sullivan reported an extremely high rate of improvement among his "schizophrenic" patients.

The reader should also be aware that many people today who appear to possess the required attributes for psychotherapy feel that current approaches to personal distress do not address the problems of alienation and existential concern that characterize twentieth-century man. Many of the individuals who have attempted traditional forms of treatment and remedial help leave these treatments more frustrated and blighted than when they entered (Goldberg, 1970a). Clearly, more refined modalities of psychotherapy are required.

Designed psychosocial experience is intended for both the individual who needs expert guidelines in recognizing, grappling with, and finally mastering misdirected urges and behavioral tendencies in himself and for the individual who wishes to develop skills for reconsidering and modifying conflictual value systems and directives in the groupings in which he has membership. Efficacious psychosocial experience provides an individual with both personal mastery and interpersonal competence.

Systems of psychotherapy are designed to come to terms with the distress afflicted on the practitioner's clients by the dilemmas of contemporary society. Accordingly, to be effective, systems of psychotherapy must be shaped heavily by the prevailing conceptions of the nature of man. The Freudian *Weltanschauung* held that man, as an object in the universe, is subject to unalterable natural and psychological laws. In sharp contrast, the world view of many present-day practitioners of group psychotherapy has placed man at the center of the universe, as much the lawmaker as he is the subject of natural and psychological laws. As lawmaker, each individual is recognized as being capable of exercising choice over his own behavior (Goldberg, 1972a).

The change in world view has brought about many changes in theory and practice. The need for societally recognized experts to decipher the strictures governing behavior is less central in the contemporary world view than it is in one in which man is perceived as subservient to a mysterious universal order. Also because of this change of perspective, emotional distress is no longer regarded as an inscrutable condition rooted within the disturbed person, a view that was the basis both for the demonological and constitutional notions of mental illness of the past and for notions of repressed libidinal urges of the psychoanalytic model. Group psychotherapy practice has focused increasingly upon interpersonal relations and the influence of contemporary interactive patterns, rather than on the participant's developmental history, which is accessible only by analysis of dreams, language slips, and other symbolic indications. Instead of depending upon such analysis, group therapeutic techniques emphasize working out conflicts by relying considerably upon the resources of peers. Many group practitioners acknowledge that it is frequently the group members, rather than the therapist, who are the most prominent therapeutic forces in the group (Goldberg, 1973).

The change in emphasis in contemporary psychotherapy reflects shifting models for examining human nature. The most salient motif in any movement concerned primarily with human welfare is the prevailing conception of the nature of man. Philosophical consideration of human nature has through the ages reflected the prevailing *Zeitgeist*. The inquiry into the conditions for human action has been prompted by the desire to explain human character in order to make it more perfect. Two existential questions have been foremost: Is man intrinsically good or inherently evil? and Does man have the capacity to choose to be whatever he wishes? These questions reflect man's interest in knowing if he possesses free will or whether his actions are determined by forces beyond his power.

In studying psychotherapeutic systems it must be recognized that such systems consist, essentially, of two interlocking dimensions. First, at the center of a therapeutic system there is an ontological notion about the nature of man and what he can become when self-actualized and notions about the interplay of intrapsychic and societal forces on the actualizing process as well. Second, a psychotherapeutic system consists of techniques and methodology, based upon the psychotherapeutic system's ontological notions, that are believed to be effective in helping the individual actualize his human potentialities. In terms of psychodynamic therapeutic practice, the ontological notions in Freud's writing stressed that removal of societally imbued neurosis would reveal an instinctually egocentric personality. This would suggest that addressing the client's conflictual nature may be necessary, but not sufficient for his self-actualization. In practice, however, psychodynamic psychotherapy appears to assume a Rousseauean type of ontology. This position conveys the notion that if a client were unfettered of his intrapsychic conflicts and distortions, he would spontaneously and naturally find a satisfying and harmonious existence. In recent years this contention has been seriously questioned both from within and from outside the ranks of psychodynamic practitioners. These practitioners contend that they frequently are not quite certain of what they wish their clients to accomplish, insofar as analytic treatment is based upon a medical model, specified in terms of aberrance and pathology, rather than rooted within a constructive and definitive model of human growth and development (Goldberg, 1975b).

The conventional individual practitioner, according to group practitioners, has been concerned primarily with the discovery and diagnosis of pathology. He operates from a genetic and constitutional bias that holds that most emotional disabilities are incurable, that the best that can be done to improve the client's condition is to transform severe pathology into less debilitating symptomatology, and that diagnosis and in-depth exploration of the client's life history are required to assess the life space parameters within which the client can successfully function. The new group movement, which will be discussed in the next chapter, has risen in protest against conventional psychiatry, which has been content to imitate the principles and practices of general medicine. Encounter practitioners regard society as essentially unhealthy and a more legitimate "patient" than the solitary individual in psychological distress. Consequently, an increasing array of practitioners has asserted that in large measure the manner in which a person is regarded and treated by society's therapeutic agents determines his present behavior, more so than does his developmental history. If he is forced into a docile and dependent patient role, that is, if he is treated as a victim of social and psychological forces, he cannot effectively deal with his situation, as Foudraine argues from his experience as an institution psychiatrist (see Chapter 4).

It is the thesis of this chapter that group psychotherapy currently requires a treatment system whose rationale and methodology are based upon a realistic assessment of the ontological conditions of contemporary man. The methodology of this system must teach clients and other concerned persons definitive skills that will enable them to minister to their own and their neighbors' loneliness and despair, to address the problems of alienation and existential exhaustion that characterize twentieth-century man.

Existential and humanistic psychology arose as a series of revolts against the image of contemporary man and his human condition embodied in the world view of conventional psychotherapy. Existential psychology has been concerned with the nature of inquiry into the human condition. In this venture, existential psychology has sought to understand the individual's behavior and experience in terms of those existential presuppositions about the human condition that existential and humanistic psychologists have claimed conventional psychotherapists tend to abuse or ignore in their treatment of ontological malaise (May, et al., 1958). Unfortunately, existential psychologists have addressed their concerns to modern practitioners in what seem to be rather poetic but unnecessarily vague terms. The quality of their terminology has resulted in considerable misunderstanding of existential concepts and intentions. This condition has exacerbated the usual difficulties of converting philosophical and theoretical concepts into viable psychotherapeutic practice. To my knowledge, existential psychologists have not been notably successful in developing a viable methodology from which to articulate their concerns. The encounter movement has arisen, as I see it, as an impatient attempt to spell out and implement the concerns of existential and humanistic psychology by focusing upon how clients and practitioners may best utilize each other as therapeutic agents. In this endeavor, the new group movement has addressed two major objections existential psychology has had with conventional psychiatry. First, group practitioners have sought to destigmatize the role of patient. Being in therapy no longer has to be associated with possessing behavioral pathology, as it did in the past. Encounter experience designed as "therapy for normals" has helped promote this revised view. Second, it has been demonstrated that in groups where peer influence is valued and permitted by the leader, the power and magic of the practitioner may be productively reduced (Goldberg, 1975b).

With an orientation toward choice, responsibility, and active participation in therapy, group practitioners have developed a myriad of provocative social technologies to accentuate the therapeutic encounter. This ever-increasing array of techniques and treatment methodologies has been an attempt to construct a model for generating positive growth and proactive development that can fulfill the vacuum left by conventional psychotherapeutic practice.

# chapter 11

# Encounter group psychotherapy

For this is the journey that men make: To find
themselves. If they fail in this it doesn't much
matter what else they find. . . .

— James Michener

Group psychotherapy has reached maturity. Treatment in groups has
come to be accepted in its own right as a decisive contribution to the
study and relief of emotional disorders. Several decades of clinical work
with clients in groups have convincingly demonstrated that experience
in well-designed therapeutic groups may make contributions to the
client's therapeutic progress that are unattainable in individual sessions
alone. Indeed, for an ever-increasing number of practitioners, group
therapy is a more viable and powerful tool for a large proportion of the
clients they treat than are dyadic sessions (Goldberg, 1973).

Treatment in groups has become such a powerful treatment vehicle
that the major challenges to group therapy have come not from other
modalities of treatment — dyadic, milieu, chemotherapy, or any other
— but from departures in treatment ideology and methodology among
the wide variety of group practices. Unlike dyadic psychotherapy,
which is historically shackled by dedication to the theory and
methodology of a few influential thinkers (Ruitenbeek, 1969), group
treatment seems relatively unlimited in its possibilities for innovation.
By means of innovative group techniques it seems possible to successfully treat persons with diverse emotional disorders that have resisted
the strategies of conventional psychotherapy (Goldberg, 1975b).

The encounter movement, seen in this context, poses a powerful
catalytic challenge to the mental health field. Encounter therapy is
both a complex and an elusive interpersonal endeavor that has stirred
excitement and anger, appreciation and sympathy in its critics, defen- 171

ders, and participants. In the United States in the last few years, there has been a profusion of innovative varieties of group experience that until now have been too recent, too complex, and too controversial to be studied carefully. As a result, it has been unusually difficult to evaluate encounter therapy with any degree of objectivity, let alone obtain the empirical evidence that evaluation requires (Goldberg, 1970b, c, and d). Recently, Lieberman and his associates (1973) have conducted an extensive investigation of encounter groups. I will report their findings in this chapter.

If taken with a healthy curiosity, the encounter movement challenges the conventional group practitioner to reconsider and seriously question his cherished beliefs about human conduct and the amelioration of emotional suffering (Goldberg & Goldberg, 1975). To do this, the practitioner must recognize the encounter movement as more than a passing social fad and a dissident social movement (Goldberg, 1970b): He must recognize it as the system of psychotherapy it essentially is.

Unfortunately, a serious consideration of these encounter models is unpalatable to many conventionally trained practitioners. These practitioners simply reject the encounter movement as a fad, destined to disappear. They maintain that encounter practitioners have failed to deal responsibly with fundamental issues of treatment and personal conduct, and they view encounter experience as callously exploiting the ravenous need for human contact in the United States today. These practitioners view with pungent skepticism any social movement that claims unabashedly that it has discovered the antidote to such resistive societal maladies as boredom, alienation, and mendacity among our chosen leaders (Goldberg & Goldberg, 1975).

I do not believe that encounter therapy can be so easily dismissed nor that the ideas and practices of its more creative and responsible practitioners can be unflinchingly ignored. Awareness of the limitations and abuses of these highly touted groups must not prevent us from critically examining and comparing their innovative practices against our own more conventional ones. To avoid operating in a social vacuum, insulated from the realities of our present culture, we all need curiously and openly to examine our particular systems of psychotherapy in comparison with the rationale, methodology, and results of innovative approaches. To view any therapy as a fad may be a denial of the needs of our clients. The psychotherapist's craft is not intended to be eternal. The individuals with whom practitioners work are finite, cast in a particular temporality, and forced to struggle with the conditions and realities of their particular period. The new group therapies have germinated and evolved in the present. As such, encounter group practices may be in greater contact with current issues of human existence in ways that therapies formulated, conceptualized, and conducted by practitioners trained in the past are not. Conventional practitioners may eventually reject the solutions the encounter movement offers them for dealing with human misery and the paths it suggests for personal and societal fulfillment. Nonetheless, the issues with which many of the encounter practitioners are struggling may be issues with which conventional practitioners have lost touch (Goldberg, 1975b).

In converting philosophical and theoretical concepts to a treatment methodology, theoretical limitations and treatment problems soon become apparent. In my concern that encounter therapy not be lost as a viable and legitimate existentially oriented treatment modality, I will explain my work with encounter groups. In it, I have attempted to bring about a rapprochement between the principles of existential psychology and what I regard as responsible therapeutic practice. A good place to begin is with the statement I make to encounter groups I have agreed to conduct. As we convene as a group, I say something to this effect:

"The focus of this marathon is on self-exploration in an interpersonal setting. Due to the pressures of time, habit, and the need to get on with the process of living, we seldom afford ourselves the opportunity to explore new modes of functioning in interpersonal encounters. We often wish that we could explore our inner potentialities. This group is designed to provide this opportunity: to explore how the individual thinks about himself and others, to explore interpersonal relationships, and to experiment with new kinds of personal strategies. In preparation for this marathon, each participant is asked to formulate goals he wishes to achieve during the two-day session by giving thought to some of the areas he would like to explore further. This group is not intended to upset anyone—although this may happen—or to make anyone feel better—this too may happen!

"What I have just said is a rather general statement. I would like to say something more personal about my work with you at this time. I am here because I want to learn something about myself and something about each of you. I assume each of you is here because you want to be and want to get something for yourself. Conceivably, each of us may be a resource for each other in this endeavor. Just how this may work out, I do not know at this moment. We do not know each other sufficiently to answer this. I do believe, however, whether you are bored or involved is up to each of you. In short, what you get out of this weekend is your responsibility. My contract with you at this moment, to the best of my awareness, is to remind you that the group is scheduled for two days. Any other aspect of our working agreement has not yet been negotiated. In any case, we have about two days to accomplish our task." Making this statement and agreeing to conduct an encounter group evokes in me certain concerns. I want to explain what they are and how I attempt to deal with them.

*An ongoing saga*
*of existential concerns*

I do not conceive of the encounter as an isolated event in time, divorced from the ongoing existence of each of the participants (though it would appear that many encounter practitioners do, else why would these practitioners be unconcerned about historical information about the participants with whom they work?). I view the behavior of each participant in the group, at any moment, as part of a process. Each behavioral event needs to be understood within the context of what has gone on before and what direction present behavior patterns portend for the next moment. Behavioral events within the encounter cannot meaningfully be explained as discrete and independent events. For each participant in an encounter group, there is a plot, as in a theatrical drama (Anthony, 1972). Working out this plot requires the cooperation of the other group members, who serve as co-actors with each participant. In developing his plot, each participant, as protagonist, reveals character attributes. The manner in which protagonist, group leader, and other participants blend the unique strengths and limitations of the protagonist's character to his human condition determines the therapeutic success of the encounter experience for each participant (Goldberg, 1975b).

Contemporary group therapists did not, of course, invent the drama as a modality for working out the human condition of the individual in quest of meaning for his existence. Playwrights and novelists throughout the ages have been concerned with drama as an arena for the struggle of reshaping the human condition (Goldberg, 1970b). In

Sophocles' plays, the protagonist is asked to come to terms with his character flaws in interface with the chorus, who represent the attitudes and sentiments of the community. Sophocles, perhaps more successfully than Shakespeare, realized that the protagonist's tragic dilemma could not be borne fruitfully through solitary struggle with his own intrapsychic processes or even in dialogue with his deity. This may be one reason why Shakespeare's tragic heroes—Hamlet, Macbeth, Othello, and Lear—are forced to collude with external forces in their own self-destruction. Sophocles' protagonists, on the other hand, appear to find meaning in their fate (Goldberg, 1975b).

Sophocles' existential arena is an encounter modality. He realized that the protagonist must come to terms with the values and sentiments of the time and place in which his human condition is situated in order to make his struggle meaningful. In this respect, a person may be regarded as acting irresponsibly, that is, disregarding his ontological responsibility, to the extent that he fails to question his socially induced roles and the sanctions that reinforce adherence to role demands and expectations. No individual can develop a durable value system and philosophy of life without coming to terms with the values and norms of the groups in which he holds membership and to which he has reference; neither can he do so without appreciating the effects these values and norms have upon others with whom he is involved. The collaborative interface of protagonist and chorus in a therapeutic encounter requires an understanding, too, of the history of the protagonist so that the other members of the encounter group can meaningfully participate in the protagonist's ongoing and proactive saga, that is, the behavioral enactment of his life contract.

The agendaless, simple structure of the encounter group, in contrast to the well-ordered and organized structure of everyday life, enables participants to come to grips with their deep-seated reasons for coming together with other people (Goldberg, 1970a; Goldberg, 1973). I focus on the existential concerns being revealed or denied by the participants. Existential concerns (see Chapter 1) are attempts by those involved in an encounter to explore—by means of dialogue, inquiry, and interaction—whether the behavior and sentiments being enacted in the encounter are in keeping with the understanding and agreement of the agents as to why they have come together and what they seek to derive from being together. Only to the extent that their interactive dialogue elicits the goals and ways of being each seeks, does an encounter constitute a therapeutic enterprise, i.e., by our definition, one that broadens the participants' willingness and ability to make informed choices in the conduct of their existence.

To know a person, I must know from whence he came. I am concerned with where each of the participants is in his own psychological development at the moment we will encounter each other in the group. I am interested in previous therapeutic experience he may have had, as well as in educational endeavors in which he has been involved. This information forms the basis for appreciating the kinds of psychosocial interventions and learning endeavors that have succeeded and the kinds that have failed in each participant's saga. Concomitantly, this information provides data on the skills each participant will bring to the encounter. Whereas I am concerned with each participant's history, I am even more interested in his proactive saga. I believe, as do many encounter practitioners, that an individual's future projection shapes his present view of himself as much or more than does what has gone on in the past. I am concerned, therefore, with how the participant has prepared himself to achieve his specific immediate and long-range goals in terms of present and future object relationships. Without these data I cannot responsibly decide whether I and the encounter weekend can be helpful for any individual who may wish to participate in an encounter group. I would not want to have a person convene with the group and, sometime during the encounter weekend, painfully discover that this group is not the place he needs or wants to be.

The conditions surrounding many encounter groups make it difficult to envision the goals for the participants in accordance with the needs of each. Nonetheless, I do not allow myself this easy excuse for repudiating clinical procedure. My therapeutic responsibility requires that prior to convening a group I make myself aware of the participants' goals and formulate a methodology to address these goals. The methodology I choose must be based on some definitive ideas about the group experiences necessary to implement these participants' goals, the risks and probabilities for success, my resources and limitations, and those of the participants as well. It is necessary, therefore, for me to speak with each of the prospective participants briefly by phone prior to accepting him in an encounter weekend.

The information I obtain prior to a face-to-face interchange I regard as preliminary data. These data constitute only the implicit, individual contracts the participants will be bringing to the encounter, as I understand them at this time. I cannot be a responsive facilitator in the actual encounter until each participant is enabled to make his contract explicit for me and the other participants. I need to know what the participant is seeking, rather than what I believe he should be seeking. Articulation of the participant's covert agenda—his assumptions, expectations, and demands about what is going to take place during the weekend—permits his hopes and fears to become public and accessible to open negotiation among the participants and myself to establish a productive modality in which to work (Goldberg, 1975a).

Although, as in Greek drama, it is the presence of other group members as community representatives that renders an encounter group an inherently real opportunity to come to terms with the values and norms of the groups in which participants hold membership, the representation of society in an encounter is not in itself sufficient to make the encounter meaningful for the participants. An intimate understanding of each protagonist as a unique individual is necessary as well. The tacit assumption that all men require the same qualities of living, in the same quantity and in the same fashion, which is underscored in many encounter groups, is antithetical to this understanding of the conditions essential to success in an encounter (Goldberg, 1975b). It is my unfortunate impression that acquiring prior knowledge of the participants' existential sagas would be regarded as unnecessarily conservative by many encounter practitioners. I gather from the presentations of many other encounter practitioners that they require no prior information about the people with whom they work in conducting an encounter group. Practitioners like Schutz (1971) and Shepard (1971), who have undaunted confidence in themselves, seem to believe that they can work successfully with anyone who finds his way into an encounter group. These practitioners would appear to have little or no concern for a specificity of the participant's psychological needs (Yalom, et al., 1970). They begin their "treatment" of the participants without initially educing what brought them to the encounter and what they want and expect for themselves during the weekend (Goldberg, 1970a).

## Composition
## of a group

It should be apparent that the motivations of persons joining encounter groups may vary considerably. Some participants may be making a sincere effort to find out what they are all about; others seek an intimate but, nonetheless, time-limited emotional adventure. Many participants regard an encounter group as an inexpensive substitute for psychotherapy, others regard it as a vehicle for getting attention for their disabilities while at the same time denying the seriousness of their difficulties. Still other participants recognize the encounter group as an opportunity to get intimately acquainted rather quickly with persons of the opposite sex or the same sex (depending upon their orientation). Also in attendance (and of the greatest concern to me) are a considerable number of participants who feel compelled to attend because of subtle or clear directives from their employer or sometimes from their spouse (Goldberg, 1970b).

Operating from a blithe ignorance of the participants' motives, many encounter practitioners inform the participants, who are strangers to them, that whereas the participants have the opportunity to try out new kinds of behaviors in the encounter, they are on their own in dealing with these new experiences: "If you want to resist instructions or group pressure, that is up to you. If you want to bow to pressure, it's your decision. If you want to be physically injured or go crazy, that too, is up to you. You are responsible for yourself" (Schutz, 1971, p. 131). It would appear that encounter practitioners like Schutz and Shepard, who use the encounter group as a platform for espousing abstract social and political ideologies, have neither the time nor the inclination to come to grips with the real concerns of the people with whom they are working.

Lieberman and his associates (1973) report, from their extensive investigation of how 206 encounter group participants functioned in 18 groups conducted by leaders using diverse styles, that encounter practitioners whose style is characterized by high aggressiveness and high charisma were particularly insensitive in identifying casualties in their own encounter groups. Indeed, these practitioners frequently indicated that the very participants the investigators report as casualties had profited considerably from the encounter experience (p. 176). Lieberman and his associates found that of the 206 participants who started in the encounter groups studied, 7.8 percent of the total number of participants and 9.1 percent of those who attended one half or more of the sessions suffered "significant psychological injury."

The important question here is whether the encounter practitioner is the participant's agent (which a participant might well assume in paying a fee) or the agent of his own social and political philosophy. I believe that it is my responsibility to concern myself consciously with the composition of the group in order to attempt to assure a productive encounter experience for all participants. I generally prefer to work with 8 to 12 participants in a weekend encounter group. I want a group that is large enough so that no one feels compelled to interact or speak and small enough so that no one needs to wait his turn to be heard. The group, in short, should be of such size and composition that interactions can freely and spontaneously ensue.

An encounter group works best for me when the membership is heterogeneous. A group composed of participants with similar vocational and personal interests frequently spends considerable time and energy in banal chatter about what they have in common outside the group with other participants, which only serves to reinforce existing behavioral patterns. Under these conditions the participants avoid exploring concerns influencing their present group behavior. Variance in the background of the participants serves to insure that the group will attend to the exploration of current group tensions and concerns, because participants will rarely tolerate the pursuit of issues of concern to only a few. The participants are naturally more amenable to exploration of the present group situation because it, not extragroup situations, is what the participants have in common. An encounter group begins serious work as an ensemble at the moment participants become aware of common feelings rather than common experiences (Goldberg, 1973).

Variance in psychological maturity is also beneficial to the unfolding of a viable encounter experience, but more so than in a therapeutic group, a fair degree of psychological maturity is necessary for a participant to profit from an encounter weekend. I have found that, to benefit from an encounter group experience, a person requires a fair degree of insight and analytic reasoning skill and a willingness to be accountable for his own behavior, but that is not all. The majority of participants who dropped out of the encounter groups investigated by Lieberman and his associates (1973) were found to be persons "who are highly conflictual about aggression, who are fearful of the expression of anger, who do not feel that it is important to express anger or to confront others directly" (p. 209). A participant must, therefore, have sufficient ego strength to form with several other persons a relationship in which he can tolerate critical scrutiny of himself and be willing to disclose to others his painful and threatening, as well as his tender and compassionate, concerns.

In planning an encounter weekend, I also address myself to the issues encounter groups raise about the participants' ("inalienable") right to know what kinds of treatment they are being subjected to, the risks involved, and the roles and responsibilities I, as an encounter practitioner, am willing to assume in the encounter experience. The terms under which the participants and I enter into a relationship to achieve some specifiable goals must be open to rational and mutual negotiation (Goldberg, 1970b). This brings me to the issue of encounter groups as influence processes.

*An influence
process*

All forms of psychotherapy, group training, and education are special cases of the more general category of influence. How people are influenced by one another is determined by the implicit and explicit agreement in their relationship. It does not matter, therefore, whether an encounter group experience is referred to as "treatment," "group training," or "education" as long as the persons involved accept the fact that it is their explicit and implicit agreement on what roles and responsibilities group leader and participants are to assume that determines what will take place. To arrive at this agreement on roles and responsibilities, the participants must understand what kinds of treatment they may be subjected to, what risks are involved, and the probabilities for success. Hence, they need some appreciation of the conditions in a group that produce psychological risk and how these risks may be reduced.

This raises the very important issue of contract negotiation. The encounter practitioner must possess, in addition to group dynamic and psychotherapeutic skills, the ability to negotiate effectively a working contract with the participants. Working parameters must be made explicit if the encounter experience is to be used as a designed, experiential, learning situation in which roles, responsibilities, skills, and procedures for working together as a group are specified (Goldberg & Goldberg 1975; Goldberg & Goldberg, in press-a). Without a clear set of objectives as to what constitutes appropriate task behavior and what constitutes resistance, statements about "irresponsible" behavior in the group are merely subjective value judgments on the part of the encounter leader and the other members of the group. Critical evaluation

and attempts to deal with dissatisfactions are difficult to render effectively without clarity about what each of the participants seeks and how
he conceptualizes the means of achieving these ends during the
weekend.

In contrast to what I regard as irresponsibility among encounter
practitioners in whose workshops and groups I have participated myself,
I insist that the group leader and the participants must concern themselves with a realistic assessment of the nature of a relationship in a
time-limited experience to assure a viable encounter (Goldberg,
1970b). They need to consider what realistically can be accomplished
in a two-day group. They need to think carefully about the nature of
disclosure and the extent of intimacy that it is reasonable or desirable to
permit oneself with people with whom a relationship may not extend
beyond the bounds of the weekend yet could, perhaps, extend beyond
the weekend into situations in which knowledge of one another's
intrapsychic struggles could be experienced as highly threatening
(Goldberg & Goldberg, 1975).[1]

In my view, for an encounter experience to be a viable therapeutic
endeavor (call it "growth experience," "influence process," or "education," if you prefer), the encounter practitioner needs to respect his
contract with the participants in terms of what they have agreed to do
and not to do. He needs to suppress his own urges to use the group as a
political arena. Too frequently, encounter leaders operate from abstract
theories of social order. By procrustean manipulation, they shape the
participants to match their theories. Though on the surface, this may
appear to be a worthy ideal with which the "liberated" client may
cooperate, on closer inspection, we should realize that manipulative
relations, regardless of the "good" they purport to serve, raise a serious
ethical concern: Where does the therapist draw the line if he doesn't
respect his contract with those with whom he works?

It even has been suggested that the encounter culture has launched a
campaign to exorcise the superego of modern man (Stone, 1970).
Sometimes skillfully, often unwittingly, core values and attitudes that
society has deemed essential to its regulation are being reshaped,

---

[1] This consideration may appear contradictory to the immediacy of experience
discussed in Chapter 4. It is, however, the struggle with apparent and inherent
paradoxes in the human condition that legitimizes existential inquiry as a
metarational endeavor.

cavalierly disregarded, or brutally removed by means of group pressure and identification with the "guilt-liberated" group leader. This subtle form of societal change doesn't appear to work; these group practitioners seem unaware that public compliance does not in and of itself lead to internalized behavioral change. I suspect that many of these practitioners are ignorant of the literature and hence unaware of what others in the encounter field and in the more established group practices have tried to do with groups and of the results of these endeavors (Goldberg, 1970b).

Instead of operating from a well-grounded and sound conceptual base, many encounter practitioners rely entirely on gut feelings. "I know I am a good leader," said one, "because I have a 'gut' feeling for people" (Goldberg, 1971). Such encounter leaders believe that their most significant contribution to ameliorative endeavors is their intuitive sense of when a technique or structured exercise is required, which technique is best, and how to engineer the technique effectively. I assume in an encounter experience that participants will expect me to bring to the group a wide assortment of structured exercises and techniques to use in difficult moments in the encounter to break through impasses and resistance. This brings me to a consideration of social technology. According to Lieberman and his associates (1973), "incorrect technology" was the fundamental problem in the encounter groups investigated (p. 451).

## Social technology

It seems to me that despite the lip service both psychotherapists and encounter practitioners give to behavioral change, most people come to a therapeutic situation not to be made different or to be compelled or taught how to act differently, but to become more accepting of what they already are. My clinical and encounter experience suggests that an individual does not change dysfunctional aspects of himself until he comes to accept and understand himself as he is. To do otherwise he would unpropitiously expend his energy in denying and defending against what he is. I have become skeptical about pervasive personality changes as the result of a single experience, no matter how intensive the encounter might have been. I have come to realize that people change when they are ready to change. This, of course, does not imply that behavioral change is entirely resistant to conscious effort or external facilitation. It does suggest, however, that efforts at behavioral change evoked (or compelled) during an encounter experience may be premature and lack durability. This contention seems strongly confirmed by the Lieberman study.

There appears to be a definite developmental progression to psychological growth (Freud's libido theory and Erikson's identity crises are but two theoretical delineations). Each developmental step requires a well-timed and relevant response from significant others in the interpersonal field of the individual in the throes of change. An effective encounter practitioner takes into account a participant's pattern of growth, as well as his style of resistance. He respects both the participant's right to proceed at his own pace and his right to remain as he is if that is his professed wish (Goldberg, 1970b).

In obviating these ethical and therapeutic considerations, encounter practitioners frequently circumvent problems of resistance by simply ignoring them or by getting the participant involved in a nonverbal exercise. They seem to feel that if they can get the participants to put their feelings into action, then there is no need to explore these feelings cognitively. Frequently in these groups, once emotion is expressed, it is dropped. These is no endeavor to explain the meaning of these feelings. The objective of the leaders of these groups is, apparently, to induce the participants to express emotion but not to learn what the emotion is all about or to attain a sense of mastery over it (Goldberg, 1970b). What these practitioners fail to realize is that experience remains largely unconscious and inaccessible to rational action unless the opportunity for cognitive processing is available. It is understandable, then, that the assumptions made by the encounter practitioners investigated by Lieberman about the accomplishments of structured exercises and other action-oriented interventions in influencing desired behavioral change in participants were not substantiated by the research. The "high learners" in Lieberman's study reported significantly more encounter incidents that involved the presence of insight and the reception of cognitive information than they did other types of group events, such as structured exercises.

I am not overly concerned with exercises and techniques. Techniques, as I have tried to indicate, are meaningless without some understanding of what is going on in the encounter. The utilization of a technique presumes the knowledge of a goal. Before suggesting exercises in a group, I need the opportunity to observe and interact with participants and consider the questions: What are their unexpressed needs? Where are they as a group? What are the normative conditions and the collusive hopes and fears of the participants at this moment and how are these factors shaping behavioral events in the group? and, most important, Where am I, as facilitator, in the group? How am I involved? How am I colluding with the participants in avoiding some of the meaningfulness of the encounter for each of the protagonists? To know this, I must ascertain what I am anxious about and have been avoiding (Goldberg, 1975b).

It is only at the moment in which I get in touch with these dynamic and therapeutic concerns that I can judiciously decide where to go in the group. By knowing what my contract is with each of the participants-as-protagonist—derived from an awareness and an agreement of how we will collaborate as authors of a specific plot in his personal saga—and by being aware of what is impeding progress at that particular moment in the encounter, I sense what needs to be done to redirect our efforts. By utilizing myself as a trained, sensitive, and responsive conductor, I sense at what moment to:

1. help induce the climate in the group in which trust and sincerity are experienced by the participants as both possible and desired,
2. not intervene in the process—for example, let the group stay with a difficult silence,
3. encourage fantasy material and associations to release repressed data,
4. induce rational discussion to process material cognitively,
5. use statements and interpretative interventions to describe the dynamics of the situation, permitting the participants to process the material as they will,
6. encourage interactions among the participants and/or participate myself in interactions with others in the group to provide relational possibilities in the group,
7. take an active and directive role in the group, suggest behavioral actions, and involve participants in nonverbal and other structured exercises to facilitate awareness of the material being avoided.

When I use the latter option, it is extremely important that the technique employed be relevant to the participant at that moment. A practitioner conveys a lack of confidence in his own clinical skills if he utilizes a technique because he or the participants are bored or threatened by existing conditions. This indicates a need to entertain and appease the group members, rather than a concern for the difficulties they are experiencing (Goldberg, 1970a).

Encounter practitioners have been particularly prolific in developing group exercises that provide participants with the opportunity to experience salient interpersonal processes that might otherwise require a long development in conventional psychotherapy. In my view, however, these techniques emphasize individual assertion and tend to regard inclination toward social responsibility as a neurotic manifestation. Lieberman found that the potency of structured exercises as a form of leader intervention was not particularly impressive. He believes that the effects of structured exercises are transitory because the participants do not experience what happens in the encounter group as being a product of their own endeavors (Lieberman, et al., 1973, p. 419). Consequently, the most important structured exercises, or *simulated situations,* as I prefer to call them, would appear to me to be those that enable each of the participants to master skills that will enable him to come to terms with his human condition by means of an interpersonally cooperative endeavor. The simulated situations described in Chapter 6 are designed to get the participants in touch with their own and their fellow participants' loneliness and despair, to take each other seriously, rather than to regard their concerns about one another as neurotic manifestations (Goldberg, 1976b).

Simulated situations are, of course, no more propitious as a modality for addressing existential concerns in an encounter experience than any of the other possible interventions at the disposal of a well-trained encounter practitioner. Each type of intervention has its proper time and place. An encounter practitioner becomes skilled when he has learned to temper his knowledge of technique and theory with intuition and interpersonal sensitivity. In my encounter practice, exercises that involve some psychological risk for participants are generally confined to the involvement of no more than two or three participants at a time. This gives me the opportunity to evaluate whether each of the participants is willing to be involved, how he needs to be involved, how he is prepared to be involved, and finally, how he experiences the exercise. When I suggest exercises that involve several participants, if not the entire group, these techniques are generally psychologically supportive rather than risky for the participants.

*Psychotherapy*
*education*

Discussion of technology to deal with resistive behavioral patterns in an encounter group raises for me the issue of psychosocial education. Analysis of resistance and transference is not sufficient to inform participants in an encounter group of the responsibilities required of them to work effectively in the encounter experience. The same holds true for psychotherapy. My experience with both encounter and psychotherapy groups has led me to believe that clients work more profitably when they are educated about therapeutic work. A number of studies have indicated that clients require a clear orientation about useful therapeutic behavior (Truax, et al., 1968; Yalom, et al., 1967; Powermaker & Frank, 1963). Nondirective approaches, therefore, work at cross-purposes to this need. Practitioners cannot avoid imposing their values in their work. Rather than trying to remain neutral, practitioners need to help shape therapeutically productive postures by reinforcing their clients for therapeutic and facilitative responses (Goldberg, 1975b). I find it fatuous to relegate all the client's rational concerns about the treatment process to the status of intellectualization and all his requests for expected psychotherapeutic behavior to the status of passive-dependent resistance. I have been increasingly impressed with the realization that much of what practitioners frequently regard as resistance is simply the client's ignorance of therapeutic behavior, as well as a legitimate reaction to inconsistent and nondirective approaches.

Because encounter group experiences are time limited, the concern for efficacious technology is perhaps more accentuated than it is in long-term therapeutic situations. In my experience, behavioral patterns and improved psychosocial functioning may be taught profitably in an encounter experience, provided that the social technology is predicated on conversance with the needs and goals of each participant involved in the endeavor.

The encounter movement, despite a wide variation in origins,[2] is based primarily upon only two, albeit rather divergent, ontological notions. Indeed, one of the most impressive things about practitioners

[2] The history of the encounter movement is well known and need not be reviewed here. The reader interested in this history should see Yalom (1970), Goldberg (1970a), and Goldberg (1973).

of encounter therapy is their willingness to borrow theory, method, and technique freely. However, in so doing, they have not been as conscientious as we might like in specifying the ontological notions and rationale behind the social technology they employ. The two ontological notions upon which encounter technology is based have not been sufficiently differentiated from each other, with serious consequences for encounter practice.

The first ontological approach is concerned primarily with teaching social technology, which will effect lasting changes in the participant's interpersonal skill and functioning after he leaves the encounter experience. The second ontological approach is an appeal to deep emotional needs that have been unsatisfied during the participant's tender years. In my view, conventional psychotherapies have failed to address adequately these two significant areas of psychological concern.

The techniques I categorize as falling within the social technology approach focus upon such skills as learning to read metacommunications; being aware of one's own body language and those of others; fighting fairly by setting up rational rules; ceasing to impose unrealistic demands upon oneself and others by checking one's irrational attitudes against psychological lists constructed, for example, by rational-emotive practitioners; and learning to interpret one's own life script and those of others by being aware of the games described by transactional analysis practitioners. Each of these techniques is based upon the assumption that there is an available model for improved interpersonal functioning. Interactive skill training and learning how to learn in an interpersonal setting teaches the participant the required steps in assuming leadership functions in the family and other natural groupings. This is an example of what Miller (1969) has referred to as "giving away psychology": changing people through education rather than therapeutic practice. Consequently, a salient characteristic of this approach is the assumption that understanding and skill in human relations can be taught. The emphasis is not on changing the psychodynamics of the participants but on teaching participants to use therapeutic, psychological, and educational concepts and principles in order to have greater influence in affecting situations outside of the group.

The second approach appears to be an answer to what the transactional analysis practitioners have referred to as the "child ego state." The emphasis is on deeply felt emotional experience generated within the group situation. In psychodynamic therapy, the emphasis appears to be on diluting and then more manageably reintroducing the psychological states that were originally experienced as traumatic by the client. In the new group approaches, the attempt appears to be to induce sudden and complete diminution of defenses against instinctual urges formulated at the client's preverbal level of functioning. The result is that the originally traumatic events are experienced again, directly and undiluted, but they are experienced in the present with the warmth and caring of the other group members rather than in the past with the rejection or indifference of the original objects. Primal scream, yelling, guided fantasies through childhood, and other such techniques are attempts to create intensive emotional experiences, as well as to circumvent impasses with resistive participants, with little or no cognitive processing of the experience.

Practitioners of both approaches must concern themselves with the style they wish to employ in having the participant experience new learning opportunities. These styles vary, of course, from "letting it happen" to "making it happen" (Lennung, 1974-75). Unlike the group leader in the first approach, the practitioner in the second approach, although he may be rather active in the session, tends to avoid taking responsibility for the learning experience. Group leaders in this position insist that they are not there to cure or to take care of participants. Instead, they are together with the participants in order to share a growth experience with them (Goldberg, 1973). Group leadership, as a result of the therapist's sharing responsibility with group members, tends to be more egalitarian than based on the authority and expertise of the therapist, as it is in the psychodynamic, or the first, approach. Where the egalitarian notion is practiced, every group member, be he client or therapist, is seen as one who heals and who is healed by others in the group. In these groups, there is stress on the group leader's openness, disclosure, and congruence of feeling, rather than on the withholding of strong affect. The group leader's role modeling of self-disclosure is designed to encourage open communication among the group members. Feedback is accentuated, in contrast to interpretation. Emphasis is on how a person is perceived by his peers and what he chooses to do about how others see him rather than on what he is and why he became that way.

The emphasis on feedback transforms the issue of countertransference to a new level. How a client fares in a group cannot be explained simply by a consideration of the pathology and psychodynamics of the participants in attendance. Examination must be directed to the role, style, and personality of the group leader (Goldberg, 1970b). There is increased awareness and attention to how group leaders subtly influence what happens in their groups (Goldberg, 1970b). Taking this into account, many encounter group leaders regard the group members as powerful counteractors to countertransferential tendencies by the group leader (Goldberg, 1975b). Those psychodynamic psychotherapists who emphasize the contamination of client perceptions due to transference, projective identification, and other distortions are less apt to utilize this monitoring capacity by group members. Generally, encounter group leaders underscore the group members' capacity for offering a perspective of process in the group that is different from, but no less valuable than, that of the group leader.

In contrasting the two approaches, it should be noted that the leadership and followership roles are defined more clearly in the social technology approach than in the deep emotional needs approach. In the former, the group leader takes considerable responsibility for the learning experience. Modalities for peer interaction must be taught in this approach, since knowledge of how to be interpersonally effective is not assumed to be an instinctual or natural tendency. In the latter approach, the group leader presents himself as being responsible for himself and insists that group members are responsible for themselves. He encourages group members to act spontaneously and on gut feelings. This would suggest that the role model for assuming harmonious and satisfying functioning is obtained by experiencing oneself in different ways—by participating in awareness exercises, processing feedback from other group members, and trying to emulate behaviors that the group leader models. Reliance upon verbal and nonactive interaction is viewed as ineffective or too slow (Goldberg, 1975b). Most encounter practitioners (most psychotherapists, for that matter) appear to emphasize one or the other of these two ontological approaches. In order to maximize available time in an encounter experience, I try to balance both these positions.

Having explored the learning technology of the encounter group, we need also to consider the dynamics and processes in a group that prompt the encounter practitioner to intervene in order to make the participants aware of their own involvement in what is occurring in the group. In all groups, there are many preconceived assumptions and expectations held by the participants about what should happen in an encounter group. I refer to these processes as the subtle aspects of a group. These predominantly unconscious notions become pooled and shared by the entire group membership, often in very subtle and obscure ways. It is on the basis of these unconscious notions that group members operate in rewarding and rejecting one another's behavior (Goldberg, 1970b). To the extent that these unconscious notions about group behavior are shared by participants, either because of similar personal orientations or through social contagion, they are referred to as *common group tensions*. These tensions are the shared, covert aspects of group process in which the needs and defenses of the group members place them at odds with one another. The manifest content of group activity may embrace any conceivable issue, but regardless of the manifest content, there always rapidly develops an underlying group tension or emotion that the participants are unaware of, but which is significantly influencing their behavior (Goldberg, 1970a).

These group tensions are composed of the divergent expectations, demands, and desires of the group members about what they intend to derive from their group experience. These tensions reveal that there are conflicts between the group's implicit and explicit working contracts. Common group tensions, if not brought to the participants' awareness, block them from working effectively on the goals for which they have convened. Knowledge of the principles of body language is crucial to the practitioner in dealing with common group tensions. Nonverbal signals often transmit powerful and urgent emotions from participant to participant or from group member to the group as a whole. One of the encounter practitioner's major tasks is to reveal these group tensions and explain their meaning for the work of the participants (Goldberg, 1970a).

If these group tensions are not revealed, a meaningful group working contract cannot be formalized. In poorly conducted encounter groups, group tensions remain hidden agendas. This aversive condition leads to group regression and depersonalization of group members. If the participants' goals are impeded because of primitive emotions evoked in pursuing these goals, and if the participants are unable to communicate these feelings to one another in an open manner, then frustration, anger, and social contagion break through with full fury (Goldberg, 1970a).

In elucidating the dynamics and processes taking place in a group, there are three general approaches to analyzing the group: (1) the Group Leader may focus on the entire group as an entity, (2) he may concentrate on a subgroup within the larger group, or (3) he may simply disregard the group as a configural reality and concern himself instead with each member of the group as an individual entity in a situation where other social objects are present (Goldberg, 1973). In conducting an encounter group, I do not maintain any one of these three perspectives exclusively; I shift focus periodically. It is incumbent upon the encounter practitioner to know when it is appropriate to work with one level of group analysis rather than another.

During an encounter experience, I select exercises and techniques to elucidate dynamics and processes at each of these levels of group functioning. I will illustrate with an encounter group workshop I conducted at the Fifth International Congress of Group Psychotherapy in Zurich a few years ago (Goldberg & Goldberg, 1975). I first sought to show how a togetherness situation, composed of strangers, is transformed into a group situation in which participants are decisively interrelating. I accomplished this by asking for volunteers early in the workshop to move chairs and tables in order to create more space in which the participants could work, then pointing out the nonverbal and symbolic expressions of the changing mood of the participants to contrast the climate of the group before and after this deceptively innocuous warm-up exercise. Following this warm-up, I used *milling* (Goldberg, 1973, pp. 194–196) to demonstrate early group sociometric configuration, a reflection of the level of relatedness and the cohesion of the group as a whole. Later in the session, I used the magic shop (see Chapter 3) to illustrate interpersonal contract negotiation among several members (a subgroup) of the group. Still later in the group, I selected *the reflected image technique*[3] to bring out repressed material and ego defenses of a participant who asked the group to help her make some behavioral changes. I suggested that before she seriously tried to make personal changes, she might wish to simply experience herself differently. This intervention takes place at the intrapersonal level of group

[3] In this technique, a participant selects another person in the group in whom he or she identifies conflict areas similar to his or her own. The two participants sit facing each other. The first participant is asked to look intently at the other as if looking into a mirror and then to relate what he or she sees in this reflected image.

analysis and is in accord with psychosocial training as an active experiential endeavor rather than as a passive cognitive experience (see discussion in Chapter 7).

## The problem
## of reentry

In my view, when appropriately involved in its task, the encounter group, like the Greek chorus, enables each of its participants to understand his personal saga (life contract)—his personal and interpersonal strategies, assumptions, expectations, wishes, hopes and fears—by which, as protagonist, he has attempted to live by and, frequently, for which he has been ready to die. Once this preliminary work has begun, the chorus and the protagonist begin to revise the saga, to express it and act it out with greater authenticity, openness, and congruent awareness of the information and sentiment protagonist and chorus have shared. The encounter practitioner may suggest techniques or provide behavioral models to facilitate resolution of areas of conflict or to develop skills that the protagonist and chorus have recognized as essential for becoming the person the protagonist seeks to become. The warmth and intimacy found in the best of encounter groups serves to reinforce the integration of the protagonist's new learning into his ongoing saga. The encouragement for developing intimate and satisfying relationships among the participants effectively serves this endeavor, provided that the practitioner and participant keep clearly in mind that lasting satisfaction is derived from relationships in the community, not from exclusive encounter group relationships that require hopping from one encounter group to the next. Within the context of community representation in an encounter group, each protagonist's revised saga can be socially validated. The other encounter participants, as representatives of present and future relationships, provide the opportunity for each participant to struggle with, contract, and negotiate for the conditions he seeks. But only within the community, where the "patient" role cannot be evoked to provide false safety, can his saga be actualized (Goldberg, 1975b).

Intensive group experiences are short-lived unless reentry is built into the methodology. Encounter practitioners, even those with psychoanalytic backgrounds, seem to believe that the working through that is such an integral part of psychodynamic therapy can be accomplished by the encounter participant on his own in the period immediately following the encounter experience. These optimistic practitioners seem to believe that if behavioral change is to occur it will happen in the immediacy of the encounter session (Schaffer & Galinsky, 1974). In this respect, encounter therapy differs markedly from conventional psychotherapy. This circumvention of the problem of participant reentry is, I believe, a major theoretical limitation and treatment problem of encounter therapy. The problem stems from a series of dubious philosophical notions that encounter practitioners assume: (1) the world outside of the encounter movement is a depriving environment, the encounter *Weltanschauung* leads to growth; (2) psychotherapy is a microcosm of the world outside, therefore, avoid psychotherapy and its conservative tenets; and (3) individual assertion is synonymous with personal responsibility, so that, if an individual feels he isn't getting what he wants from others, it is because he isn't assertive enough, and when another becomes threatened by one's assertiveness, it is the other's problem because he needs encounter experience.

I believe that in working with a participant's serious concerns about himself, I am involved in the practice of psychotherapy regardless of whether we are in an encounter group or a psychotherapeutic session. As an encounter practitioner, I am no less a psychotherapist. I do wish not to help participants insulate themselves from the world at large, but rather to enable them to develop social and personal skills for cooperatively coming to terms with other people. To foster a social modality in which each participant may effectively review, experiment with, or if he chooses, modify and revise his personal strategies and core attitudes about himself and his existential condition, the climate and composition of the group must represent the realities of the society with which he is seeking to come to terms.

A confrontation group in a Synanon program may, with some justification, brutally strip away the last remnants of defenses and reshape the character of the participants to fulfill Synanon's ethos. The goal of Synanon is to build a better self-contained subculture and not to return residents to the addictive society-at-large. On the other hand, for an Esalen-type group to do such reshaping for a weekend marathoner is both unrealistic and dangerous (Goldberg, 1975b). Encounter experience is a therapeutic experience, not a substitute for it. Paradoxically, overly "successful" encounter experience, in which the group leader and fellow participants are too reasonable, too accepting, and too caring, creates an insulation of treatment from life. Why should a participant have to risk hurt again from objects in his daily existence who lack the caring, reasonable understanding of his group leader and fellow participants? Whereas severe anxiety and depression blot out time and annihilate the future in his everyday world, the proliferation of encounter experience (or psychotherapy for that matter) guarantees the participant the security of a future as long as he continues to identify himself as in need of "encountering" (Goldberg, 1975c). Group encounter leaders and participants alike slip too easily into role relationships in which the group leader and the other group members take on the functions and responsibilities the participant and the significant others in his daily world have been assuming or should be assuming (Goldberg, 1977).

I believe it is neither responsible nor useful to leave pending serious concerns issuing from an encounter experience, and that the problem of reentry can be eased by concluding the encounter experience with an *application period*. Therefore, I conclude the encounter weekend with some exploration of how the process that evolved during the weekend can be applied to the participant's daily roles and functions. I view one of the major values of the encounter experience to be the inculcation of interpersonal knowledge that participants acquire, both on an affective and on a cognitive level, and with which they can affect conditions in their daily membership groups. Unless the encounter practitioner helps to bridge the encounter experience with the participants' daily lives, the value of an experiential group as a learning experience that can be generalized is lost. Although the encounter may be over, there are undoubtedly still participant concerns that require continuing psychological attention. I make recommendations to the participants as to how they may follow up these concerns in their everyday lives.

# chapter 12

# The therapeutic community

We live for the growing of the human spirit, and we
strive toward that growth up to the last moment of
possibility.

—R. Redfield

My starting point for applying the therapeutic partnership approach to
my work with clients is the brilliant, visionary, and existentially
oriented thinking of Trigant Burrow. Early in this century, Burrow, a
psychoanalytically trained psychiatrist, recognized that "the continuity
of the group and the isolation of the individual are processes which are
of their nature exclusive of one another" (1927). To treat the individual
patient, isolated both from the community of others whence his neurotic symptoms were derived and from those in whom he deeply desires to
elicit caring response, seemed artificial and contrary to Burrow, by
reason and evidence. He argued, apparently without much success,
with the analysts of his day:

> We need to rid ourselves of the idea that the neurotic individual is sick
> and that we psychopathologists [psychiatrists] are well. We need to
> accept a more liberal societal viewpoint that permits us to recognize
> without protest that the individual neurotic is in many respects not more
> sick than we, ourselves. For we quite lose count of the circumstances that
> the neurotic in his private substitutions and distortions has merely to
> ingratiate himself in the collective confederacy of substitutions and
> distortions which you and I, with no less eye to our self-protection, have
> had the cunning to subscribe to under the cover of our arbitrary, pseudo-
> group symptomatology.

Burrow's ideas have been furthered in theory and practical
methodology by such seminal thinkers as W. R. Bion (1961) and
Henry Ezriel (1952) and, most recently, in the concept of the therapeutic community, in which each individual entering a designed community is asked to look at his distress as part of a neurosis shared generally 195

by every other person in the community, including psychotherapists and other staff. This concept developed out of attempts to reform the age-old *total institution*, a term that encompasses residential institutions, such as prisons and mental hospitals for adults, schools for the emotionally disturbed, and training schools and orphanages for children.

### Eighteenth-century humanism

In the seventeenth and eighteenth centuries, the conditions in total institutions were deplorable. Patients were chained up, interned for life, and isolated from human company. Philippe Pinel, as director of the asylum at Bicêtre, agitated for reform and managed, in 1793, to have the psychotic patients released from their fetters. Pinel was not alone in his concern at that time. Rush, Band, and Kirkbride in North America and Tuke and Murray in England were independently carrying out their appeals for reform in the treatment of the insane. The total institutions of the seventeenth and eighteenth centuries were results of the prevailing social conditions. The inmates were forced to endure extreme abuse and deprivation before the reformers could rouse sufficient sentiment in reaction to these conditions (Zilboorg, 1941). As is always the case, intellectuals espousing social ideals had to fight public inertia to have their ideas accepted. It takes dynamic and forceful reformers, personally committed to social ideas, to awaken the public to abuses it prefers to think have been removed in decades past or will naturally disappear.

What new conception of human nature inspired the reformers of total institutions in Pinel's day? Certainly, medical science had made a large advance in understanding the conditions supporting disease. Pinel's treatment of the insane was a product of this knowledge. He believed that the fettered inmates were unmanageable because they had been deprived of fresh air, sanitation, and other natural comforts men usually take for granted (Bockoven, 1956). In addition to giving the inmates freedom of the grounds, Pinel and his associates improved the living conditions of the asylum and found activities for the inmates.

Medical science alone cannot fully account, however, for the reconsideration of institutional conditions. The social philosophy of the day was heavily influenced by a reconsideration of the rights of man. The American colonies, trailed by France, had cast off the shackles of tyranny and proclaimed that the God-given right of all men was to be free. Rousseau, Locke, Jefferson, and Paine were certainly not thinking of the mentally ill, the criminal, and the indentured child in formulating their political philosophies. Nevertheless, the prevailing philosophy of the nature of man—that he is inherently free and chooses to give up certain of his liberties to the state in return for protection from the state—had been carried into the street and been fought and died for by the populace. Men so recently redefined as free could not be entirely indifferent to the plight of the imprisoned within their own ranks.

Furthermore, it has been argued that the science of the eighteenth and nineteenth centuries held that an absolute standard of individual responsibility was impossible because human actions, like those of physical bodies, were subject to unknown forces over which the individual had little control (Bockoven, 1956). This assumption pointed up the qualities all men shared in common. The popular sentiments of the day supported this view of science, at least to the extent that it, too, emphasized the commonality of man—his inherent right and burning desire to be free. The feeling came to prevail that if the prisoner and the insane could not be set at liberty because of their danger to society, at least their life could be made as comfortable and nonpunitive as possible within the institution. However, humanitarianism, as a thread in the social movement to improve the conditions of the inmate, was not, properly speaking, a system of therapeutic treatment. Essentially, it was a reconsideration of man's worth. But, once the spirit of humanitarianism liberated the inmate from punishment for his disabilities, earnest efforts could begin to rehabilitate inmates through a movement known as "moral treatment."

So rapidly did reform take place in total institutions from the impact of moral treatment after the turn of the century that, by 1842, Charles Dickens, on a return visit to the United States, described the mental institutions as conducted on the basis of an enlightened friendship and understanding. Twenty years before in the United States, such a view would have been worse than heresy. Dickens described the patients as being as fully trusted with the tools of their trade as if they were sane men (Bockoven, 1956). The phrase, "trusted as if they were sane men," reveals the essence of the moral treatment approach. Moral treatment advocates, operating more on the basis of common sense than of empirical evidence, held the view that mental disturbances resulted from exposure to severe social and emotional stress that incapacitated the sufferer from employing his reason. There was deep conviction at the time that the inmate should be encouraged to engage himself in purposeful activity through stimulation of his friendship, arousal of his interests, and attention to his physical comfort.

Lay persons who had personal experience with the abuses of the total institutional systems, such as Clifford Beers and Dorothea Dix, did much to gain public support for the moral treatment movement. Humanitarianism, then, provided the groundwork for the influx of moral treatment, which reached its zenith in the United States and England between 1820 and 1860. Real therapeutic progress has always been impossible without the humanitarian sentiments of the populace. Without the sympathy and the aid of the public and the financial support of the state, few individuals or institutions have had the re- sources to carry on innovative programs, and, without popular urging, government until very recently has been unresponsive to humanitarian reform.

## Nineteenth-century
## pessimism

I need not go into a more detailed discussion of the moral treatment movement as it is admirably discussed elsewhere (Rees, 1957). I will touch here upon the failure and decline of the moral treatment move- ment because it helps to explain the present-day philosophy of the total institution. It is generally accepted that the use of moral treatment declined during the latter half of the nineteenth century, reaching its nadir in the first quarter of the present century. Undoubtedly, as some have claimed, the decline is partially due to the increasing size of asylums, which made it impossible for the physician to spend as much time with each patient as he had in earlier days. As the physician became more involved in administrative work, he lost touch with his patients, leaving them largely in the custody of untrained staff. The traditional role of the nonprofessional worker has been custodial rather than therapeutic. Relationships between nonprofessional staff and pa- tients and among patients themselves were seen as unavoidable by- products of custodial care rather than as important contributions to the patient's treatment. After all, it was reasoned, physicians were specially trained to cure illnesses and disease; nurses and attendants lacked this knowledge. Only a physician, therefore, was equipped to conduct therapeutic relationships with a patient. Moreover, as with contagious diseases, patient relationships, if not discouraged, would aggravate each other's morbid conditions. Therefore, as the ratio of patients to doctors increased, the amount of treatment per patient decreased proportionately (Rees, 1957).

Some have also argued that a spirit of therapeutic nihilism was perpetuated through the impact of Darwinian ideas and advances in microscopy. The idea grew in the late 1800s that mental illness and criminality were inherited due to irreversible cellular change, which could be shown under the microscope. This led to the belief that insanity and criminality were incurable, an essentially constitutional viewpoint according to which aberrant behavior is the emanation of some innate quality that causes or predisposes the victim to act in an irrational manner. The constitutional approach generally has been inversely related to social forms of rehabilitation. Thus, the leading nihilist of the day, Dr. Pliny Earle, stated pontifically that mental illness was an "inexplicable mystery" to even those psychiatrists who were best informed on the subject (Rees, 1957). The result of this gloomy attitude led to the belief that "the interests of society were best secured by segregating such people as cheaply and quickly as possible so that they did not reproduce themselves" (Rees, 1957).

With the feeling that mental illness was incurable, attempts to rehabilitate the inmate and discover curative methods were virtually abandoned. Rare exceptions to this nihilism were the voices of Dorothea Dix and Clifford Beers. Optimism about rehabilitation of persons suffering from emotional disturbance could not be effectively generated until those who were cast in the role of healers became appreciative of the vital impact of interpersonal interactions on the total social community in which resocialization endeavors were attempted. Thus, traditional attempts at rehabilitation were, at best, humane. They attempted to insulate the outcast from the "savage forces" in the external world and in himself. Because they regarded him as incapable of knowing his own mind and unable to improve his fate, they protected and nurtured him and made decisions for him. In so doing, they treated him as "sick," "insane," or "childish," and he fittingly acted in accordance with these expectations. It was only when the protective shield was removed from the inmate, when his "disease" was not used to protect him from having to take responsibility, that his "disease" could be understood as a learned response to his social reality.

The moral treatment movement in the United States did not provide an enduring treatment philosophy and methodology. It did, however, provide a strong impetus for a concept of social rehabilitation that had begun in Europe at least half a millenium before, but had, until the mid-1800s, no appreciable support in this country.

*The therapeutic*
*milieu*

This approach to rehabilitation today has come to be called by such appellations as the "therapeutic milieu," the "therapeutic community," "milieu therapy," "environmental therapy," the "total push," or some similar label. A number of such communities are described in philosophy, novels, and folk literature. A few outstanding examples are Plato's *Republic,* Francis Bacon's *New Atlantis,* Butler's *Erewhon,* and H. G. Wells's *A Modern Utopia.* These communities were the authors' conceptions of an ideal society. The Mormon and the Oneida communities were actual efforts to implement the theory and to institutionalize the dream of the ideal society based on principles of productive labor. Even earlier communities founded on this intent resulted in a system of colonies established in order to care for and treat the mentally disturbed at a time when suitable institutions were not available. The most famous of these communities for the mentally disturbed based upon self-government was at Gheel in Belgium. It came into existence in the thirteenth century.

One of the earliest and most successful schools operating under the principles of self-government and family-unit living in the United States was the House of Reformation near Boston. Established in 1826, the House of Reformation was operated for several years by the Reverend E. M. Wells, a young Episcopal minister. Wells believed that regardless of how incorrigible a boy might be, he could always be reformed while under 15 years of age, and very often beyond that age. He felt that if a child were treated as if he were incapable of such qualities as honesty and humor, he would never be able to develop a concept of himself that included these qualities. In a period where repressive and cruel treatment of children was commonplace and condoned, corporal punishments were entirely excluded from the House. By the vote of the children, the children's word of honor to behave was substituted for corporal punishment. The boys had their own self-government and their own court to handle misdeeds. Monitors were appointed among the boys at the beginning of each month, and the head monitor presided over the institution in the absence of the adult staff.

Total institutions with self-government were rare cases, however, until the influx of progressive education in the twentieth century. Exceptions were the George Junior Republic in the United States, which still exists, and the Borstal prison communities in Great Britain, begun a few years before the turn of the century and remaining in existence until World War II. The Borstal institutions were communities open to a degree unknown in the history of reformatories, and the Borstal system represented a form of amelioration generally unknown up until that time in institution reformation. Among the important features of the Borstal system were (1) a team approach by staff, (2) emphasis on productive occupation by inmates, (3) both social and vocational preparation of the Borstal resident for life outside in the community, (4) development of a positive climate with the townspeople in the community so that the Borstal residents were welcome in the community, and (5) presence of the resident at all conferences in which his progress was discussed (Brill, 1960). Due to a shortage in personnel, the Borstals were forced to close during the Second World War. As a prototype, they represent a predecessor of the rehabilitation community for psychiatric patients developed by Maxwell Jones and of other psychiatric facilities to be discussed in this chapter.

In recent times, the term therapeutic communities, under whatever names they have been called, has come to mean that the patient or prisoner is not treated in an insulated environment, set apart from the "normal," "healthy" kind of community life, activity, and people toward whom he is supposed to be rehabilitating himself. The concept of the therapeutic community holds that the process of rehabilitation parallels the process of growth and learning. Psychological treatment, if it is to be successful, cannot be set apart from the people with whom the inmate needs to develop social and emotional ties in the outside community. To improve his lot in society, the inmate first needs to improve his social skills so that he may gain the respect and admiration of those who are important to him. The inmate develops this social ability, interestingly, in the company of others, his peers, who share the same frustrations and aspirations as he does.

One of the most famous therapeutic milieus is the Menninger Clinic, which, in the late 1930s, organized therapeutic facilities "to meet the psychodynamically formulated unconscious needs of the patients, by prescribing appropriate tasks for them and personnel attitudes toward them" (Rioch & Stanton, 1953). A result of this approach was the development of a systematized hospital treatment identified as "milieu therapy" or "total push" theory (Myerson, 1939). In all of these methods, the repressed patient became the focus of a treatment plan that attempted to mobilize all possible hospital resources and refurbish his environment to motivate him to express the fears and anger that, because they became unbearable, shut him off from other people. The discerning reader will be aware that this oversimplified conception of sociotherapy dealt only with the rudiments of milieu treatment. More sophisticated theory and methodology were soon to follow.

*Current therapeutic*
*communities*

In more recent developments, the therapeutic milieu as a special movement appears split in two major directions. The first is the therapeutic milieu pioneered by August Aichhorn and exemplified most notably by Bruno Bettelheim and Fritz Redl. These practitioners work with autistic and "antisocial" youngsters. Being psychoanalytically oriented, Bettelheim and Redl institute a great deal of individual therapy and stress diagnostic evaluation of the child's psychotherapy, in addition to regulating the total environment field of the child to influence him therapeutically.

Redl, in founding his Pioneer House in Detroit, set out to treat a small group of severely disturbed youngsters. These youngsters can best be described as filled with hate. They did not have the capacity to control their aggression and were equally unable to postpone their demands for immediate gratification of primitive needs. Redl (Redl & Wineman, 1951) implemented his therapeutic program so that every child's request, every recreational activity, every argument was handled in such a way as to satisfy the child's needs while, at the same time, teaching him control. Every staff member, from the director to the gardener and chef, participated in the program, for like Aichhorn, Redl believed that affection is the indispensible core of all treatment. The child, Redl maintains, must be lavished with love and attention whether he "deserves" it or not. Unfortunately, due to the lack of financial support, Pioneer House was forced to close its doors after being in existence for only a few years.

The Orthogenic School in Chicago has been more fortunate financially. Run by Bettelheim (Bettelheim & Sylvester, 1948), it treats children with a variety of emotional disturbances. Bettelheim's therapy calls for an environment in which the child is constantly under treatment. The staff is trained to be highly permissive of deviant behavior and, like Redl's, to satisfy generously the infantile needs of the children. In so doing, the child often develops a positive relationship to the adults who provide for his well-being. Once a warm, accepting intimacy is established, the child is encouraged to amend his personality in the image of the persons who are now most important to him.

The other direction the therapeutic milieu movement has taken is that of the therapeutic community devoted to the rehabilitation of adult inmates of mental hospitals and prisons. Maxwell Jones (1956) and Paul Sivadon (1957), both psychiatrists, have been leaders in this field. Their therapeutic communities involve intensive group therapy in the form of group meetings (often the whole community convenes together) in which staff members participate equally with patients. Staff members are expected to express grievances rather than remain professionally aloof as in conventional therapy. Therapeutic community practitioners have come to realize that the type of adjustment involved in adapting to a new set of values, such as may be required to rehabilitate the patient, is best handled in the community where other patients are involved with similar problems. Correspondingly, in a therapeutic community, the responsibility for treatment is not exclusively the province of the trained staff, but is conjointly a concern of all the community members, patients, professionals, and nonprofessionals alike.

*Therapeutic partnership*
*of staff and patients*

Many psychiatric hospitals provide extensive training programs for residents in psychiatry; graduate students in psychology and social work; and trainees in nursing, the various rehabilitation counseling specialties, and pastoral counseling. Generally, the better-regarded psychiatric hospitals have the most extensive training programs. The eminent practitioners I know enjoy teaching, preferring to consult at those hospitals in which there are inquisitive students and trainees who question conventional mental health attitudes and practices. The patients in these hospitals also benefit indirectly from students and trainees questioning outmoded and ineffective practices, provided that staff is responsive to these inquiries.

For the most part, though, psychiatric patients resent the presence of students on their wards. They describe these trainees as there "to learn as much as they can from us and then go off into private practice and make a lot of money while we are still sitting here." This attitude reflects the rapid rotation of students and trainees who work with patients. A patient may be asked to work with a psychiatric resident, a clinical psychology intern, a social work student, and still another psychiatric resident in the course of 2 or 3 years because the student's apprenticeship requires rotation to several different services and, except for the psychiatric residency, the apprenticeship is rarely longer than a full year. Moreover, if a patient is regarded as an interesting case, he will have his medical history taken by several different medical students and have brief, but numerous, contacts with nursing students on each 3-week student nursing rotation on the patient's ward. Most of these data are dutifully collected in the patient's clinical folder with no real benefit to the patient. The patient is left with the feeling that each trainee has gathered a considerable amount of information about him but that he has not had the opportunity to share his deeper feelings with any of the trainees, nor has he been given the opportunity to get to know the trainees.

In addition to all this, most psychiatric hospitals do not have sufficient staff to work individually with each patient, particularly those unfortunate patients who are emotionally difficult to work with and are intellectually dull. To provide attention for patients that staff cannot work with individually in psychotherapy, psychiatric wards and units conduct patient-community meetings in which all of the patients and staff involved on the unit convene. Staff speak of these community meetings as an opportunity for staff and patients to work together to clarify misunderstandings and resolve ward tensions. I observed, however, during my own training, that these meetings were actually employed by staff to control patients who did not conform to the staff's prescriptions. Staff members would bring up specific complaints about particular patients and would encourage other patients to join the "therapeutic" confrontation of the "culprit." Patients found that they had no allies among the staff or even among their fellow patients. Staff were manifestly in concert so that each patient undoubtedly felt that he could not afford to take the part of another patient. Trainees, although encouraged to participate actively in the meetings, generally sat back and said very little. As a result, patients viewed the trainees as unsympathetic persons who were using them as guinea pigs for their own enlightenment, without any appreciable reciprocal benefit to the patients.

Later, when I served as a consultant to several therapeutic communities in a psychiatric hospital with an extensive training program, I found that the community meetings typically ran from 1 to 1½ hours. The last 15 to 30 minutes were utilized by staff and trainees to share their observations of what occurred in the community meeting. This was regarded as instructive in the trainees' learning experience. The unfortunate aspect of the post-group discussion was that the staff found it necessary to leave the patient group and to have their interchange with the trainees in private. Reactions and points of view brought up in the post-group discussion frequently had not been brought to the attention of the patients in the community meeting. Students, especially, were more candid about their impressions without patients present. Their perceptions of particular patients frequently differed from those of staff. Staff members also expressed disagreements among themselves in the post-group, which they were unwilling to express in the community meeting. Valuable information about patients was not being conveyed to patients. It was not because any of these differing perceptions were necessarily more valid than those expressed during the meeting, but because those perceptions added dimensions to a composite picture of each patient as a person, that they needed to be shared by the entire community. Frequently, these patient attributes could not be appreciated by the patient until staff first recognized them and helped the patient realize and deal with uncomfortable and threatening aspects of his personality.

I sought to modify these patient community meetings in keeping with the principles of the therapeutic community. I recommended that the patients be given the opportunity to sit in and listen to the post-group discussions. Some staff members complained that this would turn the post-group discussion into a replica of the community meeting. Some pointed out that the patients being discussed would be too resentful and argumentative to listen responsively to what was being said about them. This frequently was valid. I suggested, therefore, that we have the patients sit in on the post-group with the provision that they agree to remain silent for a set period of time. After staff and trainees had the opportunity to present their observations and perceptions, patients were given the opportunity to question or even confront staff and trainees on what was said. They were encouraged to indicate differences in how they perceived various staff members and trainees regarding them and to ask staff to try to reconcile these points of view. I served as a process consultant in order to transform threatening communication into therapeutically useful dialogue among the members of the therapeutic community. Because I did not work on the units to which I consulted, I was recognized by both patients and staff as having no vested interest in how I regarded any member of the community (Goldberg, 1970a; Goldberg, 1973).

The post-group sessions did not, of course, always run smoothly. Some of the material discussed was threatening to patients, and some of the confrontations provoked by patients were uncomfortable for staff. Yet, what happened was that the post-group sessions were dropped after a few months because staff and patients became aware that the sensitive dialogue that had initially been reserved for the post-group was now an integral part of the community meeting itself. As a by-product, there was, as well, less patient resentment of students and trainees, for now patients were receiving direct benefit from their presence on the ward.

The model of therapeutic community I have been following in this chapter focuses on the following notion of "community": A community is a social organism where people live and work, suffer frustrations and limitations, test strengths and seek resources, meet challenges and make future plans, take recreation and find communion with others. It includes all the other qualities that are important to living. There is, then, more to a community than a psyche. A community has a soul and a stomach, it has a hunger and a yearning to learn, grow, and regenerate (Goldberg, 1972a).

In creating a therapeutic community, mental health practitioner and patient alike must seek to create a modus vivendi where each community inhabitant—staff and patient—is enabled to become that which he seeks to be. This is to say, a successful therapeutic community is one that contributes toward assisting each citizen in "achieving an optimal social role in terms of his capacities and potentialities" (Wittenberg,

1968). A therapeutic community reflects this attitude by developing for all citizens opportunities to participate in the decisions and policy making of their community. Therefore, whereas an important component of the general goals of a therapeutic community is the provision of conventional therapies—group, individual, milieu, and so forth—the staff must be ready and able to provide consultation and preparation for these therapeutic modalities through role-modeling open and negotiable relationships with the patients.

A second notion in my model of therapeutic communities is as follows: The implementation of services in therapeutic communities too frequently operates from frames of reference that are both vague and poorly conceptualized. These programs will continue to be underdeveloped until they are predicated upon clearly conceptualized and theoretically specifiable premises. My attention to the concepts of equity, balance, and negotiation is an attempt to implement a treatment program based upon a basic model of interpersonal functioning.

# chapter 13

## Equity and contract negotiation in community mental health programs

The crowd has broken them
and the crowd shall heal them.

— L. Cody Marsh

In the past, psychological assistance has been viewed, paradoxically, either as a luxury for those who could financially afford it or as a necessary and an enforced treatment for those who did not conform to societal guidelines. Mental health services have never been viewed as the right of every citizen, largely because citizens themselves have in large measure denied the need for mental health services. Recent events in the public sector, such as pressures for inclusion of mental health services in the enactment of a national health insurance program, suggest a change in societal attitudes toward mental health.

Should society come to view psychological assistance as the right of every citizen, there will be serious ramifications for the psychotherapy practitioner, as a consideration of the evolution of medical practice shows: To the extent that the right to biological health has been accepted as the natural right of every citizen, medical practitioners have been restricted from carrying out with patients procedures and practices that are regarded as having dubious validity. There are stringent restrictions on the practice of legal counseling as well as on the practice of medicine. Apparently, the public has not demanded the same basic protection in the field of mental health as it has in medicine and law. Mental health services have remained relatively free of regulation of practitioners' credentials; therapists have been unrestricted in carrying out techniques and practices of limited or even nonexistent value. No state in the nation has, up to now, passed legislation to regulate those who practice psychological services for a fee unless the practitioner specifically refers to himself as a "physician" or a "psychologist." The New York State Psychological Association reports that there are as many unlicensed as licensed therapists practicing in New York State (Morgan, 1974).

National health insurance and peer review will unquestionably have a startling impact on the contemporary and future practice of psychotherapy. A national health insurance program will, for example, make the modes of treatment and the kinds of persons treated more complex for many practitioners than they are currently. It will question the practitioner's responsibility, not only to the persons he chooses to work with, but to the persons he chooses not to work with and to persons to whom he has heretofore been unavailable. Treatment through national insurance will probably be available to any citizen who wants or requires it. This will necessitate treatment modalities that may differ from those found effective with clients whom the private prac- titioner has traditionally treated.

The providers of mental health services are predominantly middle class and college educated. Their sociocultural backgrounds are highly similar to those of the clients they treat in private practice. Both come from a markedly circumscribed section of the social world, representing a high congruence of ethnic experience and religious, political, and philosophical values (Henry, et al., 1971). They share an orientation toward resolution of problems by means of rational discussion and compromise, working within and accommodating to the established social order (Goldberg & Kane, 1974a; Goldberg & Kane, 1974b). It is small wonder, then, that the middle-class mental health professional's attitudes best prepare him to provide ameliorative modalities that are insight oriented and to direct them toward clients who have a conscious philosophical stance toward life, who are capable of abstract and sym- bolic reasoning, and who have sufficiently conflict-free areas of psychological functioning to permit them to withstand day-to-day frus- trations, tensions, and problems so that they can struggle with the meaning of their existence and develop a viable sense of identity (Goldberg & Kane, 1974b).

Unfortunately, a large proportion of the persons requiring psycholog- ical services and certainly the most difficult cases, do not possess the required emotional and intellectual faculties necessary for traditional psychotherapy (Goldberg, 1973). Schofield (1964) and other investigators have documented that the younger, more attractive, better-educated, and less severely agitated client is more likely to be seen in private psychotherapy. Also, mental health education, which is heavily financed by public funds, has never been effectively linked to giving desperately needed services to those citizens who can least afford to pay for them. Psychiatrists trained in large part by National Institute for Mental Health stipends have been reluctant to treat the neglected once their training has been completed. It is rather difficult for hospitals in the metropolitan Washington, D.C., area to hire a full-time psychiatrist let alone an especially well-trained one, because insurance reimbursements make it possible for psychiatrists to treat more-preferred, less-difficult patients privately. When less-preferred clients consult a private practitioner, they are more likely than not to be seen for a short period of time and treated with chemotherapy rather than psychotherapy, if not immediately referred to a public mental health clinic or hospital. It has been estimated that one of every four hospital beds is occupied by a patient being treated for schizophrenia (Osmundsen, 1965). What is ironic and unfortunate about all this is that, whereas the less-preferred client is more likely to manifest a more serious and disabling psychological condition than the preferred client, it is the less-well-trained mental health workers in public agencies, hospitals, and institutions that find themselves having to deal with these more difficult cases. The private practitioners, who are, generally speaking, better trained and consequently better able to treat difficult clients, treat the preferred clients instead.

As mental health services come to be accepted as the natural right of every individual, the psychotherapist will increasingly be expected, if not required, to verify the validity of his practices. It is both ironic and tragic that the mental health professions, which are committed to helping those who are emotionally or characterologically disturbed, are unable to provide adequate treatment for a large number of those clients most in need of psychological assistance because their volitional disorders and other disabilities are resistive to the techniques present-day mental health practitioners have to offer (Goldberg, 1973). Innovative programs to work with difficult clients are clearly required. I will describe a specific one later in the chapter. Community mental health centers are the obvious institutions for providing such programs designed to serve the mass of people.

*The advent of community*
*mental health centers*

Community mental health, like the new therapy movement, has its impetus in humanistic and existential thought. Recognizing the importance of equity in human endeavor, a number of practitioners have sought to avoid the serious error conventional psychotherapeutic treatment has made in creating situations of inequity, imbalance, and psychotherapeutic upmanship in working with unsophisticated clients. The leaders of the community mental health movement realized that the implicit status relationship between patient and psychotherapist in the medical model treatment was one that served to increase the self-denigration of the patient rather than one that permitted the patient to learn to negotiate freely for his well-being in an effective and responsible manner.

The community mental health center movement arose in opposition to the traditional mental health clinic, which was a reactive therapeutic agent waiting patiently to be petitioned before dealing with individuals and families. There was little or no involvement of these reactive clinics in treating or dealing with the environmental forces that influence the client's daily problems and contribute to the maladies of scores of other persons being seen concurrently at the clinic (Goldberg, 1972b). Because the community mental health practitioner questioned the health of the existing normative structure in which the client lived, he assumed the role of a radical therapist.

The community mental health practitioner generally assumes that those who are called "emotionally disturbed" can be described more accurately as emotionally impoverished. Emotional disturbance is a deprivation and impediment in growth rather than an actual entity. The so-called emotionally disturbed person has been deprived of meaningful and significant relationships with others in the home and in the community. Each of these relationships serves as a lifeline that sustains and maintains the individual, keeping him alive and healthy. Many mental health practitioners are firmly convinced that the most ameliorative aspect of any therapeutic endeavor is not the insight accorded one's situation, nor the empathy and support extended to one by others, as important as these often are, but something more basic: the experience of seeking to be of help to others and finding one's efforts helpful and appreciated. Being of assistance to others is emotionally sustentative (Goldberg, 1972c). It restores lifelines with others. When a person performs needed social and emotional functions for others and is recognized for this, he becomes valued as a person. Concomitantly, he experiences a greater capacity for equity with others (Goldberg & Kane, 1974 a and b).

For example, the lives of many of the depressed middle-age women I saw as a director of a community mental health center revolved almost entirely about the home. When given the opportunity to bake a cake for a worker toward whom they felt warmly or to attend the children of other mothers who could not afford a babysitter so that they could attend sessions at the center, their depression lifted. They experienced greater satisfaction in these endeavors than, for example, in trying to help another client understand that the anger toward her husband and children might be due to unresolved conflicts with her own parents. It is these observations that in part confirm one of London's notions (1974; see Chapter 4) that for many people a meaningful involvement with others is the treatment of choice. A treatment program that excludes this opportunity while instead concentrating on intrapsychic issues completely misses the mark for these clients. What London seems to misperceive, however, is that it is frustration in the individual's inability to form meaningful interpersonal relations rather than idleness that drives many twentieth century clients to seek psychological assistance.

Viewing emotional disturbance from its interpersonal and social context, most helping professionals are no longer content today (as indicated in Chapter 11) to conceptualize the nature of emotional disturbance as a condition that is rooted *within* the distressed person. This is to say, mental health practitioners no longer regard it as appropriate to view mental illness as one would view a diseased liver or virus infection—as a disability that is housed within the body of a person. The character of present-day mental health practices has increasingly focused on interpersonal relations. The practitioner's search is for techniques to treat the patient's disturbed behavior in his daily interpersonal dealings. Correspondingly, most no longer believe that it is efficacious to remove the emotionally distressed person from the community and treat him in a separate and unfamiliar environment. The mental health practitioner who is visible in the community is also in a position to advise community agents in enriching the community, thus helping to prevent the advent of emotional disturbance and facilitating the increased psychological maturity of a community's citizens. To implement these theoretical notions about mental health treatment, community mental health centers have, since the Kennedy administration, been funded across the length and breadth of the nation.

In the past, mental health workers have pleaded for generous financial support from governmental sources. Without this support, the mental health professional has contended, viable community mental health programs could not be implemented. During the last decade, community health projects finally received a great deal of attention and support from the federal government, yet many have agreed that this support was insufficient. However this may be, the situation that now confronts the mental health workers is that funds to community mental health projects have been drastically cut; the worker must carry out his programs with much less financial support than in the past. For example, it is no longer possible to hire the large professional staffs that we have had in the past.

This situation is not necessarily a completely untoward turn of events. The concept of community mental health that many practitioners espouse but perhaps few practice requires an active involvement of community agents in the implementation of mental health programs. In my opinion, a sincere effort to involve community agents significantly in mental health services does not require large amounts of financial support. Indeed, the cost may be less in dollars than in ingenuity, creativity, blurring of professional and nonprofessional roles, radical departures from capitalistic modes of thought, implementation of barter systems of operation, and willingness to recognize strengths and resources in clients so that they may provide services to the community as "payment" for their treatment. I also want to explore in this chapter what mental health workers are currently doing to find alternatives to heavy financial support of their programs and what kinds of programs are being conducted and planned that do not require significant financial support but instead rely upon community resources.

*Failings in community*
*mental health*

Currently, mental health programs tend to regard the social and emotional problems of the urban poor as distinct rather than related entities. An example of this is treating the urban poor client in sessions dealing essentially with intrapsychic issues with little or no attention to the basis of current social stress. Living in a vermin-infested apartment is sufficient reason for a child's nightmares. This orientation has poorly served the urban poor. Studies by Hollingshead and Redlich (1958), Riesman and associates (1964), Minuchin (1967), and others have convincingly documented that mental health services to the urban poor are inadequate. It is my observation that mental health services to the urban poor operate from frames of reference that are both inchoate and poorly conceptualized. It seems evident that these programs will continue to be inadequate until they are predicated upon clearly conceptualized and theoretically specifiable premises. Without systematizing a wide array of sociological, philosophical, and psychological assumptions about the urban poor into a well-defined conceptual frame of reference, mental health services are doomed to be pervaded by contradictions and missing components.

From time to time, social systems are severely tested by inner tension and external pressures. Inevitably, breaks occur in all social systems. Deterioration of normative guidelines contributes to and further exacerbates existing conflict in the smaller units (e.g., family units) within that social system. Among the multiple-problem families frequently found among the urban poor, practitioners often find that standards and regulated exchanges among family members and with outsiders are not shared and do not function as they have been intended to by society at large.

The concept of eligibility for public welfare, for instance, was intended by concerned citizens and public officials as an adequate but temporary provision of the necessities of life for those citizens who could not secure them on their own. Welfare, however, is rarely a temporary state of existence. There have been few serious attempts to deal with the causes of poverty in this country. As a result, it is not unusual for generation after generation of a family to be on welfare. To the taxpayer, the person on welfare is regarded as leading an irresponsible life. Punitive attitudes and actions are taken toward the welfare family. Within this climate, members of welfare families experience difficulty communicating with one another, are unable to make meaning of their existence, and fail, subsequently, to function harmoniously.

The practitioner finds that in such families under conditions of social deprivation, the ever-present situational crises are compounded by inadequate social skills for dealing with these concerns. Lacking social skills and resources, the individual in a multiple-problem family feels incapable of freely and effectively negotiating in a fair manner with others. He feels that he can survive only by depending upon others to care for his needs, so he feels forced to assume the role of patient or child.

It is my observation that persons who seek mental health services are essentially concerned with establishing equitable relationships with significant others. It is my contention that in order to develop this capacity, the client needs the opportunity to experience three essential roles in the ameliorative process (Goldberg, 1972c). The role most ubiquitously sought by clients is that of *patient*. A patient is a person who, because he regards himself as sick or disabled, is unable to be of help to himself or others. A second role that many clients may assume is that of *student*. A student does not regard himself as having emotional problems; he convenes with a professional worker and is quite comfortable in a psychotherapy group or other group modalities in order to learn about what happens in therapy and to accelerate what he regards as his normal psychosocial development. He is generally too intent upon observing interesting events in psychotherapy processes to be of much help to others. Finally, there are clients who seek the role of *healer*. The healer tries to demonstrate that he understands and can deal with his own problems. In group or family therapy situations, he takes the role of assistant therapist and tries to compete with or win favor from the therapist by demonstrating his ability to be helpful to other group members.

It is important to realize that not only do clients assume all of these roles but that each of the three is essential to healthy psychological functioning at appropriate times. The patient role suggests that without the emotional recognition of dysfunctional aspects of his own behavior, an individual cannot ameliorate problem areas. In keeping with the conceptual scheme I have been presenting in this book, a major focus of mental health services should be to point out how the individual is seeking to achieve, maintain, or avert a position of equity with significant others in his life, that is to say, to indicate to the client how he uses the equity issue, in the form of justification, rationalization, illness, and weakness, to assume positions of inferiority, passivity, irresponsibility, or on the other hand, domination, oversolicitude, and overresponsibility.

The role of student suggests that without utilizing the cognitive skills of the student, an individual cannot generalize from one life situation to the next or learn from the experience of others. If equity is an essential dimension in effective psychosocial functioning, then the client must be taught directly how to negotiate for fairness in his interpersonal and societal transactions. It is not sufficient simply to seek out reasons why the client is not obtaining equitable object relations.

Finally, the healer role suggests that without the experience of being of assistance to others and being recognized and appreciated for these efforts, an individual's interpersonal relations would remain sterile and ungratifying. An ex-psychiatric patient has said it succinctly: "What patients want is some recognition of themselves as individuals . . . being recognized and appreciated as an individual who may have something positive to contribute" (Agel, 1971, p. 50). In the case of the Blunt family, who will be discussed in the section on results, the mother was encouraged by the therapist to assume a healer role. It appeared that she had required permission from someone other than herself to take this role. In it, she served as a reinforcer of certain concepts the therapist had been trying to get the family to deal with, and she gained, as well, increased status from the other family members.

Each one of us potentially is a patient; similarly, each one of us potentially is a healer. Persons in emotional distress are experiencing difficulty in their everyday functioning not because they have assumed one of these roles, but because they persevere in maintaining one role to the exclusion of others. Effective mental health programs provide ameliorative experiences for their clients insofar as these programs foster a realistic integration of learning experience in which the client: (1) is enabled to let others be of help to him (i.e., to be a patient), (2) experiences himself as being of help to others and learns to accept others' appreciation (i.e., to be a healer), and (3) acquires the cognitive skills needed to be an effective psychosocial agent in negotiating for himself and for the goals of others (i.e., to be a student).

Dumont, a community psychiatrist, finds it fascinating that studies of mental illness reveal that the incidence of psychiatric disorders is highest among the poor in all diagnostic categories except psychoneurosis—the condition most responsive to middle-class oriented psychotherapy. "Psychiatry has generated a middle-class treatment for middle-class patients" (Dumont, 1971, p. 27). In short, the urban poor client is neither oriented toward nor prepared to undergo the intellectual and emotional endeavors required by a middle-class worker and a middle-class treatment modality.

This serves to exacerbate an already inequitable and unbalanced interpersonal relationship. An effective therapist must give considerably of himself to help a client come to terms with his difficulty. Ethically, he can receive only a fee for his services. The poor client cannot afford to pay a fee. In relation to the mental health professional, he assumes an underdog, patient role, either passively or complainingly presenting his daily concerns to the professional as a perceived authority figure and waiting in turn to be told what to do. The practitioner, on the other hand, by training and preference, is prepared for the client to take a student role, which means, in middle-class thinking, that the client takes an intellectual interest in his problems and is willing to solve them himself, having once derived the necessary general principles in working with the practitioner.

It is no surprise, then, that the urban poor have been regarded by the mental health professional, in no small part in the defense of his professional integrity, as resistive and untreatable (Goldberg, 1973). These difficult clients are shunted off either to minority-group professionals who are patronizingly told that they "understand these people better than the rest of the staff," or to a middle-class professional with a lower threshold for guilt than other staff members, or to a nonprofessional who finds himself specializing in urban poor clients.

In short, mental health services to the urban poor are oriented toward middle-class values and middle-class levels of comfort and anxiety. As a result, these clients are forced exclusively into the role of patient. Urban poor clients being served by traditional middle-class mental health services have little or no opportunity to experience student and healer roles.

Those community mental health practitioners who question the health of the existing normative structure in which the urban poor live, provide an opportunity for their clients to assume a second therapeutic role. In recognizing that immediate physical needs must take precedence over intellectual strivings, the radical therapist chooses to act as an advocate and teacher who brings citizens together with institutional representatives and instructs these citizens in skills in which the roles and responsibilities of citizens and their leaders may be explicitly negotiated. The advent of community mental health, therefore, has provided the urban poor with the opportunity for a second essential ameliorative experience—the role of student.

Mental health professionals have been trained for the role of providers of psychological service. Unfortunately, both for the average layman and most mental health practitioners, this role has become synonymous with that of providing psychotherapy. Consequently, in attempting to widen their spheres of influence from the reactive clinic, where they dealt with patients with serious psychological disabilities, to the community itself, many mental health professionals have only been prepared to offer psychotherapy for the variety of problems of living found in the community. The community, however, has refused to accept the community mental health professionals on these terms. For example, many of the existing community social agencies believe that they perform the same help-and-care services for which comprehensive community mental health centers have been financed. They reject as absurd the notion that all social and human problems can be resolved by psychotherapy just as the man in the street has long done. Consequently, as long as the mental health clinic is willing to offer psychotherapy only, it will be regarded as a local sanitation service and receive for treatment only those whom the community has discarded.

Only when the mental health practitioner is willing to admit that there are types of help and enabling often better suited to the community's needs than psychotherapy (as psychotherapy is presently constituted) will the mental health center and the community be able to attain a rapprochement and begin to work together in a concerted manner. Only when the community is involved in the care and treatment of those persons with whom the community mental health center works and is convinced of their "cure," will these clients cease to be marginal and alienated figures in their own community. This is to say, unless the community is willing to accept back again those for whom the informal community help-and-care system has failed, these persons will not be able to make successful community integration (Goldberg, 1972a).

*Implementing a community mental health program based on services-in-kind*

One experiment in running a community mental health center in such a way as to avoid the typical failings described was the Laurel center, of which I was director.[1] The staff of the Laurel center recognized that the opportunity for many clients to be healers of others had been neglected in other mental health programs. Though group therapy and other group modalities have given many clients the opportunity to help themselves by encouraging their contribution to the amelioration and well-being of others, it is generally the middle-class clients who are able to benefit because the rewards of being helpful to others in group psychotherapy are at best indirect and inferential. The urban-poor client's orientation is toward concrete rewards. He needs to see a direct relationship between his efforts and the reactions of the persons toward whom he is directing his efforts. He is more comfortable and skillful in performing actions than in discussing and trying to express thoughts and feelings. So, we decided to develop a program that would provide the opportunity for clients to help themselves by contributing to the amelioration and well-being of others through active services.[2] In providing opportunities for urban poor to experience the role of healer, we would facilitate our general goals of helping clients to establish equity and balance in their existences.

The program at the Laurel center provided the opportunity for our clients to compensate the center and the community by contributing services-in-kind for others. For example, some of our clients who

---

[1] The mental health agency described in this chapter is the Laurel Comprehensive Community Health Center. The Laurel center is the administrative and service center of the Northern Mental Health Team of Prince George's County, Maryland. The overall responsibility of the center was to provide comprehensive mental health services to a highly diversified population of about a quarter of a million people. Even though this region is not an urban area, it has many of the problems and characteristics of the two metropolitan centers in whose corridor it is situated. Poverty is not a major problem for most of the citizens of the area. Nevertheless, there are a number of poverty pockets in this part of the county whose mental health needs have not been adequately met.

[2] I have found only one other community mental health center that utilizes the concept of services-in-kind, the Harborview center in Seattle, Washington. At about the same time as the Laurel center, the Harborview independently developed an experimental program called "Payment for Services-in-Kind" (PSK), which was initiated with a small number of clients. In the PSK program, clients gave services to the center or the community to make up for that portion of the standard fee they could not afford to pay directly (Sata, 1972).

received marital counseling compensated the community by tutoring students who were having problems in school, instead of paying a fee to the center. Housewives attended the children of other mothers who were being seen, or offered transportation to clients who had no transportation of their own.

The services-in-kind program was an experimental treatment modality. Patients were not selected in a systematic way. There were several reasons for this. First, the program was an innovative one; we had no empirical data that would suggest which clients might best profit from the program. Our theoretical assumption, which has already been discussed, was that clients who experience themselves as having little or no opportunity to enact the role of healer, either in their life in the community or in other treatment modalities, would most benefit from this program. Second, not all of the Laurel center staff were sufficiently comfortable with the concept of services-in-kind to employ it with their clients. The selective factor, therefore, was the therapist rather than the client.

In implementing the program we felt that the client's commitment to giving services was a more important therapeutic ingredient than the economic value of the service. Therapist and client therefore discussed the client's vocational skills and experiences, his interests and avocations, as well as areas of service required in the center or, in some instances, in the community. Therapist and client came to some agreement about a specific assignment and the approximate amount of time the client would spend in giving the service. The client was then directed to a staff person, usually a secretary, to receive an orientation for the assignment. Problems the client experienced on the assignment were discussed with the therapist.

In the services-in-kind program were persons who do not earn sufficient income to pay a fee and who might otherwise feel guilty and self-denigrating for getting something for nothing. There also were persons who could afford fees but whom we thought would benefit more from giving of themselves than through paying a fee. When the poor pay fees, they know that their fees are adjusted to their incomes and this reveals quite baldly their economic inferiority. If the client chooses to render service in return for services rendered him, it is likely that he can demonstrate skills and abilities of which he is proud and for which he can be admired. This serves to balance his relationship with those who are assisting him with problems of which he is less proud.

As would be expected with any experimental program, there were certain difficulties to overcome in implementing it:

1. *State and county health systems' objections.* It was difficult to sell the concept of a services-in-kind program to state and county health systems that had grown accustomed to collecting fees. There are two basic reasons for these systems to resist this concept: (1) A services-in-kind program results in loss of money to the state. All fees collected by the center are sent to the state treasury and are therefore unavailable to the center or the community. (2) The state and county health systems view their clients as totally lacking in resources, in other words, as there to be served but capable of nothing in return. The staff of the Laurel center strongly disagreed with this view. We dealt with the systems' objections simply by initiating the program, writing it up in our program plans and progress reports as a therapeutic program, and giving considerable effort to specifying its ongoing effectiveness for our clients.

2. *Staff discomfort.* In any community mental health center, there is a continual struggle between staff who emphasize direct, traditional services and those who wish to encourage indirect services including non-traditional relationships with clients. All of the Laurel center staff seemed to agree with the concept of services-in-kind, but some staff were more comfortable with the implementation of the program than others were. This was evidenced by the fact that several staff members frequently involved their clients in services-in-kind while others continued to employ the traditional sliding pay scale with their clients. I now realize it was a mistake to make implementation of the program with particular clients a staff option because, if a program is efficacious, it needs to be implemented uniformly, making foremost client needs, not those of staff. Each client must have the opportunity to participate in the program if he so chooses.

3. *Appropriate assignments.* Because Laurel was a new center with much to learn, finding appropriate assignments for every client was nearly impossible. Although therapists were offering the services-in-kind program to their clients, little creative thought had been given to what services could be used by the agency and community. Consequently, more clients than could be adequately handled were sent to the secretaries, who were frustrated because they had too few jobs for the number of people being sent. In addition both clients and therapists were frustrated because many of the tasks assigned fell in the realm of busywork and did not take advantage of the creative abilities of the

clients. To make a services-in-kind concept work in a creative and rewarding manner, it is necessary to have one person who will define areas where contributions can be made by patients and to match patients with areas of service. We eventually hired a coordinator of volunteers to serve in this capacity, as well as to coordinate other volunteer programs.

4. *Supervision of services.* It was not always clear who would supervise and work with the clients on their service assignments. Frequently, nonprofessional staff, e.g., secretaries, assumed this responsibility. They often felt uncomfortable in this role. Some of the clients were difficult to work with, and in these instances, the nonprofessional staff felt that the therapists should have been working more closely with their clients on their assignments. The therapists, in turn, maintained that attending to their clients' service assignments would take valuable time from their therapeutic work with other clients. I concluded that to insure that service assignments have their intended therapeutic implications, professional staff must be available to orient and supervise their clients on their assignments.

5. *Community acceptance.* A services-in-kind program is a rather innovative way of viewing community resources. The public generally views lay volunteers to a mental health program as people of generous spirit who are without serious emotional difficulties. The general public needs to be educated to realize that each of us, professional mental health worker and citizen alike, potentially is both a patient and a healer. We attempted to inform the community about our programs by writing weekly mental health columns in the local newspaper, appearing on several radio shows, and conducting open houses to the community. We tried as well to have staff visible. Being involved with several civic organizations in the community provided staff members with occasions to discuss our programs rather informally with interested citizens.

6. *Maintaining an adequate staff.* The Laurel center was mandated to serve a rather large area with a limited budget, resulting in a limited number of professional staff. We were, of course, not unique in this. In the Southern region of the county a mental health team of seven full-time staff was mandated to cover approximately 200,000 people. There were numerous conflicts among staff in regard to the kinds of services to offer. Though these conflicts were due in part to ideological differences among the practitioners, a more immediate and practical

cause for the conflict was the lack of sufficient, let alone competently trained, staff. The lack of trained staff was in part attributable to rapid turnover. Practitioners who remain on a community mental health project for more than 2 years generally experience the "burned-out" syndrome. The staff of such a center usually consists of essentially two types: young, enthusiastic recent mental health graduates and older, tired, and overly compromised workers. In my experience, the gifted professional soon leaves (especially if he can fill a private practice), while the mediocre practitioner remains until retirement. To keep the more gifted practitioners at the center as long as we could, considerable emphasis was given to staff development. While I was director, I probably spent more time in this area than in any other clinic function.

To acquire more mental health resources than our budget allowed us, we had to depart from capitalistic modes of operation. We used a barter system. We trained students from all the mental health disciplines except psychiatry, including candidates for a mental health associate degree, at the Laurel center. The students in return worked directly with our clients. We supervised students in groups so that they could profit from both peer supervision and professional supervision. More students could be placed at the center in this way than would be possible if individual supervision were utilized exclusively. We obtained the services of a group dynamics trainer from a local university who served as a process consultant to our weekly staff development group. In exchange, I gave several seminars and talks at the university and provided training to its students. To add further to our staff resources, a senior staff social worker at the center trained a small group of select volunteers from the community to work with multiple-problem families. These volunteers reported that as a result of their work with these troubled families, there were positive changes in their own families.

*Results*
*of the program*

Center staff found countless opportunities in day-to-day therapeutic encounters to bring the concepts of balance and equity into the relationship between client and therapist. The following examples from the program indicate the wide range of such experiences—from the brief, spontaneous response that brought about balance in a relationship to a planned therapeutic endeavor—and also show how services-in-kind worked in one instance. There were failures, too, but they are evidence, I believe, of instances of staff inability to do adequate planning and follow-through rather than of a lack of validity of the concept of balance and equity. No systematic study of the services-in-kind program in terms of the concepts of balance and equity has been undertaken. However, I do believe that such a study would yield valuable data.

1. *A brief, spontaneous response that brought balance to a relationship between a therapist and a parent of a child patient.* Mr. Thomas was a parent without a partner rearing three children, two boys and a girl. The girl, 11 years of age, had been referred to us because of her acting-out behavior at school and some concern that she might be experiencing rejection from her father. Mr. Thomas was a late-middle-aged laborer who was at this time unemployed and thus available to transport his child and to involve himself in her therapy. Once during a therapeutic hour the subject of fresh fish came up. The staff worker shared the fact that she did not know where in the area to go to purchase fresh fish, a matter of concern to her because she had a child who "loved" fish and was restricted because of diet to eating only freshly caught fish. Mr. Thomas seized upon this opportunity to offer to the worker something of obvious value to her. This contribution permitted Mr. Thomas to let down his guard and be more open in revealing himself, which produced material that revealed areas in which the worker was able to proceed in attempting to strengthen his relationship with his daughter.

2. *The use of the concepts of equity and balance in a planned therapeutic endeavor.* Mr. and Mrs. Blunt were clients of lower socioeconomic status who were seen at the Laurel center upon court referral. They had three latency-age children of their own. In addition, they had accepted into their nuclear family three nieces of Mrs. Blunt. They had discovered that the children's mother had exposed them to socially unacceptable behavior and to considerable emotional and physical deprivation and then decided to give them to "friends." Though the Blunts scarcely had enough money to meet their nuclear family's needs, taking care of one's own blood relatives was a part of the family's system of values.

In spite of their own problems, which were complicated by poor economic status and a history of social rejection, the Blunts were able to use their own natural gifts, one of which was Mrs. Blunt's tremendous ability to nurture others, to provide the nieces with excellent resocialization. With support from the school community, the children made unbelievable progress. The problems they brought with them began to disappear. There was no more feces smearing, their enuresis ceased, and they began to practice some of the social graces (e.g., table manners, courtesy) that were part of the Blunt family's system. They also made some adjustment to the school environment. Then one of the children went to school appearing to be physically abused. Unfortunately, the school initiated court procedures. The court allowed the children to remain in the home and awarded the Blunts custody; however, it stipulated that they were to be involved in family therapy.

As they presented themselves to the center for court-ordered family therapy, the Blunts expressed frustration, resentment, and acting out behavior. They later shared their feelings that the court decision was confusing because it carried a conflicting message and that to be brought into court in the first place was grossly unfair (i.e., lacking in equity).

Mrs. Blunt contended that the court had no jurisdiction over her own family and refused family therapy, but she did agree that two of her nieces did need help. Recognizing Mrs. Blunt's right to have some say in what happened to her family, the practitioner began play therapy with the two nieces. Though these children had improved in many ways under Mrs. Blunt's care, there was a most definite need to work with them to establish ego boundaries. Mrs. Blunt later shared with us that she felt the other niece and her own three children could also benefit from the therapeutic goals, so all of the children became part of the group.

Though the relationship between Mrs. Blunt and the agency appeared improved, she continued to behave to a great degree as though the agency's expectations and values were the only ones of importance. For example, she once telephoned to *ask* if she might cancel the therapeutic session as one of the children was sick and she had no one to babysit while she brought the others to the center. The center helped her to claim her authority in this situation.

Eventually, Mrs. Blunt shared the concern that though she saw some improvement in the children's behavior at home, it did not equal their improvement at the center. The worker responded by offering to hold the therapy sessions in the home. The worker and Mrs. Blunt worked out that the sessions in the home would begin following Christmas when the children would receive new toys. They agreed initially to have six sessions. However, the Blunts (Mr. Blunt having also become actively involved in the home sessions) expressed a wish to have the sessions extended to assure that they had a firm grasp on helping the children to respect boundaries. The worker later learned that the Blunts had also experienced some fear about how the school and court would respond to the ending of the sessions. Finally, the Blunts were confident enough to claim their gains and end the sessions.

Several months passed and Mrs. Blunt telephoned the agency, leaving an urgent message to have her call returned. The worker returned her call the next day upon her return to the office. Mrs. Blunt at first seemed aloof but upon learning that the worker had been out until shortly before returning her call and was not showing a lack of interest in the urgency of her call, she went ahead to share her reason for initiating the contact. She wished to bring one of the children into the agency again, and an appointment was set up. During the appointment, Mrs. Blunt stated that the child had discussed with her experiences from the child's early life with her natural mother. Mrs. Blunt wished to know the significance of this material and how she should handle such disclosures in the future.

First, the worker helped Mrs. Blunt with the fears she shared concerning this incident. Then Mrs. Blunt and the worker saw the child briefly together, with the worker attempting to create an atmosphere of: It's safe to share with us and we will help you deal with what it is you are sharing, if we can. The child was then returned to the waiting area while Mrs. Blunt discussed what her own response in the home had been. Her response revealed warmth and sensitivity, which the worker helped her to affirm. When the worker asked her if she felt another appointment was needed, she did not believe it was necessary, but said she would call the agency if she needed help in the future.

In this situation, the therapist was actively attempting to establish a sense of equity and balance in this client's relationship with the center. It was a planned therapeutic endeavor based on the belief that the Blunts' creativity in relation to their family could not be realized until they regained a sense of balance in their relationships with the center, the school, and the court, i.e., the world-at-large. Frustrations experienced in their encounter with the center were likely to have a negative effect on their relationship with the children, the cause of their relationship with the center in the first place. Therefore, the practitioner struggled diligently to bring balance into the relationship with the

Blunts. Comments made by Mrs. Blunt before termination indicated that having experienced a balanced relationship with us had helped her to assert herself in establishing a more balanced relationship with other social agencies.

3. *Services-in-kind:* Mrs. Whitmore's husband was being seen at the Laurel center on a regular basis for a chronic emotional problem. She then presented herself to the agency in frustration because of what she believed to be our lack of concern about what she was experiencing in a difficult marital situation. Consequently, the center brought her and her husband together for marital therapy. The husband was unable to tolerate the degree of intimacy in their relationship that Mrs. Whitmore craved; he preferred to have the relationship remain stagnant. When the wife continued to experience a thrust toward growth, he showed signs of being extremely threatened and withdrew from therapy.

Mrs. Whitmore had earlier begun to play guitar for church services. She continued to do this and also began to prepare for her high school equivalency examination. Mr. Whitmore's behavior became increasingly more physically violent toward her. Thus, she was forced to move out of the home prematurely, though she had hoped to wait until she had completed her high-school equivalency and found a job. Nevertheless, she did find a job, secured an apartment, and renewed a relationship with her father, which had been broken while she was in her teens following his desertion of the family. She declared her readiness to end the therapeutic relationship, and we agreed that she was ready.

When Mrs. Whitmore expressed a desire to repay the agency for its contribution to her, we told her of the services-in-kind program. She expressed a desire to use this service, as finances were more of a problem for her now than ever in the past. She had shown in therapy that she was an extremely sensitive person and her mothering relationships reflected this, so we offered her an opportunity to serve as co-therapist in a play therapy group. She was enthused and visibly moved by the confidence she realized we had in her ability to give of herself to others. We offered Mrs. Whitmore some minimal training and urged her to use herself in whatever creative way seemed right to her.

Without a doubt, Mrs. Whitmore made a meaningful contribution in numerous ways to the children who received help through the group. Her most memorable contribution came about through her use of her guitar and singing. She took special interest in one hyperactive child who showed an interest in learning to play the guitar and singing with her. Her special interest in this youngster did wonders for his self-esteem. Moreover, Mrs. Whitmore learned a lesson about terminating relationships when the child finished with the group.

This involvement in the play therapy group seemed to add also to Mrs. Whitmore's self-esteem as well because she realized along with us that our agency could not have begun to help this group of children as early as it did without her assistance. Though the value of this service—ours to her and hers to us—is immeasurable, we are confident that payment in dollars from her for our service would have had far less value than the service she rendered in return.

Though in this example the client's assignment involved contributing to a therapy group, the largest number of services-in-kind contributions were in the area of secretarial services. The value of these services in a center with many community programs operating on a case-formula budget is not hard to imagine. Thus, those performing such services soon realize their importance in the workings of the center.

In working with multiple-problem families and the urban poor, the practitioner must avoid falling into the trap of bifurcating mental health problems as either social or emotional problems. If the practitioner is concerned about the plight of the poor, he must first discern the issues that predicate their place in the social order. Having done this, the practitioner needs to ascertain the conditions that threaten as well as advance their place in society.

The issue of equity is a rather significant issue for a community mental health center. The question the community mental health practitioner needs to ask himself is whether the client who petitions the center is asking for help in changing himself, is asking simply to be understood, or is asking for justice (in terms of societal institutions) and fairness (in terms of interpersonal relations). Studying the role of fairness forces the practitioner out of the world of fantasy and the unconscious and into the interpersonal world of social reality, negotiation, and compromise. It forces the mental health practitioner out of his role of armchair observer of intrapsychic process and into the community to deal with social problems that are not necessarily best resolved (and are often exacerbated) by conventional therapeutic practices.

The eventual goal in my community mental health work was to move further and further from the reactive clinic model and toward contributing to the community as a whole. As a mental health specialist the community mental health worker can contribute more to a community and to the development of its autonomous resources by providing consultation and training to the traditional caretakers and other community agents than by emphasizing and specializing in direct services.

The following is a consultation assessment inventory that I devised for our staff members to assess the extent to which our services to community agencies could, by means of contract negotiation, result in refurbishment and increased resource to the community.

### Consultation Assessment Inventory

This inventory is intended to help provide the Northern Mental Health Team and an agency requesting consultation with relevant information necessary to determine if consultation or some other service is required.

Please be brief and concise. If information on some items is not currently available, specify what would be necessary for gathering this data.

1. Identify agency or group requesting services.
2. Name, title, and role designation of person who made the initial contact with us.
3. How did they hear about us?
4. What did they hear about us?
5. Why is the request being made?
6. Brief account of past and existing relationship between consultee agency and consultant agency (or consultant agent).
7. Quality of the request—was it a demand, a plea, or a solicitous request?
8. a) Is the "problem" chronic, reactive, a current crisis, proactive, or preparatory?
   b) Some history of the identified issue.
9. Does the requester identify himself as part of the problem or situation or does he claim to be noninvolved?
10. Who else in the system is involved?
11. Briefly, how do the others in the system see the situation?
12. Is there any discrepancy in system accounts of the problem? If yes, how do you account for this discrepancy? Please be brief.
13. Type of service—advice, treatment, training, objective feedback, or other?
14. Who in our agency would perform the service?
15. What is your estimation of the duration of the service required?
16. In your estimation, will our service lead directly or indirectly to changes in the larger system? Briefly identify changes.

17. Briefly, in your estimation, what is the system willing or able to do as a result of our service?
18. Overall evaluation:
    a) What are the advantages and benefits of rendering this service?
    b) What are the problems and drawbacks of rendering services?
    c) Should we agree to perform service?
    d) If yes, under what conditions should we provide services?
    Consultant's Name: _____

(Developed by Carl Goldberg, Ph.D., Laurel Comprehensive Community Health Center, January 1972.)

In the model I have proposed in this chapter, the mental health practitioner must work with other community agents such as teachers, ministers, volunteers, and other citizens in planning and implementing community projects. The central mandate of the community mental health center is to find ways and means of educating the community to respond to the needs of its citizens. Therefore, whereas an important component of the general goals of a center is the provision of prompt and effective direct services, the staff must be ready and able to provide consultation and education. Through discussion and involvement with local groups and programs, the center must seek to be fully cognizant of the concerns and challenges facing the community. Only in this way can the center provide intelligent means for eradication of community stigmas, barriers, and fear of participation in mental health services. Only in this way will mental health services be available to all, "sick" or "well." As long as the community mental health center is in the "sickness-cure" business, it will not be happily regarded by the community. Under this regime, the center will only be permitted to function as a narrow, circumscribed service.

Mental health practitioners should stress opportunities for citizens in the community where continuous growth and refurbishing experiences may be obtained. They should encourage holistic experiences rather than the narrowly circumscribed and fragmented services that present mental health programs provide. They must discourage long-term dependence upon a clinic that insulates the patient from the demands and challenges of the community with which he needs to cope in order to become a fully functioning person. Working within this framework, a center's philosophy of treatment should aim at helping clients assume responsibility for their improvement. There should be an emphasis on the shared responsibility of the client and therapist in working through problems stressed from the first contact through termination. The center can contribute to self-generative strivings of the client by facilitating and encouraging significant and meaningful relationships by the client with natural and self-help groups in the community. As soon as possible after his crisis has ebbed, the center should refer the client to existing community groups that serve as half-way steps toward full community integration.

The treatment plan should, therefore, be short-term, with specific goals, on a contractual basis. The mental health practitioner should help the client clarify from the onset what it is he is seeking help for, what roles and responsibilities he and the practitioner are willing to assume, and how together they can implement the client's goals. Having once reached these goals, client and practitioner can decide together the next step in the client's quest for maturity.

# Epilogue

The truth is one, but sages
call it by various names.

— Gita

If psychotherapy is to be more than the conclave of a select few, if it is to be available as the right of every individual, then we, as practitioners, must immediately and realistically confront the limitations of our craft. When mental health services are seen as the right of the individual there will be a greater reliance upon research, because the pressure for specified treatment outcomes will raise the issues of both definition and measurement. It should be apparent that, as practitioners of an applied art, we must design psychological modalities, whether based upon treatment, education, or something else, that have the advantage of greater economy of time and money and that are suitable for the specific disabilities of those who require psychological services (Goldberg, 1973). In order to do this, there are serious philosophical, ethical, and scientific questions and issues with which practitioners must grapple.

In order to develop better-conceptualized treatment modalities, we need well-designed research. This should be a problem for all of us, as therapists, because we all share as our foundation a body of information about the practice of psychotherapy that, with few exceptions, currently consists of unverified theory, scholastic exhortations, case histories (with an $n$ of 1), clinical observations, and anecdotes. For example, despite the current, zealous enthusiasm for group approaches to the amelioration of personal and societal distresses, there is little or no empirical data to substantiate the lasting effects of group treatment (Goldberg, 1973), encounter groups (Lieberman, Yalom, & Miles, 1973), or sensitivity training (Goldberg, 1970a).

Despite the lack of empirical verification of their effectiveness, we cannot afford to discard existing techniques. There are too few established techniques in psychotherapy. This is due in part to the general immaturity of the social sciences, particularly the applied aspects. Social science has not yet established a venerable history or tradition. To say, for example, that a concept in social science is respectable is to

233

say that it is a concept borrowed from the physical sciences; "individual," "group," "system," and "process" are all such terms. They have proven their usefulness in the discourse of the older sciences. In recent years, psychologists and other social scientists, in whimsical deification of the precision of method and theory exhibited by the physical scientists, have exerted their efforts perhaps too exclusively in the development of precision tools. As a consequence, there has been a great advancement in theory and practice of measurement. Unfortunately, however, unless we know more about the variables we are supposedly measuring, the results of our elaborate measurements are rather sterile.

Fortunately, there is a growing awareness that psychiatric disorders are not illnesses and that man's proclivity for aggression and hatred is not an inevitable result of his inherent nature. There is hope for improving human personality. It is now accepted by most mental health practitioners that aggression and hatred, like feelings of tenderness and compassion, are developed from socioemotional concert of the individual with his significant others. If the practitioner can effectively demonstrate to the emotionally distressed person that treating others sympathetically and fairly is socially rewarding and relevant, clients will have the opportunity to unlearn dysfunctional responses to other people.

I have explored in this book a therapeutic system derived from the principles of productive interpersonal relations and based upon a contractual model. Contractual psychotherapy is a valuable component in the development of the therapeutic relationship. Yet, this aspect of psychotherapy has been either neglected, poorly developed, or generally unrecognized in the psychotherapy literature. It is true that there have been attempts by several practitioners (discussed in Chapter 3) to develop a contractual approach to psychotherapy. These approaches have emphasized practical considerations, such as how contractual approaches militate against misunderstanding and therapist abuse in the therapeutic relationship. On the other hand, these approaches have, for the most part, lacked a philosophical foundation for contractual relations, other than the contention that contractual relationships are in accord with the principles of democratic living. These approaches, consequently, have not been able to remove the therapeutic relationship from its pseudolegal and political arena to one in which the client is best provided with the opportunity to meaningfully explore his being-in-the-world.

Unfortunately, practitioners with more' philosophical orientations, who have recognized that a therapeutic partnership depends on a climate in which both therapist and client seriously grapple with their reasons for being together with others, have not developed specific guidelines or methodologies to articulate this indispensible existential consideration. In this book, I have attempted to address this problem by combining the concepts of responsibility, self-respect, egalitarianism, openness, and congruence with a specific theoretical and therapeutic model.

# appendix A

# Client guide to selecting
# a therapist and formulating
# a therapeutic contract

Even superior talents will be obscured, defeated and
destroyed if a man does not recognize the limits of
his power.

—Johann Wolfgang von Goethe

Practitioners realize that there is considerable variation in therapeutic
approaches and in the quality of available practitioners. For a prospective client, however, any port in the storm may appear more secure than
the crisis and confusion he is experiencing in his search for psychological assistance. Clients, as a consequence, quite frequently select practitioners and subject themselves to treatment programs that are expensive and psychologically (and sometimes physically) risky without
realizing or carefully considering the options available to them. Shar-
land Trotter (1975), in a report to the members of the American
Psychological Association, has summarized a number of salient concerns encountered by prospective clients in selecting practitioners and
treatment programs:

> The current psychotherapy scene is, for most of the lay public, a jumble
> of conflicting schools, theories, methods and techniques. Anyone seek-
> ing professional help is confronted with a confusing smorgasbord of
> therapies ranging from orthodox psychoanalysis to drug therapy; from
> client-centered, existential, humanistic, gestalt, rational-emotive or
> family therapy, to biofeedback, hypnosis, megavitamin therapy, or
> transactional analysis—or some combination of these. Requesting a
> referral from professional associations will usually net one a list of
> therapists' names and addresses—but to avoid possible bias, information
> about the kind, quality, or price of treatment is scrupulously not in-

237

cluded. These things the consumer must find out the hard way—by costly and time-consuming trial and error.

Friedson (1976) has argued from his study of doctor-patient relationships that the patient's reluctance to question the doctor's judgment and his subsequent acceptance of poor quality and ill-conceived treatment is due to certain "myths of the medical mystique." Patients tacitly assume that: (1) doctors must tailor to each patient such complicated judgments that no one except another doctor who has gone through the case step by step can judge the validity of the diagnosis and treatment rendered by his doctor, (2) the quality of medical care is assured by the long and rigorous course of training a doctor must undergo to secure his degree and pass his licensing examination, and (3) doctors are always responsible professionals who are dedicated to the welfare of the patients they treat and the public they serve. Friedson and others seriously question the validity of these assumptions. Indeed, this book should serve clients, as well as practitioners, by dispelling the myths and mystique of psychological amelioration.

It is to serve clients that I add this guide written for the reader who is in treatment or is seeking psychological assistance. It is beyond my scope here to indicate to the reader why he should seek therapy. Actually, much has been written about that already (see brief bibliography at the end of this appendix). Moreover, the person who listens deeply and respectfully to himself will know at once whether or not to seek psychotherapy. The more important question is whether the individual in distress will respond to his own intuitive sense.

Too many people enter psychotherapy without giving due consideration to the complex concerns this important decision raises. Selecting an appropriate therapist is one of the most crucial dimensions in therapeutic outcome. Practitioners vary considerably in their training, styles of practice, fees, and so forth. It is essential that the prospective client be aware of these differences in order to select an appropriate therapist. Although mental health practitioners may be certified or licensed, they are essentially unregulated in terms of the fees they charge and the quality and style of their practice. Appropriate information about the therapist's practice is often difficult to obtain. The Health Research Group in Washington, D.C., a consumer advocacy organization sponsored by Ralph Nader, has reported an extraordinary amount of resistance from professional mental health societies toward those collecting data on the practices of their constituents (Adams &

Orgel, 1975). This evidence underlines Torrey's complaint (1974) that it is easier to obtain information about the qualifications of a plumber than of a psychotherapist.

In providing a guide for prospective clients, the selection of a therapist needs to be explored on several different levels. First, there are the most practical considerations: *location, fee,* and *schedule of appointments.* The prospective client may wish to consider whether a therapist's office is located conveniently to his home or place of business. This must be an initial consideration for a client who doesn't have a dependable mode of transportation.

Many practitioners refuse to discuss fees over the phone. They prefer to deal with fees in the larger context of the client's orientation toward treatment, or only after an indepth exploration of the client's financial situation. These are reasonable practices, especially if the practitioner utilizes a sliding scale to set fees. Nonetheless, it is unreasonable for a prospective client to attend more than a session or two without finding out whether or not he can afford to continue seeing the therapist. If the practitioner's custom is to set fees after face-to-face discussion, then the prospective client would be wise to reach an initial agreement about the fee for the first session before scheduling an appointment. A practitioner's unwillingness to divulge his range of fees (and other administrative practices as well) before the prospective client makes a commitment to work with him should cast some doubts in the client's mind about the practitioner's openness on other issues vital to the client.

Practitioners vary in the promptness they require for payment of fees. For a client with health insurance coverage, it is necessary to ascertain whether or not the practitioner is covered for his services on the client's policy and whether the practitioner requires to be paid directly by the client or is willing to wait for third-party reimbursement. These considerations are of considerable importance if the client has little available cash. For some practitioners, fees have definite status value, but, as with restaurants, there is probably no direct correlation between cost and quality. In most instances, fees reflect the going rate in a particular geographical area among the various mental health disciplines, with a practitioner who regards himself as a psychoanalyst generally charging the highest fee, a nonpsychoanalytic psychiatrist somewhat less, a psychologist still less, and a social worker or a psychiatric nurse the least (with obvious overlaps and notable exceptions).

A therapist's schedule of appointments should be such that, within reasonable limits, he is available to the client when he needs him. He should have times available that are convenient for the client. Some practitioners work best in the morning, others in the afternoon or evening; the same is true for clients. Although I don't ever remember being asked by my clients when I work best, it does seem to be a reasonable and significant consideration in scheduling sessions. The conventional therapy session is 45 to 50 minutes, and practitioners with busy schedules generally prefer regular, conventionally scheduled sessions. If a client feels he can work better with an infrequent but longer session than with a typical weekly or semiweekly session, he may do better with a practitioner with a more flexible schedule. Having said all this, I caution the prospective client to weigh these considerations along with the psychological and dynamic ones discussed below. In most instances, the psychological factors should, of course, be given greater weight.

The prospective client should not permit himself to be discouraged from inquiring to ascertain for himself information about all concerns of importance to him in entering a psychotherapeutic relationship. He should be prepared to ask questions that seem intrusive: for example, whether a practitioner he contacts has both adequate training and experience dealing with the sort of concerns the prospective client has. Of course in many instances, the prospective client may not know how to evaluate the practitioner's qualifications. He may, in these instances, confer with a mental health referral service for this information. He should ask as many direct questions as he needs to in order to be assured that he is being referred to a practitioner whose work the referring professional has adequate knowledge of, rather than merely to a name the referring professional chooses from a list of practitioners in the community. Each of the mental health disciplines issues a directory of its members. Some of these directories provide professional biographies, listing the places of education and training, licenses, certifications, and areas of specialty. Each of the professional mental health disciplines also has a committee for standards and ethics. The prospective client may inquire of representatives and of these professional associations whether a practitioner is a member in good standing and further, whether the practitioner has had complaints lodged against him and, if so, the nature of these complaints. But the client should bear in mind that the information that a member is in good standing in a professional association is only useful for avoiding practitioners who have been found to employ dubious professional practices. Of course no client needs physician-induced problems added to those from which he seeks relief.

That a practitioner is a member in good standing of his professional association does not necessarily indicate that he is a capable and effective psychotherapist, however. This decision the client must ultimately make for himself. For while it is helpful to consult another professional for referral to a psychotherapist, it is eminently wise in making a commitment to work with a practitioner to consult your own senses. For example, a family physician frequently refers his patient to a psychotherapist for concerns with which he feels unwilling or untrained to deal. As Adams and Orgel (1975) validly indicate, "Physicians like anyone else tend to refer to people with whom they are familiar, but their familiarity is not always based on knowledge of the other professional's practice." Moreover, a physician is likely to make referrals to another physician who is a classmate or social acquaintance and happens to practice psychiatry, though a nonmedical practitioner might be a more appropriate and less expensive therapist for the client.

Naturally, it would be helpful for a prospective client to speak with the former clients of a practitioner to whom he has been referred to find out how useful their therapeutic experiences were, but unless he personally knows people who have worked with a particular practitioner, there is no feasible way to secure this data. He may ask a friend or relative for the therapist with whom they are consulting, but unless they have had previous therapy or have shopped around for a practitioner they may lack a sufficiently comprehensive frame of reference with which to evaluate their therapist.

Some professionals prefer to refer clients to practitioners who have attained some professional distinctions, such as board certification in psychiatry and neurology, or have become diplomates of the American Board of Professional Psychology. It is my impression, nonetheless, that there probably is no correlation (positive or negative) between such attainments and proficiency as a psychotherapist. These distinctions are indicative of knowledge of theoretical principles and of professional standards and practices, and as such, they evince diagnostic and teaching competence rather than the sensitivity, intuition, personal adaptability, and the meaningful life experiences required of an effective psychotherapist. Many well-trained mental health practitioners with many years in the field as diagnosticians and educators have had relatively little actual experience as psychotherapists. They may have done a considerable amount of short-term counseling of students in regard to their academic course work or career planning, but have conducted little or no intensive or long-term psychotherapy. Their temperament may not be suited for therapeutic practice. It is important for the prospective client to ascertain how much direct clinical and therapeutic experience the practitioner with whom he confers has had. Many states license and certify their mental health practitioners. Certification and licensing do not, unfortunately, guarantee psychotherapeutic skill. However, if a practitioner is not licensed or certified, the prospective client should inquire into the reason for this.

Certification of postgraduate training at an outstanding psychotherapeutic or psychoanalytic institute is generally a better reflection of psychotherapeutic acumen than board certification, diplomate status, or state licensing and certification. Here, too, the match is hardly perfect. In qualifying for postgraduate institutes, a certain degree of loyalty to the school of psychotherapy promulgated by the institute is required. This results in varying degrees of dogmatism among its graduates (see Chapter 4). Moreover, depending upon the emphasis given to theoretical acumen as compared with interpersonal sensitivity and intuitive skills, practitioners who are theoretically sound but are personally poorly suited to therapeutic work may slip through even the best training institutes (see Chapter 6).

Making the client's choice even more complex is the fact that a good therapeutic experience cannot be guaranteed even by referral to an outstanding practitioner. The temperament and personality of both agents must be congruent. The most important single consideration in selecting a therapist is the quality of the interaction between client and therapist. The client must evaluate for himself whether the practitioner seems to understand that with which he is struggling. Many therapists are capable of offering clients empathy, comfort, and reassurance (see Chapter 4), but these qualities are not alone sufficient for a meaningful therapeutic encounter. The therapist must be able and willing to enable the client to articulate his concerns in such a way that the client can understand, come to terms with, and gain mastery over his own struggles. Discomfort arises over time in any meaningful interpersonal encounter. The crucial issue is whether both agents are able, in their being together, to deal openly with their discomfort.

Every psychotherapeutic belief system from which practitioners operate is based upon certain ontological and philosophical assumptions and value orientations (see Chapter 11). Is the therapist willing to articulate his orientation so that the client is clear about what is expected of him in treatment, and most important for the client, are these values and assumptions consistent with the kind of person the client is seeking to become?

A meaningful therapeutic relationship involves a partnership between client and therapist. Does the client feel like a collaborator in formulating a working (treatment) plan, or does the therapist unilaterally inform him what he thinks the client should be working on? Is there open and effective negotiation for roles and responsibilities necessary for attaining the client's objectives in treatment?

With this general orientation for selecting a psychotherapist in mind, you the consumer should also consider a number of specific concerns and suggestions to be aware of in choosing and working with a therapist:

1. Don't fly blind in seeking psychotherapeutic assistance. Give the consideration at least as much thought as you would buying a house or a car. Before launching into therapy, give considerable thought to why you are seeking treatment. Having clarified this for yourself or having at least become in touch with the questions and concerns about yourself you want to address, you can more efficaciously decide which kind of psychological experience is best for your deeper needs, rather than your more transitory ones. But, if you're seriously hurting, don't put off getting help. Strupp and his associates (1969) have found that the more successful therapy client is typically a person who has sought help rather promptly after recognizing that something was wrong.

2. In choosing a psychological program, be wary of practitioners to whom the mass media give considerable attention because of their "innovative," special techniques and their nonconventional lifestyles. In general, be cautious of practitioners who spend considerable time on television shows or promotion tours for their books or for their "radical" new psychotherapy institutes. At best, these practitioners have little available time for careful work with clients. Moreover, many of them, as self-promoters, may be more concerned with selling you a technique and a lifestyle than with helping you come to terms with where you're at.

3. Be wary of a practitioner who makes promises to enact a particular emotional state of being with you, e.g., to be caring, uncritically

accepting, emotionally intimate, or even just a good friend, before he has had a sufficient opportunity to get to know you. No therapist is able to guarantee interpersonal goodies.

4. In entering therapy, if you have doubts about the therapist's ability to help you or about how motivated you actually are to undergo intensive work, ask for a short-term arrangement. Knowing that the commitment is for a specific period, you are in a better position to recognize your unwillingness to get deeply involved in therapeutic work if you experience an intense desire to terminate therapy before the time you agreed to stop (Clark, 1975).

5. Anyone who considers entering psychotherapy should immediately divest himself of the fictions that therapy is a science and that the practitioner is essentially objective and value free. "Clients must maintain a skeptical but fair attitude toward everything the therapist suggests explicitly and implicitly" (Clark, 1975, p. 23). Be wary of practitioners who appear to have axes to grind. Steer clear of therapists with a doctrine to sell. Avoid therapists who try to coerce a reluctant client to be "honest" and "open" rather than enable the client to develop sincere dialogue and a free give-and-take with them. "Clients must identify the therapist's world view as quickly as possible. Any competent therapist will attempt to minimize the forcefulness his or her values may be expressed with simply because of the therapist's role and authority, but the client's best protection against emotional damage and unnecessary conflict with a therapist is to select a person or method which is largely congruent with the client's own value system" (Clark, 1975, p. 24). After all, once therapy has ended, the client will be living his own life, not that of the therapist. The therapist's value system should be one that gives at least as much attention to what you consider your healthy attributes as to your disabled ones. In addition to his ability to work with conflict and pathology, the practitioner needs to have a definitive model of human growth and development. It is a dubious assumption that once a client is unfettered of his intrapsychic conflicts, he will spontaneously and naturally find a satisfying and harmonious existence (see Chapter 11).

6. Be suspicious of the therapists who wish to have more than one kind of relationship with you. A therapist who assumes more than one hat with a client seriously impedes his effectiveness as a psychotherapist. (On the other hand, the client who is looking for a love affair would be wise to look elsewhere. Why pay an expensive therapy bill for

a lover when there is no reason to believe that therapists are more responsive lovers than persons of any other walk of life!) Take with skepticism any practitioner's statement that as a result of psychotherapy he will make you a competent psychotherapist or an assistant therapist or enable you to take on mental health responsibilities for which you have not been trained. If you don't have the credentials for being a practicing therapist, any promise a practitioner makes about his ability to do so is a rather dubious and, probably, unethical offer.

7. In a decisive study of the therapeutic relationship, Strupp and his associates (1969) report that the composite image of the "good therapist" drawn by their respondents on the basis of their own therapy experience is that of "a keenly attentive, interested, benign and concerned listener—a friend who is warm and natural, is not averse to giving direct advice, who speaks one's language, makes sense and rarely arouses one's intense anger" (p. 117).

8. Nonverbal communication and body language may be excellent sources of information about the therapist. Be aware of your own bodily reactions to the therapist. If you are uncomfortable, attempt to ascertain if there are discrepancies and contradictions between what the therapist is communicating bodily and what he is stating in words.

9. An effective psychotherapist should make sense to you. He should be someone who doesn't hide behind a therapeutic mask. He should be someone who is willing to share with you his own reactions to you (Viscott, 1973). He should be someone who is able to lay out your issues in such a way that you and he can work together. Be aware of the therapist's unwillingness to accommodate his own behavior to the goals of therapy. For instance, does he do things, like answer the phone during the session, that are irritating or uncomfortable for you? How does he respond to your objections to these behaviors? Does he take personal responsibility for his behavior and demonstrate a willingness to deal with it, or does he make it your problem by suggesting that his behavior shouldn't bother you? Does he make up appointments he is forced to break at a time of mutual convenience? In short, does he take you seriously as a person or does he treat you simply as a patient? Each therapist conducts his practice to suit himself, but if his behavior is getting in the way of helping you, he must be willing to explore his own involvement in your discomfort. Instead, he may refuse to do so. He may indicate that you are concerned because this kind of upset is the problem that brought you to see him; he may suggest that as a trained

professional he knows better than you what should and should not be explored in therapy; he may even tell you that the kind of psychotherapy he practices (his system of psychotherapy) precludes his discussing his behavior with you. He may inform you that he fully explores his therapeutic work with a supervisor, consultant, or control analyst but not with his clients. In any of these cases, you would be wise to wish him well and find a more responsive therapist who makes sense to you.

10. I have left for last perhaps the most important initial consideration in seeking psychological assistance. Psychotherapy is an expensive way to deal with problems, and it may indeed be a rather inefficient way to resolve problems. Consequently, you need to explore whether there are less expensive and more efficient ways to come to terms with the problems for which you are asking help. Ethically, a therapist must be open to this kind of exploration. Steinzor (1967) has stated this issue succinctly. In his discussions with his clients, he asks: " 'Why are we discussing this complaint and why are you not describing your feelings to your friend, your lover, your supervisor?' [Steinzor explains that] if the therapist does not raise this question, the implication conveyed to the patient is that only through the therapist will true revelation appear, like a miracle vision in the desert. The patient must be confronted with his choice in bringing any thought or feeling before the doctor rather than elsewhere" (p. 9).

Clark's (1975) distinction between therapeutic experience and therapeutic relationships has bearing here; the quest for meaning and for a greater sense of being-in-the-world may lead people into therapeutic experiences as well as into psychotherapy. Therapeutic experiences may be renewing family ties; developing new, or reestablishing former, friendships; or joining in social, political, and educational pursuits. The quest for meaning and sense of being-in-the-world may be explored in time-limited, goal-limited therapeutic experiences such as carefully chosen encounter and growth-oriented workshops and weekends. Moreover, for certain types of psychological problems, hardcore drug addiction or serious alcoholism, for example, self-help groups and residential treatment programs are frequently more effective than private psychotherapists. In instances in which the client will only accept removal of "the problem" (see Chapter 6), circumscribed therapy techniques such as behavioral modification, sex therapy, or psychosocial training may be best. You as a prospective client should confer with a practitioner who is knowledgeable about a wide range of treatment options and has no special vested interest in selling a particular technique.

11. After having been involved in psychotherapy, you should ask yourself the following questions to help you review the therapeutic relationship:

a) Does the therapist seem to listen?

b) Does the therapist regard your objections and negative feelings about the therapeutic relationship as negotiable concerns or does he reduce them to manifestations of your problem?

c) Does the therapist explore by initiating options, that is, is he willing to try more than one way of reaching you or does he only react to your initiations?

d) Are you regarded as a collaborator or as a patient?

e) Does the therapist share his feelings as well as his thoughts (including doubts) about the relationship?

f) Do you have more clarity about the concerns that brought you into treatment than you did when you began?

g) Do you experience more viable options than when you began psychotherapy?

h) Do you feel more optimistic and experience more constructive energy (emotionally, intellectually, and physically)?

i) Are you now able to connect and emotionally appreciate the interrelationship between your concerns and conflicts that, prior to entering psychotherapy, seemed isolated, vague, or irreversibly fused?

j) Have the events of the past, present, and future strivings taken on new meaning?

12. If you have not experienced yourself making progress on these dimensions after a reasonable amount of time, seek consultation. Not all therapists click with every client. A competent practitioner generally senses this before the client does and should himself suggest consultation. It makes no sense to remain in therapy to avoid an unpleasant confrontation with one's therapist or to avoid hurting his feelings. Even when you sense that the serious underlying conflicts in your interactions with your therapist are emanating from your personality, it may make sense to leave therapy, should you feel that your therapist, after a reasonable time, has not been able to help you get at these issues effectively. It is important to recognize that a client's resistance is not

entirely related to his intrapsychic makeup. In such a case, however, you should be prepared to follow up this unsuccessful therapeutic relationship with another therapist who may be of greater help to you. The right to terminate a therapeutic situation you experience as noxious is your major source of protection (Clark, 1975) and should in no way be denied by a practitioner, regardless of how much he thinks you still need treatment.

For the reader who is interested in further information about seeking psychotherapy, here is a list of recent books written for laymen about the practice of psychotherapy:

*Basic concepts in psychotherapy*

Cameron, D. E. *Psychotherapy in Action.* Grune & Stratton, New York, 1968, $8.50.

Ruitenbeek, H. M. *Psychotherapy: What It's All About.* Avon Books, New York, 1976, $1.95.

*Description of psychotherapy approaches*

Harper, R. A. *Psychoanalysis and Psychotherapy: 36 Systems.* Prentice-Hall, Englewood Cliffs, N.J., 1959, $2.45.

Harper, R. A. *The New Psychotherapies.* Prentice-Hall, Englewood Cliffs, N.J., 1975, $2.95.

*Experience of psychotherapy*

Freeman, L. *What Happens in Psychoanalysis.* McGraw-Hill, New York, 1958, $1.75.

Freeman, L. *Farewell to Fear.* G. P. Putnam's Sons, New York, 1969, $6.95.

Stanford, G. & B. *Strangers to Themselves: Reading on Mental Illness.* Bantam Books, New York, 1969, $6.95.

*How to utilize psychotherapy*

Adams, S., & Orgel, M. *Through the Mental Health Maze: A Consumer's Guide to Finding a Psychotherapist,* including a sample consumer/therapist contract. Health Research Group, 2000 P Street N.W., Washington, D.C. 20036, $3.00.

Clark, T. *Going into Therapy.* Harper & Row, New York, 1975, $1.95.

Collier, H. L. *What's Psychotherapy and Who Needs It?* O'Sullivan Woodside, Phoenix, Arizona, 1975, $5.95.

Horney, K. (Ed.). *Are You Considering Psychoanalysis?* Norton, New York, 1963, $2.45.

Korel, J. *A Complete Guide to Therapy: From Psychoanalysis to Behavior Modification*, Pantheon, New York, 1975, $10.00.

Lazarus, H. R. *How to Get Your Money's Worth Out of Psychiatry*. Sherbourne Press, Los Angeles, 1972, $6.95.

Park, C. C., with Shapiro, L. N. *You Are Not Alone*. Atlantic Monthly Press Book, Little, Brown, Boston, 1975, $15.

Wiener, D. N. *A Consumer's Guide to Psychotherapy*. Hawthorn, New York, 1975, $3.95.

Wittenburg, R. *Common Sense About Psychoanalysis*. Funk & Wagnalls Publishing Company, New York, 1968, $1.25.

you slow
... ... your
... ...

How do you ... ...
to sleep ...

# appendix B

# Consultation
# as a dimension of
# contractual psychotherapy

Today science brings the individual a double
protection from illusion, it enables him to
scrutinize both the subjective and objective
source of his ideas.

— Lancelot L. Whyte

Conferring with a senior or expert colleague is regarded as necessary for
the practitioner who, though trained as a psychotherapist, is less experienced than his practice requires. The relationship that ensues
between the practitioner and his senior colleague is referred to as
*supervision.* Supervision is part of a defined didactic model in which the
senior colleague is the teacher and the less-experienced practitioner is
the student. There is generally implied, if not stated, an element of the
supervisor as permission-granter for the supervisee's behavior, conduct,
and performance in his therapeutic encounters with clients. The concept of consultation overlaps that of supervision, though the roles of
consultant and consultee are generally more vaguely defined and the
element of permission, which characterizes supervision, is generally
absent. The consultant is brought in as an advisor. As an outsider
without administrative responsibility for the practitioner's work, his
advice and point of view may be rejected or not acted upon without any
consequence to the consultee other than disapproval and possible
termination of the relationship. In this agreement, the consultee
theoretically has as much influence over the consultant's behavior as
the consultant has over his.                                            251

*Consultation to assess progress
and impasse in psychotherapy*

We labor to make a fine distinction between supervisory and consulta-
tive relationships because the model represented by the consultation
relationship has direct bearing on the psychotherapeutic relationship: It
approximates the therapeutic partnership I have endorsed in this book.
In contrast, the supervisory-relationship model parallels the majority of
current therapeutic relationships today. The use of consultation, unfortunately, generally is poorly understood, largely neglected, and frequently misused in the psychotherapy enterprise. Just as the consultee is
free to decide how or whether to use a consultant's advice, the client
should be entitled to dismiss the therapist's influence or hold it in
abeyance while he obtains a second opinion if he has serious questions
about the practitioner's influence on him.

The value of consultation is better understood, better accepted, and
in my view, more functionally utilized in medicine, legal counseling,
and other professions than it is in psychotherapy. When a client confers
with another therapist about problems he is experiencing with "his
own" therapist, without his therapist's explicit permission, this consultation is generally treated as acting out behavior. The client is frequently accused by the therapist of trying to avoid dealing with painful
material he is experiencing with the therapist that is, according to the
practitioner, in actuality, a transferential reexperience of unresolved
conflict with others in his life. Yet the practitioner considers consultation as appropriate for himself. At his own discretion, he may confer
with a consultant or may even be in supervision or control analysis with
a senior colleague. The client is rarely informed of this situation. This
suggests that therapists frequently use their power to secure support,
objectivity, and redirection through consultation, while at the same
time not informing their clients of its potential usefulness to them and
even actively preventing them from its use. This state of affairs is an
obvious contradiction of an egalitarian partnership.

Separate consultation for client and therapist is a useful adjunct to
viable psychotherapy. Consultation for both together is, I believe, an
idea worthy of consideration, though to my knowledge it is seldom
employed.[1] Conjoint consultation would tend to demystify the process

[1] I would appreciate hearing from any reader who has direct experience with or
knowledge of this type of consultation.

of psychotherapy and reduce the omnipotence of the therapist. Some practitioners may object that it would also result in breach of confidentiality and loss of the valuable exclusive relationship of the patient and his doctor. These objections are invalid to the extent that consultation and supervision are acceptable practices even though they, too, "violate" confidentiality and diffuse the therapeutic relationship.

I propose a model that approximates conjoint marital therapy, which is a partnership model in contrast to concurrent treatment or treatment of one spouse but not the other. In a conjoint consultation the client feels part of a collaborative endeavor in which problems, tensions, and strains are not his alone to deal with nor are they the therapist's prerogative to resolve; rather, they are part of a process in which both the client and his therapist-as-partner are intimately involved. By demystifying the therapeutic process and reducing the therapist's omniscience, each agent is permitted to recognize the limitations of his own knowledge and personal resources. This realization frees them to secure appropriate assistance. Through conjoint consultation, therapeutic progress can be objectively assessed, treatment can be productively redirected and, when indicated, rationally terminated or meaningfully referred elsewhere, all without the anger and misunderstanding attendant upon consultation sought by the client on his own. Not infrequently, a result, or at least a subsequent condition, of consultation is that the client terminates treatment with the first therapist and enters therapy with the consultant or another practitioner recommended by him. Conjoint consultation may make this result less of a threat to the therapist because he is present and involved in the consultation process. There are, of course, numerous practical issues involved in conjoint consultation that require careful consideration, such as who is to pay for the consultation—the client who is getting additional professional services, or the therapist who is getting consultation.

# References

Abrahams, J. Group Psychotherapy: Remarks on Its Basis and Applications. *Medical Annals of the District of Columbia* 1947, *16,* 612-616.

Abse, D. W. *Clinical Notes on Group-Analytic Psychotherapy.* University of Virginia Press, Charlottesville, Vir., 1974.

Adams, S., & Orgel, M. *Through the Mental Health Maze.* Health Research Group, Washington, D.C., 1975.

Adler, J., & Berman, I. R. Multiple Leadership in Group Treatment of Delinquent Adolescents. *Intern. J. Gr. Psychot.,* 1960, *10,* 213-225.

Agel, J. (Ed.) *The Radical Therapist.* Ballantine Books, New York, 1971.

Alberti, R. E., & Emmons, M. L. *Stand Up, Speak Out, Talk Back!* Pocket Books, New York, 1975.

Anthony, E. J. The History of Group Psychotherapy. In H. I. Kaplan & B. J. Sadock (Eds.), *Sensitivity Through Encounter and Marathon.* E. P. Dutton, New York, 1972, 1-26.

Bach, G. F. The Marathon Group: Intensive Practice of Intimate Interaction. *Psychol. Reports,* 1966, *18,* 995-1002.

Bach, G. F., & Wyden, P. *The Intimate Enemy.* Avon Books, New York, 1968.

Bailis, S. S., & Adler, G. Co-therapy Issues in a Collaborative Setting. *Amer. J. Psychot.,* 1974, *28* (4), 599-606.

Baker, D. P. Group Therapy "Joke" Wins Release of 10-Year Inmate. *The Washington Post,* 1974.

Bales, R. F. *Interaction Process Analysis.* Addison-Wesley, Cambridge, Mass., 1950.

Bergin, A. E. When Shrinks Hurt: Psychotherapy Can Be Dangerous. *Psychology Today,* 1975, *9* (6), pp. 96-100, 104.

Bergler, E., & Roheim, G. Psychology of Time Perception. *Psychoanalytic Quarterly,* 1946, *15,* 190-206.

Berne, E. *Games People Play.* Grove Press, New York, 1964.

Bettelheim, B., & Sylvester, E. A Therapeutic Milieu. *Amer. J. Orthopsychiatry,* 1948, *19,* 191-206.

Bindram, P. A Report on a Nude Marathon. *Psychotherapy: Theory, Research and Practice.* 1968, *5,* 180-88.

Bion, W. R. *Experiences in Groups.* Tavistock Publications, London, 1961.

Blatte, H. Evaluating Psychotherapies. *Hastings Center Report,* (September) 1973, 4-6.

Bockoven, J. S. Moral Treatment in American Psychiatry. *J. Nerv. Ment. Disorders, 124,* 1956, 167-194.

Bonaparte, M. Time and the Unconscious. *Intern. J. Psychoanalysis,* 1940, *21,* 427-468.

Breggin, P. R. The Second Wave. *Mental Hygiene,* 1973, 57 (1), 11–13.

Brill, H. *Research Conference on the Therapeutic Community.* Charles C Thomas, Springfield, Ill., 1960.

Brock, T. C., & Buss, A. H. Dissonance, Aggression and Evaluation of Pain. *J. Abnorm. Soc. Psychol.,* 1964, 68, 403–412.

Broom, L., & Selznick, P. *Sociology.* Harper & Row, New York, 1955.

Burrow, T. The Group Method of Analysis. *Psychoanalytic Review,* 1927, 14, 268–280.

Calet, V. Justice and the Arbitrator: Some Clinical Observations Concerning the Concept of Justice. *Amer. Imago.,* 1950, 7, 259–277.

Camus, A. *The Myth of Sisyphus.* Knopf, New York, 1955.

Carkhuff, R. R., & Berenson, B. G. *Teaching As Treatment.* Human Resource Development Press, Amherst, Mass., 1976.

Chodoff, P. The Effect of Third-Party Payment on the Practice of Psychotherapy. *Amer. J. Psychiatry,* 1972, 20, 122–123.

Clark, T. *Going into Therapy.* Harper & Row, New York, 1975.

Demarest, E. W., & Teicher, A. Transference in Group Therapy: Its Use by Co-therapists of Opposite Sexes. *Psychiatry,* 1954, 17, 187–202.

Dreikurs, R. The Techniques and Dynamics of Multiple Psychotherapy. *Psychiatric Quarterly,* 1950, 24, 788–799.

Dublin, J. E. A Further Motive for Psychotherapists: Communicative Intimacy. *Psychiatry,* 1971, 34, 401–409.

Dumont, M. P. *The Absurd Healer.* Viking Press, New York, 1971.

Egan, G. *Encounter: Group Processes for Interpersonal Growth.* Brooks/Cole, Monterey, Calif., 1970.

Enelow, M. L. Discussion of Papers of Gadpaille and Gelb. In J. H. Masserman (Ed.), *The Dynamics of Power,* Grune & Stratton, New York, 1972.

Erikson, E. *Life History and the Historical Movement.* Norton, New York, 1975.

Ezriel, H. Notes on Psychoanalytic Group Therapy: II. Interpretations and Research. *Psychiatry,* 1952, 15, 119–126.

Fenichel, O. *The Psychoanalytic Theory of Neurosis.* Norton, New York, 1945.

Fiske, D. W., & Maddi, S. P. (Eds.). *Functions of Varied Experience.* Dorsey, Homewood, Illinois, 1961.

Foudraine, J. *Not Made of Wood.* Macmillan, New York, 1974.

Foulkes, S. H., & Anthony, E. *Group Psychotherapy.* Penguin Books, New York, 1957.

Frankl, V. *The Will to Meaning.* World, New York, 1969.

Freud, S. Lines of Advance in Psycho-Analytic Therapy. *The Standard Edition of the Complete Psychological Works of Sigmund Freud.* Hogarth Press, London, 1919.

Freud, S. Analysis Terminable and Interminable (1937). *Collected Papers V.* Basic Books, New York, 1959, 316–357.

Freud, S. Recommendations for Physicians on the Psycho-analytic Method (1912). In *Freud: Therapy and Technique.* Macmillan, New York, 1967, 117–126.

Freud, S. Further Recommendations in the Technique of Psycho-analysis: Observation on Transference-Love (1915). In *Freud: Therapy and Technique,* Macmillan, New York, 1967, 167–179.

Friedson, E. *Profession of Medicine:* A Study of the Sociology of Applied Knowledge. Dodd, Mead, New York, 1976.

Fromm-Reichmann, F. The Philosophy of Psychotherapy. Hunter College Lecture, The William Alanson White Psychiatric Institute, New York, 1953.

Gadpaille, W. J. The Uses of Power: A Particular Impasse in Psychoanalysis. In J. H. Masserman (Ed.), *The Dynamics of Power,* Grune & Stratton, New York, 1972, 173–183.

Gans, R. W. Group Co-therapists and the Therapeutic Situation: A Critical Evaluation. *Intern. J. Gr. Psychot.,* 1962, *12,* 82–88.

Gelb, L. A. Psychotherapy as a Redistribution of Power. In J. H. Masserman (Ed.), *The Dynamics of Power,* Grune & Stratton, New York, 1972, 184–195.

Gendlin, E. *Symposium on Psychotherapy.* Sponsored by Friends of Psychiatric Research, Baltimore, October 18, 1974.

Gillis, J. S. Social Influence Therapy: The Therapist as Manipulator. *Psychology Today,* 1974, *8* (7), pp. 90–95.

Glass, D. C. Changes in liking as a means of reducing cognitive discrepancies between self-esteem and aggression. *J. of Personality,* 1964, *32,* 531–549.

Glasser, W. *Reality Therapy.* Harper & Row, New York, 1965.

Goldberg, C. Responsibilities of Heterosexual Relationships—A Look at Single Adult Hang-ups. Address given at the Jewish Community Center Coffee House, Washington, D.C., February, 1968.

Goldberg, C. *Encounter: Group Sensitivity Training Experience.* Science House, New York, 1970a.

Goldberg, C. Encounter Group Leadership. *Psychiatry and Social Science Review,* 1970b, *4* (11), 2–8.

Goldberg, C. Group Sensitivity Training. *Intern. J. Psychiatry,* 1970c, *9* 165–192.

Goldberg, C. Reply to Discussants. *Intern. J. Psychiatry,* 1970d, *9,* 226–232.

Goldberg, C. An Encounter With the Sensitivity Training Movement. *Canada's Mental Health,* 1971, *19* (5), 10–17.

Goldberg, C. A Community Is More Than a Psyche. *Canada's Mental Health,* 1972a, *20* (3–4), 15–21.

Goldberg, C. Reply to Dr. Hoffer. *Canada's Mental Health,* 1972b, *20* (5), 36–37.

Goldberg, C. Group Counselor or Group Therapist: Be Prepared. *Psychotherapy and Social Science Review,* 1972c, 26 (8), 24–27.

Goldberg, C. *The Human Circle: An Existential Approach to the New Group Therapies.* Nelson-Hall, Chicago, 1973.

Goldberg, C. Courtship Contract in Marital Psychotherapy. *Journal of Family Counseling,* 1975a, 3 (Spring), 40–45.

Goldberg, C. Peer Influence in Contemporary Group Psychotherapy. In L. R. Wolberg & M. L. Aronson (Eds.), *Group Therapy 1975,* Stratton Intercontinental Medical Books, New York, 1975b, 232–241.

Goldberg, C. Termination—A Meaningful Pseudodilemma in Psychotherapy. *Psychotherapy, Theory, Research and Practice.* 1975c, 12 (4), 341–343.

Goldberg, C. Existential Oriented Training for Mental Health Practitioners. *J. Contemp. Psychot.,* 1976a, 8 (1), 57–68.

Goldberg, C. Existentially Oriented Training for Group Therapy Practitioners. In L. R. Wolberg & M. L. Aronson (Eds.), *Group Therapy 1976.* Stratton Intercontinental Medical Books, New York, 1976b, 52-61.

Goldberg, C. Patient-Therapist Partnership in Co-therapy—A Systems Perspective. *Proceedings of Conference on Systems Science and the Future of Health.* Groome Center Publication, Washington, D.C., 1976c, 153-155.

Goldberg, C. Encounter Therapy As An Existential Saga. In H. Grayson and C. Loew (Eds.), *Changing Approaches to Psychotherapy,* Spectrum Publications, New York, 1977.

Goldberg, C., & Goldberg, M. Encounter Group Experience Workshop. *Proceedings of the International Group Psychotherapy Congress.* H. Huber, Zurich, 1975, 663–667.

Goldberg, C., & Goldberg, M. The Psychodramatic Magic Shop as a Technique in Contract Negotiation. In Ira Greenberg (Ed.), *Psychodrama: Old Dynamics and New Dimensions,* in press-a.

Goldberg, C., & Goldberg, M. The Psychodramatic Magic Shop As A Technique in Contract Negotiation. *Proceedings of the International Congress of Social Psychiatry.* Athens, Greece, in press-b.

Goldberg, C., & Kane, J. D. A Missing Component in Mental Health Services to the Urban Poor: Services-in-Kind to Others. In D. A. Evans & W. L. Claiborn (Eds.), *Mental Health Issues and the Urban Poor,* Pergamon Publications, New York, 1974b, 91–110.

Goldberg, C., & Kane, J. D. Services-in-Kind. A Form of Compensation for Mental Health Services. *Hospital and Community Psychiatry,* 1974a, 25, (3), 161–164.

Gorman, W. *Dynamic Psychotherapy and the Sense of Justice.* Warren H. Green, St. Louis, 1974.

Haigh, G. V. Psychotherapy as Interpersonal Encounter. In J. F. Bugental

(Ed.), *Challenges of Humanistic Psychology*, McGraw-Hill, New York, 1967.

Haley, J. *The Power Tactics of Jesus Christ.* Avon Books, New York, 1969.

Halleck, S. L. *The Politics of Therapy.* Harper & Row, New York, 1971.

Halpert E. The Effect of Insurance on Psychoanalytic Treatment. *J. Amer. Psychoanal. Assoc.,* 1972, *20,* 122-133.

Havighurst, H. C. *The Nature of the Private Contract.* Northwestern University Press, Evanston, Ill., 1961.

Heider, F. *The Psychology of Interpersonal Relations.* John Wiley, New York, 1957.

Hellwig, K., & Memmott, R. J. Co-therapy: The Balance Act. *Small Group Behavior,* 1974, *5* (2), 175–181.

Henry, W. E., Sims, J. H., & Spray, S. L. *The Fifth Profession.* Jossey-Bass, San Francisco, 1971.

Hoffer, A. The Flight from the Patient: An Exchange. *Canada's Mental Health,* 1972, *20* (5), 34–35.

Hollingshead, A. B., & Redlich, F. *Social Class and Mental Illness.* John Wiley, New York, 1958.

Hollister, W. H., & Holloway, M. M. *Change Now: An Introduction to Contractual Group Treatment with Transactional Analysis.* Midwest Institute for Human Understanding, Akron, Ohio, 1973.

Homans, G. *The Human Group.* Harcourt Brace Jovanovich, New York, 1950.

Horney, K. *The Neurotic Personality of Our Time.* Norton, New York, 1937.

Hosch, D. *Use of Contractual Approach in Public Social Services.* Regional Research Institute in Social Welfare, University of Southern California, 1973.

Howard, J. *Please Touch.* McGraw-Hill, New York, 1970.

Irmscher, W. F., & Hagemann, E. R. *The Language of Ideas.* Bobbs-Merrill, Indianapolis, 1963.

Jones, M. The Concept of a Therapeutic Community. *Amer. J. Psychiatry.* 1956, *112,* 647–650.

Jordan, M. Behavioral Forces That Are a Function of Attitudes and of Cognitive Organization. *Human Relations,* 1953, *6,* 273–287.

Jourard, S. M. *The Transparent Self: Self-Disclosure and Well-Being.* Van Nostrand Reinhold, New York, 1971.

Kaplan H. S. *The New Sex Therapy.* Brunner/Mazel, New York, 1974.

Kiresuk, T. J., & Sherman, R. E. Goal Attainment Scaling: A General Method for Evaluating Comprehensive Community Mental Health Programs. *Community Mental Health Journal,* 1968, *4* (6), 443–453.

Korda, M. *Power! How to Get It, How to Use It.* Random House, New York, 1975.

Kregarman, J. J., & Worchel, P. Arbitrariness of Frustration and Aggression. *J. Abnorm. Soc. Psychol.* 1961, *63* (1), 183–187.

Laing, R. D. *The Divided Self.* Penguin Books, New York, 1965.

Lake, M., & Levinger, G. Continuance Beyond Application: Interviews at a Child Guidance Clinic. *Social Casework,* 1960, *41,* 303–309.

Lazase, A., *et al.* The Walk-in Patient as a "Customer." *Amer. J. Orthopsychiatry,* 1972, *42* (5), 872–883.

Lecky, P. *Self-Consistency: A Theory of Personality.* Doubleday, New York, 1969.

Lennard, H. L., & Bernstein, A. Dilemma in Mental Health Program Evaluation. *American Psychologist,* 1971, *26,* 307–310.

Lennung, S. A. Implicit Theories in Experimental Group Practices—A Pedagogical Approach. *Interpersonal Development,* 1974-5, *5* (1), 37-49.

Lerner, M. J., Evaluation of Performance as a Function of Performer's Reward and Attractiveness. *J. Personality and Soc. Psych.,* 1965, *1* 355–360.

Lerner, M. J., & Simmons, C. H. Observer's Reaction to the "Innocent Victim": Compassion or Rejection? *J. Personality and Soc. Psych.,* 1966, *4,* 203–210.

Levinger, G. Continuance in Casework and Other Helping Relationships: A Review of Current Research. *Social Work,* 1960, *5* (6), 40–51.

Lieberman, M. A., Yalom, I. D., & Miles, M. B. *Encounter Groups: First Facts.* Basic Books, New York, 1973.

Linthorst, J. The Transactional Dimension of Action. *Psychotherapy: Theory, Research and Practice,* 1975, *12* (2), 160–163.

Loeffler, F. J., & Weinstein, H. M. The Co-therapist Method: Special Problems and Advantages. *Group Psychotherapy,* 1953-4, *6,* 189–192.

London, P. *The Modes and Morals of Psychotherapy.* Holt, Rinehart and Winston, New York, 1964.

London, P. The Psychotherapy Boom: From the Long Couch for the Sick to the Push Button for the Bored. *Psychology Today,* 1974, *8* (1), pp. 62-68.

Lundin, W. H., & Aronov, B. M. The Use of Co-therapists in Group Psychotherapy. *J. Consult. Psychol.,* 1952, *16,* 76–80.

Maclennan, B. W. Co-therapy. *Intern. J. Gr. Psychot.,* 1965, *15,* 154–166.

Mainord, W. A. Operant Group Psychotherapy in a Total Institution Setting. *The Dis-coverer,* 1968, *5* (1, 2).

Manus, G. I. Marriage Counseling: A Technique in Search of a Theory. *Journal of Marriage and the Family,* 1966, *28,* 449–453.

Marin, P. The New Narcissism. *Harper's Magazine,* 1975 (October), *251* (1505), pp. 45–70.

May, R., Angel, E., & Ellenberger, H. *Existence.* Basic Books, New York, 1958.

Meade, G. H. *Mind, Self and Society*. University of Chicago Press, Chicago, 1934.

Meerloo, J. A. Justice as a Psychological Problem. *Arch. Crim. Psychodynamics*, 1959, *3*, 7–51.

Meltzer, M. L. Insurance Reimbursement: A Mixed Blessing. *American Psychologist*, 1975, *30* (12), 1150–1156.

Menninger, K. *Theory of Psychoanalytic Technique*. Harper & Row, New York, 1955.

Michels, R. Ethical Issues of Psychological and Psychotherapeutic Means of Behavior Control. *Hastings Center Report*, 1973, (April).

Miller, G. A. On Turning Psychology Over to the Unwashed. *Psychology Today*, 1969, *3* (7), pp. 53–54, 64–74.

Minitz, E. E. Special Values of Co-therapists in Group Psychotherapy. *Intern. J. Gr. Psychot.*, 1963a, *13*, 127–132.

Minitz, E. E. Transference in Co-therapy Groups. *J. Consult. Psychol.* 1963b, *17*, 34-39.

Minitz, E. E. Male-Female Co-therapists. *Amer. J. Psychot.*, 1965, *19*, 293–301.

Minuchin, S., *et al.*, *Families of the Slums*. Basic Books, New York, 1967.

Morgan, T. Inside the Therapy Subculture. *New York Magazine*, 1974, pp. 38–44.

Mowrer, O. H. Conflict, Contract, Conscience, and Confession. Unpublished paper, University of Illinois, 1968.

Mullan, H. Transference and Countertransference: New Horizons. *Intern. J. Gr. Psychot.*, 1955, *5*, 169–180.

Myerson, A. Theory and Principles of the "Total Push" Method in the Treatment of Chronic Schizophrenia. *Amer. J. Psychiatry*, 1939, *95*, 1197–1204.

Neufeldt, A. H. Planning for Comprehensive Mental Health Programs. *Canada's Mental Health*, 1967, Supplement 67 (March-April).

Osmundson. New Unit Formed on Schizophrenia. *The New York Times*, November 27, 1965.

Overall, B., & Aronson, H. Expectations of Psychotherapy in Patients of Lower Socioeconomic Class. *Amer. J. Orthopsychiatry*, 1963, *33* (4), 426.

Pastore, N. The Role of Arbitrariness in the Frustration-Aggression Hypothesis. *J. Abnorm. Soc. Psychol.*, 1952, *47*, 728–731.

Paulson, I., Burroughs, J. C., & Gelb, C. B. Co-therapy: What Is the Crux of the Relationship? *Intern. J. Gr. Psychot.*, 1976, *27*, 213–224.

Perelman, C. *Justice*. Random House, New York, 1967.

Pfeiffer, E. (Ed.). *Sigmund Freud and Lou Andreas-Salome' Letters*. Harcourt Brace Jovanovich, New York, 1972.

Pine, I., Todd, W. E., & Boenheim, C. Special Problems of Resistance in Cotherapy Groups. *Intern. J. Gr. Psychot.*, 1963, *13*, 354-362.

Pirandello, L. *Naked Masks: Five Plays.* E. P. Dutton, New York, 1952.

Polsky, H. W., Claster, D. S., & Goldberg, C. *Dynamics of Residential Treatment.* North Carolina University Press, Chapel Hill, 1968.

Polsky, H. W., Claster, D. S., & Goldberg, C. *Social System Perspectives in Residential Institutions.* Michigan State University Press, East Lansing, 1970.

Powermaker, F., & Frank, J. *Group Psychotherapy: Studies in Methodology of Research and Therapy.* Harvard University Press, Cambridge, Mass., 1963.

Pratt, S., & Tooley, J. Contract Psychology and the Actualizing Transactional Field. *Intern. J. Soc. Psychiatry,* Congress Issue, 1964, 51–59.

Rabin, H. M. How Does Co-therapy Compare With Regular Group Therapy? *Amer. J. Psychot.*, 1967, *21*, 244–255.

Rawls, J. *A Theory of Justice.* Harvard University Press, Cambridge, Mass., 1971.

Redl, F., & Wineman, D. *Children Who Hate.* Free Press, New York, 1951.

Redlich, F., & Mollica, R. F. Overview: Ethical Issues in Contemporary Psychiatry. *Amer. J. Psychiatry,* 1976, *133* (2), 125–136.

Rees, T. P. Back to Moral Treatment and Community Care. *Journal of Mental Science,* 1957, *103,* 330—313.

Riegel, K. F. The Dialectics of Human Development. *American Psychologist,* 1976, *31* (10), 689-700.

Riesman, F., Cohen, J., & Pearl, A. *Mental Health of the Poor.* Free Press, New York, 1964.

Ringer, R. *Winning Through Intimidation.* Funk & Wagnalls Publishing Company, New York, 1975.

Rioch, D. M., & Stanton, A. H. Milieu Therapy. *Psychiatry,* 1953, *16,* 63-72.

Rogers, C. R. *Client-Centered Therapy.* Houghton Mifflin, Boston, 1951.

Rosenquist, C. M. Differential Responses of Texas Convicts. *Amer. J. Sociology,* 1932, *38,* 10–21.

Ruitenbeek, H. M. *Group Therapy Today: Styles, Methods and Techniques.* Atherton, New York, 1969.

Ruitenbeek, H. M. *The New Group Therapies.* Avon Books, New York, 1970.

Sager, C. J., Kaplan, H. S., et al. The Marriage Contract. In C. J. Sager & H. S. Kaplan (Eds.), *Progress in Group and Family Therapy.* Brunner/Mazel, New York, 1972, 483-497.

Sata, L. S. A Mental Health Center's Partnership with the Community. *Hospital and Community Psychiatry,* *23,* 1972, 242–245.

Schaffer, B. P., & Galinsky, M. D. *Models of Group Therapy and Sensitivity Training.* Prentice-Hall, Englewood Cliffs, N.J., 1974.

Schaffer, R. Talking to Patients in Psychotherapy. *Bulletin of the Menninger Clinic*, 1974, *38* (6), 503–515.

Schatzman, M. Madness and Morals. In J. Agel (Ed.), *The Radical Therapist*. Ballantine Books, New York, 1971, 65–96.

Schief, P. Sex Therapy Situation is "Chaotic." *Montgomery County Journal*, 1975.

Schmidt, J. The Use of Purpose in Case Work Practice. *Social Work*, 1969, *14* (1), 80.

Schofield, W. *Psychotherapy—The Purchase of Friendship*. Prentice-Hall, Englewood Cliffs, N.J., 1964.

Schutz, W. C. *Here Comes Everybody*. Harper & Row, New York, 1971.

Schwitzgebel, R. K. A Contractual Model for the Protection of the Rights of Institutionalized Mental Patients. *American Psychologist*, 1975, *30* (8), 815–820.

Seabury, B. A. The Contract: Uses, Abuses and Limitations. *Social Work*, 1976, *21* (1), 16–21.

Sharfstein, S. S., Taube, C. A., & Goldberg, I. D. Private Psychiatry and Accountability: A Response to the APA Task Force Report on Private Practice. *Amer. J. Psychiatry*, 1975, *132* (1), 43–47.

Shepard, M. *Games Analysts Play*. G. P. Putnam's Sons, New York, 1970.

Shepard, M. *Marathon 16*. Pocket Books, New York, 1971.

Shore, M. F. Introduction. In M. F. Shore & S. E. Golman (Eds.), *Current Ethical Issues in Mental Health*, Department of Health, Education and Welfare Publication No. (HSM) 73-9029, 1973.

Sivadon, P. Techniques of Sociotherapy. *Psychiatry*, 1957, *20*, 1–11.

Slater, P. E. Role Differentiation in Small Groups. *Amer. Sociol. Rev.*, *20*, 1955, 300–310.

Slater, P. E. Cultures in Collision. *Psychology Today*, 1970, *4* (2), pp. 31–32, 66–68.

Small, L. *The Briefer Psychotherapies*. Brunner/Mazel, New York, 1971.

Solomon, A. F., Loeffler, J., & Frank, G. H. An Analysis of Co-therapist Interaction in Group Psychotherapy. *Intern. J. Gr. Psychot.*, *3*, 1953, 171–180.

Spotnitz, H. Comparison of Different Types of Group Psychotherapy. In H. I. Kaplan & B. J. Sadock (Eds.), *New Models for Group Therapy*. E. P. Dutton, New York, 1972, 3–34.

Steinzor, B. *The Healing Partnership*. Harper & Row, New York, 1967.

Stone, A. A. The Quest of the Encounter Culture. *Inter. J. Psychiatry*, 1970, *9*, 219–226.

Strupp, H. H., Fox, R. E., & Lessler, K. *Patients View Their Psychotherapy*. Johns Hopkins University Press, Baltimore, 1969.

Stuart, R. B. Operant—Interpersonal Treatment for Marital Discord. *J. Consult. and Clin. Psych.*, 1969, *33* (6), 675–682.

Sykes, G. M., & Matza, D. Techniques of Neutralization: A Theory of Delinquency. *Amer. Sociol. Review*, 1957, 22, 664–670.

Szasz, T. S. *The Myth of Mental Illness*. Harper & Row, New York, 1961.

Szasz, T. S. *The Ethics of Psychoanalysis*. Dell, New York, 1969.

Szasz, T., & Hollender, M. H. The Basic Models of the Doctor-Patient Relationship. *Archives of Internal Medicine*, 1956, 97, 585–592. Also in H. W. Polsky, D. S. Claster, & C. Goldberg (Eds.), *Social System Perspectives on Residential Institutions*. Michigan State University Press, East Lansing, Mich., 1970.

Thibaut, J. W., & Kelley, H. H. *The Social Psychology of Groups*. Wiley, New York, 1959.

Torrey, E. F. *Plumbers and Psychiatrists: A Consumer's View of Mandatory Evaluation*. Presented at the meetings of the American Psychiatric Association in Detroit, May 8, 1974.

Toussieng, P. W. Child Psychotherapy in A New Era. *Amer. J. Orthopsychiatry*, 1971, 41 (1), 58–64.

Trotter, S. Nader Group Releases First Consumer Guide to Psychotherapists. *American Psychological Association Monitor*, 1975, 6 (11), 11.

Truax, C. B., Shapiro, J. G., & Wargo, D. G. Effects of Alternate Sessions and Vicarious Therapy Pretraining on Group Psychotherapy. *Intern. J. Gr. Psychot.*, 1968, 18, 186-198.

Viscott, D. S. *The Making of A Psychiatrist*. Fawcett Crest, New York, 1973.

Walster, E., & Walster, G. W. Equity and Social Justice. *J. Soc. Issues*, 1975, 31 (3), 21-43.

Warkentin, J., Johnson, N. L., & Whitaker, C. A. A Comparison of Individual and Multiple Psychotherapy. *Psychiatry*, 1951, 14, 415-418.

Webster, B. Menninger's Clinic: The Dream That Cures Minds. *Moneysworth*, March 1, 1976, 12.

Weigert, E. Contribution to the Problem of Terminating Psychoanalysis. *Psychoanalytic Quarterly*, 1952, 21, 465–480.

Wittenberg, C. A Community Mental Health Program in an Urban Slum. *Mental Health Reports No. 2*, U. S. Department of Health, Education, and Welfare, Public Health Service, February, 1968, 185–200.

Wolfe, L. The Question of Surrogates in Sex Therapy. *Reflections*, 1974, 9 (4), 23–33.

Yalom, I. D. *The Theory and Practice of Group Psychotherapy*. Basic Books, New York, 1970.

Yalom, I. D., et al. Preparation of Patients for Group Therapy. *Archives of General Psychiatry*, 1967, 17, 416–427.

Yalom, I. D., et al. Encounter Groups and Psychiatry. *Task Force Report*, American Psychiatric Association, Washington, D.C., 1970.

Zilboorg, G. A. *A History of Medical Psychology*. Norton, New York, 1941.

Zimet, C. N. A Register of Health Service Providers in Psychology: A Reality. *The Clinical Psychologist*, 1974, 28 (1), 10.

# Author index

# Subject index